Theatre of Real People

Methuen Drama Engage offers original reflections about key practitioners, movements and genres in the fields of modern theatre and performance. Each volume in the series seeks to challenge mainstream critical thought through original and interdisciplinary perspectives on the body of work under examination. By questioning existing critical paradigms, it is hoped that each volume will open up fresh approaches and suggest avenues for further exploration.

Series Editors

Mark Taylor-Batty
Senior Lecturer in Theatre Studies, Workshop Theatre, University of Leeds, UK
Enoch Brater
Kenneth T. Rowe Collegiate Professor of Dramatic Literature & Professor of English and Theater, University of Michigan, USA

Titles

Brecht in Practice: Theatre, Theory and Performance
by David Barnett
ISBN 978-1-4081-8503-2
Postdramatic Theatre and the Political
edited by Karen Jürs-Munby, Jerome Carroll and Steve Giles
ISBN 978-1-4081-8486-8
Theatre in the Expanded Field: Seven Approaches to Performance
by Alan Read
ISBN 978-1-4081-8495-0
Ibsen in Practice: Relational Readings of Performance, Cultural Encounters and Power
by Frode Helland
ISBN 978-1-4725-1369-4
Rethinking the Theatre of the Absurd: Ecology, the Environment and the Greening of the Modern Stage
edited by Carl Lavery and Clare Finburgh
ISBN 978-1-4725-0667-2

Howard Barker's Theatre: Wrestling with Catastrophe
edited by James Reynolds and Andy W. Smith
ISBN 978-1-4081-8439-4
The Contemporary American Monologue: Performance and Politics
by Eddie Paterson
ISBN 978-1-4725-8501-1

Theatre of Real People

Diverse Encounters at Berlin's Hebbel am Ufer and Beyond

Ulrike Garde and Meg Mumford

Series Editors
Mark Taylor-Batty and Enoch Brater

Bloomsbury Methuen Drama
An imprint of Bloomsbury Publishing Plc

B L O O M S B U R Y
LONDON · OXFORD · NEW YORK · NEW DELHI · SYDNEY

Bloomsbury Methuen Drama

An imprint of Bloomsbury Publishing Plc

Imprint previously known as Methuen Drama

50 Bedford Square	1385 Broadway
London	New York
WC1B 3DP	NY 10018
UK	USA

www.bloomsbury.com

BLOOMSBURY, METHUEN DRAMA and the Diana logo are trademarks of Bloomsbury Publishing Plc

First published in 2016

© Ulrike Garde and Meg Mumford, 2016

Ulrike Garde and Meg Mumford have asserted their rights under the Copyright, Designs and Patents Act, 1988, to be identified as authors of this work.

British Library Cataloguing-in-Publication Data
A catalogue record for this book is available from the British Library.

ISBN:	HB:	978-1-4725-8022-1
	PB:	978-1-4725-8022-1
	ePDF:	978-1-4725-8024-5
	ePub:	978-1-4725-8023-8

Library of Congress Cataloging-in-Publication Data
A catalog record for this book is available from the Library of Congress.

Series: Methuen Drama Engage

Typeset by RefineCatch Limited, Bungay, Suffolk
Printed and bound in Great Britain

To our families

David, Dennis, and Vera
and
Paul, Imogen, and Tom

Contents

List of Figures

Acknowledgements

Like much Theatre of Real People, this book is the outcome of a long preparatory process characterized by numerous forms of collaboration, dialogue, and networking. Many aspects of this process would not have been possible without institutional support for: research leave in both 2010 and 2014, resource materials, conference travel, rehearsal attendance, transcription, and publication subsidy. For this support we are indebted to both Macquarie University and The University of New South Wales in Sydney, Australia. We are also grateful to former and current staff at Berlin's Hebbel am Ufer (HAU) production house. In particular, we would like to thank Kirsten Hehmeyer, head of press and marketing and a curator for the HAU (2003–12) for her generous engagement with our project through discussions and an interview, and through providing access to the house archive. We would like to thank also Maria Magdalena Schwaegermann, formerly acting artistic director of the Hebbel Theater (now HAU1), for her interview with us about Theatre of Real People at the HAU, and for introducing us to Mobile Academy's *Blackmarket for Useful and Non-Useful Knowledge and Non-Knowledge* format. We are also indebted to the HAU office staff, who have swiftly and helpfully responded to an array of inquiries and requests throughout the research process.

For their important contributions to an influential mode of socially engaged performance, and for their willingness to share their ideas and production materials with us, we warmly thank the following artists whose work at and with the HAU has been a major source of inspiration for this book: the Rimini Protokoll performance collective Helgard Haug, Stefan Kaegi, and Daniel Wetzel, as well as dramaturg Sebastian Brünger; dramaturg for *X-Wohnungen* (2004), Arved Schultze; and Mobile Academy founder and curator Hannah Hurtzig. We also thank the following 'real people' who featured as performers in some of the HAU productions we analyse and gave of their time to speak to us:

Anton Griffith and Rochelle Humphrey (*100% Melbourne*), and Madhusree Mukerjee (*Call Cutta: Mobile Phone Theatre*). For their invaluable contribution to our research into *100% Melbourne* we would like to give special mention to two City of Melbourne Arts and Participation Programme staff: Vicky Guglielmo (Project Manager) and Bec Reid (Associate Director and Casting). Our access to *100% Melbourne* was greatly assisted by Goethe-Institut Australia, which not only supported the presentation in Australia of this and other work by Rimini Protokoll during our research process, but also hosted two public discussions instigated by ourselves on the subject of both the company and Theatre of Real People. In particular, we received support for both panel events from the Institut Director, Arpad Sölter, and Gabriele Urban, Cultural Office Melbourne. Our understanding and presentation of Berlin-based Theatre of Real People has also been shaped by our discussions with artist-scholars Gudrun Herrbold and Anna Scheer.

Our thanks also to the many people who have helped us with image permission and reproduction, including: Nino Medas (HAU); Helgard Haug, Heidrun Schlegel, and Caroline Gentz (Rimini Protokoll); Cristina Navarro (Mobile Academy); Anna Wille and Elke Weber (She She Pop); and Shona Johnson (City of Melbourne). For feedback on our book proposal, sample chapters, and final manuscript we are indebted to Bloomsbury's Methuen Drama Engage series editors, Mark Taylor-Batty and Enoch Brater, and to the book proposal reviewer David Barnett. Senior Commissioning Editor Mark Dudgeon and Assistant Editor Emily Hockley have provided prompt, informative, and professional advice on numerous occasions throughout the process. Our colleagues Caroline Wake and Johannes Birgfeld have generously cast their astute eyes over our Introduction and Conclusion, respectively. People who have been instrumental to the proofreading process are John Golder and James Lane, and we thank also Dennis Garde for his assistance with bibliographic matters.

And, finally, a heartfelt thanks to our immediate family members – David, Dennis, and Vera, and Paul, Imogen, and Tom – for making our juggling of multifaceted work, home and theatre worlds both physically possible and emotionally rich. Last but not least, a thank you to each other for a sustained sharing of passion, wit, honesty, care, and stamina throughout a rewarding collaboration.

Introduction

Setting the scene

Lit by a spotlight, captured in live-feed close-up, and speaking into a microphone positioned in front of a large revolving stage, Thomas Gerlach introduces himself as a real-life employee of the German Federal Statistical Office. He states that he represents one per cent of Berliners and explains that the casting process for the show he is now opening was based on a 'chain reaction' in which each selected inhabitant of Berlin had twenty-four hours to choose the next performer according to statistically relevant categories. He then welcomes to the microphone the performer he was responsible for casting: his young daughter Annemarie Gerlach, who carries a soft-toy black sheep as an object of personal significance. The revolve begins to move, slowly, in a clockwise direction, and only stops when all 100 diverse Berliner cast members and their chosen objects have been introduced and, like beads on a string, occupy the entire circumference of the revolve. This is the opening of *100% Berlin*, a production that featured as one of the main events in the 2008 centenary celebrations for Berlin's Hebbel Theater, and an exemplar of the mode of performance that we refer to as, 'Theatre of Real People'. The production was conceived by the performance collective Rimini Protokoll, and its transportable *100% City* (*100% Stadt*) format, a conceptual and organizational framework, has now been adapted to and performed in over twenty cities across the world.

During *100% Berlin*, Rimini Protokoll were artists-in-residence at the Hebbel am Ufer. Known as the HAU, this award-winning production house operates across three neighbouring theatre buildings, which, prior to the inception of the HAU in 2003, were known as the Hebbel Theater (HAU1), the Theater am Halleschen Ufer (HAU2), and the Theater am Ufer (HAU3). From 2003 until 2012, the HAU was strongly shaped by the leadership of its artistic director, Matthias Lilienthal, and his self-declared 'hysterical yearning for the real'[1] (hysterische Sehnsucht nach Realität: Behrendt 2004). Earlier in the period of Lilienthal's leadership, the HAU had already invited 100 real people into HAU1 and HAU2 for three separate iterations of Mobile Academy's format *Blackmarket for Useful Knowledge and Non-Knowledge* (*Schwarzmarkt für nützliches Wissen und Nicht-Wissen*). At each of the *Blackmarket* events at the HAU (2005–7), 100 'experts' from a diverse array of social, ethnic and occupational backgrounds – the vast majority of whom were not professional performers – took turns operating at rows of small tables, each table atmospherically lit by a hanging light bulb. In the case of the March 2007 performance evening, the experts delivered a narrative on topics relevant to the theme of mobility pioneers and functionaries to each audience member lucky enough to occupy a seat opposite them, as well as those onlookers who accessed the talks via headphones. To date, the *Blackmarket* format has been applied to performance events in at least fourteen cities across Europe and in Israel.

Even earlier in the HAU's history, Lilienthal had introduced a format that also featured real and unfamiliar people when he further developed his own *X-Apartments: Theatre in Private Spaces* (*X-Wohnungen: Theater in privaten Räumen*), a format premiered in Duisburg in 2002. In the 2004 event in Berlin – others would follow in 2005 and 2008, and the format has been adapted subsequently to many cities across the world – audience members placed in pairs journeyed through a series of urban site-specific performances. These events took place in private flats across Kreuzberg, the ethnically diverse suburb where the HAU theatres are located, as well Lichtenberg, a former satellite town in the German Democratic Republic. During the multiple short performances, participants met performers who seemed to be local residents, people who seemed to be trained actors, and people whose status as performers was unclear. *100% City*, *Blackmarket*, and *X-Apartments* are not only some of the key objects of our analysis in this study, but also exemplify the kind of engagement with both Theatre of Real People and cultural diversity that was memorably developed at the HAU under Lilienthal, and which has given significant impetus to the lines of inquiry at the heart of this book.

Recent socially engaged Western theatre has shown an intense fascination with Theatre of Real People, a mode of performance that presents contemporary people, who tend not to be trained theatre performers. These people often appear live in person, or via an audio and/or visual recording. In the case of relevant genres such as verbatim and documentary theatre, these performers are usually made manifest via a scripted text based on real-life interviews and documents, and delivered either by themselves or by actors. As we will show, recent Theatre of Real People has addressed numerous pressing contemporary social issues, including increased mediation of human interaction and a consumerist culture of self-optimization. In this book, our focus is on the way in which innovative versions of this mode that have emerged from Germany are addressing the current situation of intensified cultural diversity. To this end, we consider how one of the most prominent types of socially engaged performance today is representing the complex identities, and encounters with the diverse, that characterize the intercultural nature of much contemporary everyday life (Leggewie and Zifonun 2010: 14). Drawing on our combined expertise in Theatre Studies and Intercultural (German) Studies, we turn the spotlight on how specific forms of this performance represent cultural diversity and unfamiliar people. By 'unfamiliar' we mean not only people who are perceived by the participants in the theatre event as different, foreign or insufficiently known due to their occupational, class, and ethnic background, but also 'theatre strangers', those who do not usually perform their everyday activities within the theatre or as theatre. Engagement with such culturally diverse unfamiliar people is a characteristic feature of the theatre productions explored in this book, all of which were hosted by the HAU.

The three theatres constituting the HAU consortium brought with them a rich history of socially engaged and experimental approaches to theatre, a history we address further in Chapter 2. Since the merger, the HAU has programmed a variety of local, national, and international performance events across an array of theatre and non-theatre spaces. During Lilienthal's time, it specialized in particular in presenting an experimental Theatre of Real People that is often referred to as *Reality Theater* in Germany, or 'Reality Theatre' in English-language discourse (Boenisch 2008; Forrest 2008; Pailer and Schößler 2011). This theatre develops or diverges from documentary theatre through its *foregrounding* of non-professional theatre performers who present aspects of themselves or of their lives. The HAU has fostered Theatre of Real People through its support for important contributors to this mode of performance (for example, Nurkan Erpulat, Constanza Macras, Gob Squad, Rimini Protokoll, She She Pop, and Tamer Yiğit), as well as for new formats, such as the *Blackmarket* events and *X-Apartments*. Under Lilienthal, the HAU also developed a responsiveness to its location in the suburb of Kreuzberg, the cosmopolitan city of Berlin, and a globalized world. This responsiveness was expressed in its lively exchange with local communities, its creation of performances that can be staged beyond the HAU and travel the world, as well as its expansion of international networks, an approach that had been fostered by Nele Hertling and Maria Magdalena Schwaegermann prior to Lilienthal. In this book, we focus on theatre productions developed and/or presented at the HAU that have addressed the unfamiliar, both within and between cultures, as a significant part of their overall socio-political engagement. We define that engagement as characterized by an attempt to grasp, illuminate, and disturb habitual modes of perception and behaviour.

One of the main issues addressed in this book is the potential of Theatre of Real People to facilitate encounters with culturally diverse people, in particular as that potential has been explored at the HAU. We approach that issue by asking the following question: 'How and in what contexts can the key aesthetic feature of Theatre of Real People – its generation, and in many cases its destabilization, of a *sense* of the authentic – invite fresh ways of perceiving diverse and unfamiliar people?' Here 'authentic' is a synonym for one or more of the following: 'sincere', 'genuine', 'truthful', 'actual', 'unmediated' (Knaller and Müller 2005: 42, 52). Through pursuing this question, we address a paradigmatic interplay of aesthetics and social engagement that, in our climate of mediatization and cultural diversity, continues to represent an important challenge for theatres both within and beyond Germany.

The Theatre of Real People mode and Authenticity-Effects

The key source of a sense of authenticity in the mode of performance explored in this book is its foregrounding of what seem to be 'real people' – that is, contemporary people who have a verifiable physical existence, and who usually have not received institutional theatre training and have little or no prior stage experience. These real people literally appear on stage or are represented – through techniques such as verbatim text, film, pre-recorded or live-feed video – and figure as *consensual* protagonists in specific theatre forms and genres. By 'real people' we also mean those people in a theatre context who present aspects of their own selves – their perspectives, personal histories, narratives, knowledges, skills, environments, social worlds, and/or socio-economic categories – rather than those of fictional or devised characters. Occasionally, Theatre of Real People may include trained actors or performers, who represent aspects of their own selves, often alongside people who are not professional performers. While many real people on the stage may perform in a manner that has much in common with those forms of amateur theatre that are concerned with the staging of dramatic texts (by children, students, local theatre club members etc.), the real-people performers are distinguished by the self-representational and either fully or partially self-devised nature of their presentations.

Currently, Theatre of Real People is a prevalent performance mode that exists across diverse and emergent genres, including: autobiographical theatre, *Bürgerbühne* (Citizens' Stage), community-based theatre, delegated performance, documentary theatre, ethnographic performance, participatory performance, refugee theatre, reality theatre, re-enactments, testimonial theatre, theatre of everyday experts, and verbatim theatre. A further defining feature of Theatre of Real People is that it works and/or plays with the assumption underpinning realist epistemology, namely that 'knowledge is available through sense perception and cognition linked to objects/documents' and that such aspects of a performance can put spectators in contact with 'the reality they are trying to experience or understand' (Reinelt 2009: 9). When using the term 'reality' in this book, we draw on the pragmatic approach adopted by Pam Morris and define it as that which, in intersubjective communication, is agreed to exist (Morris 2003: 6). When using the term 'real', we draw on Carol Martin's observation in her recent study of what she calls 'theatre of the real', that it is difficult to maintain the real's ambiguity when writing about it: '"Real" in quotation marks insinuates that the real is not real. Real (without quotation marks) insinuates that the real is real' (Martin 2013: 177). Following Martin's practice, we have elected not to present the real and reality in quotation marks, but to clarify our understanding of the complexity of these phenomena through our discussions.

A number of other components of Martin's conceptualization of 'theatre of the real' have also been influential in our coinage of the term 'Theatre of Real People'. According to her, the 'phrase "theatre of the real" identifies a wide range of theatre practices and styles that recycle reality, whether that reality is personal, social, political, or historical' (Martin 2013: 5). Such recycling involves the explicit citing, quoting, simulating, and summoning of the world outside the theatre through a variety of means that may include: verbatim text, archival photos, film, audio recordings, set pieces and objects, real clothing, and also the use of 'actual people to perform narratives of their own lives' (2013: 80). Martin's phrase also seeks to draw attention to 'theatre's participation in today's addiction to and questioning of the real as it is presented across media and genres' (2013: 5). While she does not rule out the possibility that explicit recycling of reality has existed since the inception of Western theatre, she points to early twentieth-century popular culture forms such as dance marathons and the theatre of Piscator and Brecht as the important precursors of and influences on today's theatre of the real (2013: 15–16).

Our coinage of the phrase 'Theatre of Real People' deliberately echoes Martin's phrase for two reasons: first, in order to connect the mode of performance we have identified, with the broader field of cultural activity devoted to using theatre to access 'the real thing' or to engage with the representation of reality (Martin 2013: 4); and second, to draw attention to a recurrent mode of performance in contemporary theatre of the real, one that is partially acknowledged, but not explored further, in Martin's scholarship to date. This mode not only contributes to theatre of the real's participation in 'how we come to know and understand what has happened' through a staging of memory and history (2013: 5, 17), but also to the ways in which we experience and understand what is happening *now*. While Martin chooses not to capitalize her phrase, an approach that evokes for us a sense of a fluid concept and of diverse and shifting practices, our decision to capitalize 'Theatre of Real People' seeks to convey a more containable or discrete (if by no means fixed) type of theatre-making.

Our analytical focus on how this more discrete field destabilizes a sense of authentic encounter with real and unfamiliar people is one further reason why we use the phrase 'Theatre of Real People'. In the emergent discourse about aspects of this mode of performance, terms and labels usually express particular critical frameworks. For example, in her thought-provoking appraisal of lineages and types of contemporary art that involve people as the medium or material, Claire Bishop refers to such work as 'participatory art', and, for occasions when non-professional performers are hired by artists 'to perform their own socio-economic category' (Bishop 2012: 5, 219), she uses the term 'delegated performance'. Bishop's use of both phrases draws attention to both her own analytical concerns, and those of some of the artists whose projects she investigates. One of these concerns is the way in which artistic practice can or does engage with the ethics and aesthetics of contemporary labour (2012: 220). For example, Bishop argues that her preferred versions of delegated performance transgressively reiterate contemporary forms of precarious labour, such as offshore outsourcing, an economic practice that became prominent in the early 1990s: '[I]f the aim of outsourcing in business is to decrease risk, artists frequently deploy it as a means to increase unpredictability' (2012: 231). She also argues that delegated performance embodies and can alert attention to 'a service industry that increasingly relies upon the marketing of certain qualities in human beings' and to what, in their assessment of contemporary capitalism, Luc Boltanski and Eve Chiapello call the 'commodification of the authentic' (2012: 231) – that is, the extraction of profit from the uniqueness of a given place, person or service. While Bishop's considerations have informed, for example, our analysis of how our case studies negotiate encounter with real and unfamiliar people, the phrase 'delegated performance' does not adequately express the issues at stake within our critical framework.

'Theatre of Real People' is a phrase that more clearly positions our objects of study in relation to dominant theatre conventions and traditions that are often important elements in the generation and/or destabilization of a sense of the authentic. Such positioning should not obscure the way experimental theatre from the HAU in particular often delights in blurring boundaries between arts disciplines. By 'experimental', we mean here theatre that plays with the limits of (theatre) form, 'putting pressure on certain conventions and prescribed rules in order to stretch or invent others' (Bailes 2011: 13). The way the HAU's experimental theatre blurs disciplinary boundaries is in many respects indistinguishable from contemporary art forms such as delegated performance. However, the HAU's productions are usually framed on an institutional level as theatre rather than visual art (e.g. hosted by theatre producers and funders, created by performance practitioners, and often presented in theatre buildings and similar public performance spaces). They are thus often consciously set in relation to established theatre conventions and horizons of expectation. For example, when Theatre of Real People foregrounds contemporary people and self-representational materials associated with them, it frequently does so in a way that plays with expectations that theatre will present characters in a form of drama.

With regard to the term 'reality theatre', in addition to its use as a label for experimental relatives of documentary performance, it has also been used to designate, for example, ethnographic drama and performance (Saldaña 2005), and the public enactment of prior therapy sessions by a real client and his or her psychologist (Lerner website). In this book, we categorize these various forms of reality theatre as strands of the overarching mode of performance we call Theatre of Real People. While in past publications we ourselves have used the term 'Reality Theatre' to refer to both the mode and the experimental theatre strand, we now use 'Theatre of Real People' to better distinguish the mode from its various manifestations.

The Theatre of Real People mode is characterized by: (1) a focus on representing or literally putting contemporary real people on stage; (2) an interest in extending public understanding of these individuals and their social environments; and (3) the utilization of what we call 'Authenticity-Effects'. These effects, discussed in detail in Chapter 3, are, on the one hand, theatre techniques and modes of representation, and, on the other, the resulting perceptual experiences. The techniques are characterized by their capacity to generate, and sometimes also to destabilize, a *sense* of one or more of the following: the sincere and genuine; referential truthfulness and veracity; and unmediated and intimate contact with people. As we also discuss in Chapter 3, our conceptualization of Authenticity-Effects both relates to and diverges from Roland Barthes' concept of the reality effect as well as Bertolt Brecht's *Verfremdungseffekt* (defamiliarization or distantiation effects).

At various points in this book, especially Chapter 1, we interpret Theatre of Real People's emphasis on Authenticity-Effects as partly a response to a society impacted by industrialization and the increased levels and types of mediation it has made possible through new communication and representation technologies; and a society that is now mediatized in the sense that it is permeated by the products of mass media or media and information technology (Auslander 2008: 4–5). In Chapter 3 in particular, we present this emphasis as complex, encompassing both idealizing assertions of sincerity, facticity, and unmediated access to original speech and bodies, as well as more philosophically sceptical and destabilizing oscillations between, or simultaneous combinations of, a *sense* of the authentic and inauthentic. Following Susanne Knaller and Harro Müller (2005) and Julia Straub (2012), we endorse the idea, one sometimes overtly expressed in these more sceptical manoeuvres, that the authentic is not a given and stable entity, but rather the product of framing practices, and of a contract between performers and spectators that has to be renewed for each 'authenticating act' (Garde 2011).

In the case of experimental Theatre of Real People from the HAU, we demonstrate that it is often characterized by a playful use of Authenticity-Effects that destabilizes perceptions relevant to our encounter with the familiar and unfamiliar. In particular, this approach to authenticity can destabilize a sense of how the people and events being experienced are connected to reality, representation, and fiction (Lehmann 2006: 99–104). Elsewhere, we have argued that such destabilization ruptures the fictional cosmos and coherent self-contained reality typical of dramatic representation and that it can, therefore, be regarded as manifesting a usage of theatrical signifiers typical of postdramatic theatre (Garde and Mumford 2013: 148). Some commentators, Frank M. Raddatz in particular, have presented German Theatre of Real People productions, and what he refers to as 'Theatre of the Authentic' (Das Theater des Authentischen), as synonymous with postdramatic theatre (Raddatz 2010: 139, 159), and therefore as a major contributor to a supposed reduction in the literariness of theatre. We, by contrast, view our case studies as working in idiosyncratic ways with various practices and traditions, including both the dramatic and postdramatic and agree with Johannes Birgfeld (2015) that literariness can exist in both postdramatic and Theatre of Real People forms.

Authenticity-Effects and the unfamiliar

Just as the use of Authenticity-Effects and diverse real people can be read as responses to the proliferation of forms of mediation and mediatization, they also can be viewed as responses to the intensified voluntary and forced mobility of people – both geographical and social – resulting from the manifold impacts of globalization. In his discussion of the emergence of 'the problem of authenticity, of naming "the real thing"' in mid-nineteenth-century America, Miles Orvell explicitly links the idea of authenticity with increases in forms of social complexity and mobility:

> One might imagine that the concept of authenticity begins in any society when the possibility of fraud arises, and that fraud is at least possible whenever transactions – whether social, political, commercial, or aesthetic – routinely occur, especially when the society becomes so large that one usually deals with strangers, not neighbours. (Orvell 1989: xvii)

The relationship between the concern with authenticity and increased contact with strangers – including people marked by occupational, class, and ethnic difference – may be one reason why Theatre of Real People has frequently been characterized by an attentiveness to culturally unfamiliar people and theatre strangers.

Just as Theatre of Real People and the critics who experience it can make apparent the way authenticity is the product of framing and construction rather than a given and stable entity, we argue that it also can demonstrate effectively that what is regarded as familiar and unfamiliar within and between cultures and subjects, is not a stable, fixed entity, but rather the result of processes of mutual positioning during encounters (Gutjahr 2010: 26). Having the capacity to disrupt perceptions that fix strangers in oppressive ways seems all the more important in the context of a globalized world, where everyday life, especially in urban contexts, is marked by constant interaction with complex, fluid, and unfamiliar cultural identities. The people who are perceived as unfamiliar, in this broad sense, we often refer to as 'strangers'. That is, we put 'strangers' forward as a synonym for 'unfamiliars' in order to avoid this unwieldy neologism, and to denote phenomena that have the potential to become better known.

In many performances that put contemporary strangers on the stage, techniques that destabilize our sense of the nature of what is before us invite audiences to reflect critically on their ascriptions of the categories of familiar and unfamiliar. Therefore, this book is guided by the following three hypotheses. First, while many types of Authenticity-Effect have the potential to open up new ways of encountering the unfamiliar and viewing cultural difference, they are more likely to do so when they serve to destabilize our sense of what is authentic and staged, familiar and unfamiliar. Second, they are also more likely to be effective if guided by a careful attention to the nature and effects of proximity to and distance from strangers. And third, that any analysis of engagement with the authentic and/or (un)familiar through theatre must consider the expectations and pre-knowledge of the individual participants – including artists, real-people performers, and audience members. These expectations are shaped by schemata, which are in turn influenced by local (theatre) histories, collective and personal memories.

A new approach to Theatre of Real People and its social engagement

Our interest in Theatre of Real People's artistic approach to the unfamiliar at the HAU offers a unique response to the issue of that mode's capacities and strategies for social engagement. To date, research into related theatre forms and the issue of staging authenticity and real people, particularly in today's context, has considered, for example: the cultural reasons for and/or socio-political goals of prevalent and new genres (Brown 2010; Paget 2007, 2009; Tiedemann and Raddatz 2007, 2010; Wake 2013a); the politics of company organization and working methods (Dreysse and Malzacher 2007; Mumford 2011); the impact of and responses to recent media culture and/or capitalist spectacle (Diederichsen 2012; Hammond and Steward 2008; Irmer 2006; Weiler 2006); the self-conscious acknowledgment of the performative nature of the everyday, complexity of reality, and staged nature of authenticity (Bottoms 2006; Fischer-Lichte 2008; Fischer-Lichte, Horn, Pflug and Warstat 2007; Forsyth and Megson 2009); the aesthetics, ethics, and labour politics of art that uses non-professional performers as its medium (Bishop 2012; Karschnia 2007a; Keim 2010); the way in which theatre of the real participates in how we come to understand our personal, social, and political lives (Martin 2013); and historical and philosophical shifts in the way the relationship between theatre and the real has been understood and practised, particularly in Western theatre from 1990 to 2010 (Tomlin 2013).

One of the springboards for our fresh approach to Theatre of Real People's transformative capacities has been Derek Paget's observation that new hybrid forms of docudrama are emerging that 'challenge audiences to adjust their views of fundamental ways of making sense of the world, of organizing knowledges of self and other/self and the external world' (Paget 2007: 172). This book supplements the investigations of Paget and other performance scholars, including the aforementioned, through its consideration of the ways in which Theatre of Real People is mobilizing Authenticity-Effects in order to challenge normative modes of encountering strangers (Garde 2013a; Garde and Mumford 2013). It also considers this approach to performance in the context of the HAU under Lilienthal, an institution that was a major driver for 'a different notion of aesthetic and social diversity in [German] theatre' (Weiler 2015: 224).

Recent insights into the 'intercultural condition' of current societies (Terkessidis 2010), as well as forms of multiple belongings (Şenocak 2011), inform this book's investigation of how Theatre of Real People is addressing the complex nature of cultural identities and intercultural encounters. Our attention to complexity on stage goes beyond an earlier approach in Intercultural Theatre Studies (such as that of Pavis 1992) that has been criticized for focusing on foreign theatres and cultures rather than on intercultural interaction. Instead, we respond to the still-pertinent call in the German journal *Theater heute* to develop new criteria for intercultural work (Mündel and Mackert 2010: 43) by supporting the ongoing discussion of such criteria by ventures such as the Berlin-based Interweaving Cultures Project (Fischer-Lichte 2014). We do so by analysing how a theatre with a renewed interest in depicting real people can engage with and possibly shape our changing sense of identity and habits of intercultural interaction.

Conceptual frameworks and methods

This book investigates the use of Authenticity-Effects in Theatre of Real People by focusing on the presentation and reception of performers and texts, and their theatre production and social contexts, in post-millennial Berlin. Our analysis of performers and their relations with the unfamiliar applies, for example, poststructuralist theory with regard to authentic speech and presence, and feminist scholarship into encounter, in order to consider how performances unsettle notions of the unfamiliar other as a fixed entity. Our analysis of the way audiences engage with Theatre of Real People protagonists and their narratives is informed by theory derived from reception studies and the cognitive sciences. This theoretical framework enables an analysis of how spectators co-author performances and generate a sense of the sincere, genuine, truthful, actual, unmediated, and/or intimate.

Our analysis is also informed by our shared expertise in past and contemporary artistic endeavours to combine innovative aesthetic approaches on stage with a clear commitment to socio-political engagement. Since the mid-twentieth century, discussion about how social reality can be staged so that fresh ways of engaging with the status quo are generated has been especially influenced by the legacy of Bertolt Brecht. According to Brecht, literally mimetic art was incapable of mastering and transforming social reality. Successors have claimed that realist mimetic drama is often limited in its ability to 'question and destabilize the spectator's construction of identity and the "other"' (Jürs-Munby, in Lehmann 2006: 5). Brecht advocated that the defamiliarization of blindingly familiar and oppressive social phenomena could be achieved through a combination of literal mimesis and distantiating artistry (Mumford 2001). His *Verfremdungseffekte* were informed by the belief that causal laws underpinned reality and that these could be known and managed via Marxist modes of analysis (Mumford 2000). More recently, discussions about the nature of postdramatic theatre have reignited the debate about how performance can change audience perception (Deck and Sieburg 2008; Fischer-Lichte 2006; Lehmann 2006; Roselt 2008; Stegemann, in Raddatz 2014a). In this debate, the Brechtian model, which assumes that social contradictions can (in theory) be resolved, and that the ever-changing world is governed by deducible and constant social laws, has been challenged by the insight that, in contemporary performance, changes of perception are not guided by a stable understanding of social reality.

In the following chapters, we analyse in detail seven theatre productions, many of which sit within the context of three key performance formats: *100% City*, *X-Apartments*, and *Blackmarket*. In general, our production analysis focuses on artistic and social contexts, format and dramaturgical concepts, performances, and audience reception. It investigates approaches to: casting and modes of performance; the choice and presentation of various types of written and spoken text, including elements such as literary devices and foreign language; managing authorship and editing; exploring the roles and physical positioning of performers and spectators, as well as relationships between observer and observed; and the organization of time, space, and location. It also takes into account the seminal role played by audiences in creating a sense of being in the presence of real people through a complex engagement with the multiple strands of authenticity.

Objects and structure of the analysis

Since its inception, the HAU has curated and produced a vast number and diverse array of productions and events (Behrendt 2012; Wille 2012). We, however, focus only on those experimental Theatre of Real People works that literally place what seem to be contemporary non-professional theatre performers on some form of stage, and that incorporate subjects (for example, polycultural city-dwellers, (post) migrants and their witnesses) who manifest the intercultural condition of our globalized world. In cases such as the *Blackmarket* format, the real-people performers consist not only of the experts cast by Mobile Academy, but also those audience members who become dialogue partners. While audience members often become a form of real people in contemporary performance when they are invited to physically participate, particularly in participatory art, this book concentrates on theatre in which pre-prepared real-people performers play a key role. The focus on work that seems to foreground pre-cast real people enables an in-depth investigation of our chosen mode of performance. However, such a focus also necessarily entails exclusions. For example, we do not pay close attention to acclaimed works featured at the HAU that engaged with the subjects and encounters of a culturally diverse world but which did not employ the Authenticity-Effect of a 'theatre stranger' – as is the case with the documentary work of Werner Kroesinger or the semi-documentary works by Nurkan Epulat, Tamer Yiğit, and Feridan Zaimoglu.[2] Furthermore, while we acknowledge the relevant contributions of practitioners such as Constanza Macras in the fields of dance and physical theatre, their work requires forms of analysis that are beyond the scope of this book's focus on theatre that foregrounds spoken text.

This book considers works that usually do not foreground the stranger as the exotic outsider, except when it comes to their status as inexperienced theatre performers. Instead, it predominantly features diverse people who appear culturally unfamiliar due to a variety of factors, including socio-economic status and different lived experiences.

It thereby looks to extend Intercultural Theatre Studies beyond a focus on migrant and foreign theatres. At the same time, it makes a contribution to our capacity more broadly to understand and respond effectively to a world where interaction with complex unfamiliar identities has become part of everyday life. This negotiation is crucial in the national German, transnational European, and global context where 'human mobility [continues to represent] one of the most complex issues facing the world today' (UN Human Development Report 2009).

Our unfolding of concepts and findings is organized into two interrelated sections. The first section, which comprises the opening four chapters, provides contextual information and theoretical frameworks. The second section and remaining chapters feature analyses of individual case studies. The opening chapter of the first section provides the reader with a history of Theatre of Real People in Western theatre, a history that illuminates both the mode of performance itself and the broader context that informed its post-millennial explosion at the HAU. When addressing causal factors, manifestations, and implications of the mode within German theatre and beyond, the chapter foregrounds how it has been characterized by an engagement with social reality. More particularly, it draws attention to how that engagement has been marked by two parallel and often overlapping concerns: first, cultures (both on- and off-stage) of imitation, illusion, artifice and spin, and counter-cultural forms of (play with) authenticity; and second, the representation of diverse culturally unfamiliar people. Chapter 2 introduces the artistic and institutional impulses, principles, and initiatives that underpinned the Theatre of Real People at the HAU under Lilienthal. These include a realist credo and commitment to engaging with contemporary society and pressing social issues, and a model of a 'city district theatre' (Stadtteiltheater) that worked with culturally diverse artists, real people, participants, and locations. It also introduces relevant formats, theatre-makers, productions, and genres fostered or featured at the HAU.

Chapters 3 and 4 unfold the conceptual and contextual terrain with regard to our exploration of authenticity and the unfamiliar. The focus of the former is authenticity discourse in contemporary Western theatre, in particular the paradoxical concept and stage phenomenon of Authenticity-Effects. This chapter introduces prevalent types of such effects, and focuses on what we refer to as 'idealizing' and 'sceptical' (or 'destabilizing') approaches to authenticity. It also establishes our interest in the sceptical approach to Authenticity-Effects, considers its potential to generate productive forms of uncertainty about the nature of people, actions, and artistic representations, and briefly compares Authenticity-Effects with Barthes' reality effect and Brecht's *Verfremdungseffekte*. Chapter 4 investigates the openness of the HAU under Lilienthal to the unfamiliar, to cultural diversity and complexity, and to exchange. It begins with a clarification of our use of key terms such as 'unfamiliar', 'diverse', 'culture', 'transcultural', and 'intercultural', and of two forms of cultural encounter: in the first, what is unfamiliar has the potential to become better known, both within one's own culture and beyond; and in the second, something thought to be well known loses its sense of familiarity. We then proceed to outline some key features of the HAU's approach to cultural identity and migration, and new approach to intercultural theatre. This chapter also explores authenticating behaviour and its tendency to obscure the complexity of difference, and raises the issue of the potential and pitfalls of Authenticity-Effects for challenging habits of perception and cognitive schemas concerning the familiar and unfamiliar.

Chapters 5–8 apply our conceptual framework to a range of case studies. Chapters 5 and 6 focus on *100% City* and *X-Apartments*, typical and successful production formats at the HAU that continued to be adapted and performed after Lilienthal moved on in 2012. In Chapter 5 the analysis of *100% City*, subtitled *A Statistical Chain Reaction* (*Eine statistische Kettenreaktion*), compares two of the format's incarnations, the first production in the series, *100% Berlin* (2008), and its evolution, as exemplified by *100% Melbourne* (2012), an Australian adaptation that occurred towards the end of Lilienthal's directorship. The chapter demonstrates how Rimini Protokoll developed the original show, which showcased Berlin's diverse population in an inclusive and cheerful atmosphere, into *100% Melbourne* – and other iterations of the format – which used a sceptical approach to Authenticity-Effects in order to destabilize spectators' expectations of seemingly familiar home towns around the world. While both incarnations of *100% City* worked with referential truth and a sense of personal authenticity, the Australian version destabilized audiences' impressions of the statistical 'truths' presented to them in a more complex way. The Authenticity-Effects also became a stronger component of the individual presentations on stage, particularly of the short narrative segments interspersed throughout the evening, resulting in a more diversified concept of personal identity.

Like *100% City*, *X-Apartments* exemplifies the HAU's typical engagement with the cultural complexity of Berlin and the frequently playful approach towards Authenticity-Effects that marked many productions under Lilienthal's leadership. Chapter 6 engages with several of the brief five- to ten-minute performances that artists, film and theatre directors, and professional and non-professional theatre performers developed in a number of private flats located in Kreuzberg and Lichtenberg for the 2004 version of *X-Apartments*. Using Ayşe Polat's production as a case study, the chapter illustrates how playing with frames of reference and cognitive scripts invite audience-participants to confront their cultural stereotypes and to change their ways of seeing a particular Berlin district and its residents. By taking into consideration the format's premiere in 2002 in Duisburg – part of the Theatre of the World Festival – and its adaptation to the Berlin district of Neukölln in 2008, the chapter provides an insight into how Lilienthal, his dramaturge Arved Schultze, and some of the other artists engaged with the issue of voyeurism. This issue represents a challenge inherent in a format that foregrounds the 'private' encounter of small audiences with local residents, and/or people whose status as professional performers remains unclear.

Like the case studies analysed in Chapters 5 and 6, Rimini Protokoll's *Call Cutta: Mobile Phone Theatre* (*Call Cutta. Mobiles Telefontheater*), examined in Chapter 7, also exposes audiences to moments of uncertainty, by both delivering and undermining a sense of authentic contact with the real people featured in the performances. However, it differs from the previous case studies in that it enables an intensive one-on-one encounter, with participants spending about an hour talking on the phone to an unfamiliar person situated in an Indian call centre, who acts as his or her personal guide and directs the participant on a city tour through the lesser-known areas of the district surrounding the HAU. The analysis focuses on the second and final version of this theatre *parcours* in Berlin (2005), showing how this journey through the district of Kreuzberg offered a complex engagement with the unfamiliar by disturbing any notion of authenticity, and carefully interweaving notions of the unfamiliar both beyond and within the borders of culture perceived as one's own. The chapter also addresses issues that arise from the ambiguous status of the call-centre performers due to the performance's reliance on a dissimulation game that is part of both their globalized professional life, and of their performance in Rimini Protokoll's project.

The final case-study chapter offers an analysis of two productions, which, through their focus on the subjects and subject matter of migration and other forms of human mobility, invited encounter with people and/or their expertise that are foreign or insufficiently familiar due to cultural differences and geographical locations. The first production is the seventh *Blackmarket* event, subtitled *Routes and Sites of Mobility Pioneers and Functionaries* (*Routen und Orte der Mobilitätspioniere und funktionäre*), that Mobile Academy presented at the HAU in 2007. The second is Rimini Protokoll's *Mr Dağaçar and the Golden Tectonics of Trash* (*Herr Dağaçar und die goldene Tektonik des Mülls*, 2010–), a production that foregrounded rubbish recyclers of Kurdish and Greek Gypsy background who had travelled from various parts of Turkey to Istanbul in search of work. Co-produced by the HAU, the show premiered in Istanbul and Essen and then toured to HAU2 in 2011. Drawing on Sarah Ahmed's theorization of ethical communication as involving an attempt to get closer to the other while simultaneously acknowledging the other as beyond one's grasp (Ahmed 2000: 139, 148, 157), this chapter draws attention to the way both productions offered only partial proximity for audience members to unfamiliar people and invisible knowledges. That is, the access provided by the productions was openly incomplete, flawed or subjective, biased and mediated. Such partial proximity was invited through the interweaving of Authenticity-Effects with both destabilizations of a sense of the genuine and unmediated, *and* overt artistry, an interweaving that has the capacity to challenge the masterful gaze that is potentially desired by both theatre artists and spectators.

In the conclusion, we provide our findings with regard to the key questions raised by our study: how and when can creating a sense of the authentic in the theatre invite fresh ways of engaging with the culturally unfamiliar, including the unfamiliar within one's own supposedly familiar culture, city, neighbourhood or self? And how did Theatre of Real People at the HAU mobilize Authenticity-Effects in ways that invite modes of relating to the unfamiliar that avoid clichés, voyeurism or authoritarian hierarchical social relations, and instead encourage understanding of complexity and ungraspability? We locate these conclusions within the ongoing debate regarding the future of the reality trend, especially its postdramatic manifestations, both within Germany and beyond.

Notes

1   Unless otherwise indicated, all translations from the German quoted in this book are our own. In the case of our translations, we provide the original in brackets.

2   Throughout this book we endeavour to use the original spelling of names, complete with diacritics, whenever it is frequently used in a person's artistic work or academic publications. Like Tom Cheesman and Karin Yeşilada, we believe that diacritics express the recognition 'of cultural difference'. However, we are aware that Zaimoglu 'seeks the status of a German without alien diacritics', so have spelled his name accordingly (Cheesman and Yeşilada 2012: 3–4).

1

A Historical Perspective on Theatre of Real People

Since the 1990s, there has been a marked rise in the cultural prominence of performance that foregrounds the texts, voices, and/or bodies of 'real people' and the 'facts' of their lives and social reality – that is, in theatre that focuses on non-professional and self-representing theatre performers as both its material and subject matter. In Western performance, the literal incorporation of non-trained performers or their texts is not a new phenomenon. However, it was not until the early twentieth century that their involvement in professional theatre as consensual self-representing figures began to gain momentum. In this chapter, we offer a history of Theatre of Real People, a mode of performance that focuses on non-fictional contemporary people, extends public understanding of these individuals and their social worlds, and uses techniques and modes of representation that we call 'Authenticity-Effects'. We define these effects as both the artistic strategies that generate and/or destabilize a sense of contact with the sincere, truthful, unmediated, and intimate, and as the perceptual experiences arising from such techniques and representations.

The following history unfolds some of the main reasons for the emergence of the mode as well as its varied manifestations and political implications, and its particular prominence over the last two decades. It is a mapping that confines itself, for the most part, to developments in theatre performance rather than in related media such as film, radio, and television. Through drawing attention to the appearance and functions of this mode within Western theatre in general and German theatre in particular, it seeks to illuminate not only Theatre of Real People and its operations across diverse genres, but also the context that informed the Hebbel am Ufer (HAU) practitioners and productions featured in this book. This history draws upon scholarship into the histories of related theatre phenomena, such as autobiographical theatre (Heddon 2008), (German) documentary theatre (Barton 1987; Favorini 1994a; Irmer 2006), participatory art including delegated performance (Bishop 2012), theatre of the real (Martin 2013), and verbatim theatre (Garde et al. 2010; Paget 1987, 2007; Wake 2013a). However, it extends this scholarship through its focus on plotting developments in Western theatre's incorporation of what we term 'real people'. Moreover, it attends to how these developments often have been characterized by a concern with not only theatre's relation to social reality – including what some would regard as the reality of capitalist spectacle – but more particularly with its relation to cultures of imitation, illusion, artifice, and spin, a relation often played out through a counter-culture of authenticity. And finally, it demonstrates that a concern with authenticity has not only pervaded historical developments in the Theatre of Real People mode, but has also been paralleled by a concern with theatre's representation of diverse socially marginalized and culturally unfamiliar people.

In the broader realm of performance, there are many historical precedents for the involvement of non-professional performers in staged events. In a number of cases, the involvement of the participants was non-voluntary, or involved a degree of exploitation. Such precedents include the gladiatorial games of ancient Rome, the various forms of freak show that first became popular during the European Renaissance, and the ethnographic displays that became prominent in the nineteenth century and continued well into the twentieth century that featured the imperialist exhibition of live humans in 'authentic' settings within museums and world fairs. Higher levels of voluntary and self-determining participation were more evident in forms such as the popular culture entertainments of the early twentieth century, including the American dance marathons and roller derbies of the 1930s that Carol Martin includes in her account of antecedents for today's theatre of the real (2013: 12–13). We position Theatre of Real People as a subset of the latter, which Martin has defined as a diverse field that encompasses 'a wide range of theatre practices and styles that recycle reality, whether that reality is personal, social, political, or historical' (2013: 5).

In the realm of European theatre, recorded instances of using non-professional performers date back to, for example, medieval mystery plays, which on occasion featured the brutal practice of casting a real criminal as Christ and then crucifying and killing him during the performance (Favorini 1994a: xiv). Since the early nineteenth century, a variety of forms of dramatic theatre have existed in which contemporary people and their lives are represented in a literally mimetic or quasi-documentary way, though usually through characters and actors rather than non-trained self-representing performers. These forms include forerunners of the docudrama such as Georg Büchner's plays *Danton's Death* (1835) and *Woyzeck* (1836–37), and the Naturalist theatre that featured contemporary characters whose language, clothing, comportment, and environment reproduced that of real contemporary people (Garde, Mumford and Wake 2010: 9–11). One of the forces that shaped the emergence of dramatic theatre dedicated to the recycling of contemporary reality was the advent of new technologies for observing, archiving, and communicating, including the printing press, photography, phonographic recordings, and film.

First wave: socially useful art and cultures of authenticity

The first wave in the practice of using voluntary and sometimes self-representing non-professional performers intersected with, and was partly driven by, the surge in European political and documentary theatre in the early twentieth century. As part of their response to the social turmoil brought about through modernization, political instability, and war, German theatre-makers Piscator and Brecht both experimented with socialist-inspired theatre that incorporated amateur performers. In his groundbreaking version of documentary theatre, Piscator spearheaded the incorporation of photos, newsreels, and other forms of footage of contemporary people and events into live performance, as well as using amateur actors. In the late 1920s, Brecht and his collaborators introduced the Learning Plays (*Lehrstücke*), which, although they could be and were performed by professional actors, were conceived as educational vehicles to be fully or partly performed by participants such as radio listeners or school children. Brecht declared these experiments to be 'art for the producer, not art for the consumer' (Brecht 2015: 123).

In most cases, the non-professional performers involved in Piscator and Brecht's experiments presented historical or imagined characters rather than their own lives and expertise. Instead of delivering self-devised, fully or partially autobiographical narratives, the text they delivered was authored typically by, for example, theatre-makers, journalists or historical figures. However, on occasion Piscator included performers with minimal theatre training whose personal life experience was similar to that of the character(s) they portrayed. For example, the two-hundred-member cast he used for the political revue *In Spite of Everything!* (*Trotz alledem!*, 1925), and which was tasked with portraying characters from recent post-war history such as citizens of Berlin and proletarians, included Berlin-based members of proletarian choirs and sports clubs as well as members of the Red Front action committee (Favorini 1994b: 1). In the production of *The Kaiser's Coolies* (*Des Kaisers Kulis*, 1930), Piscator cast the author of the playscript, Theodor Plivier, to play the First World War sailor Köbis, whose first-hand naval experience apparently did not quite make up for his lack of acting skills (Willett 1986: 103). Some of Piscator's productions also integrated moments when expository material was delivered by people with relevant expertise rather than professional actors, such as the short lecture given by the journalist and economist Alfons Goldschmidt in *Tai Yang Awakens* (*Tai Yang Erwacht*, 1931) (Willett 1986: 103–6). Such instances have much in common with the experts of the everyday showcased on stage at the HAU, particularly in the work of Rimini Protokoll.

One of the goals that informed both Piscator and Brecht's work with amateurs, and that of other post-war artists in the 1920s who were similarly interested in social utility, was to create opportunities for the participation of the working class and other culturally marginalized groups in the production of art, social and scientific knowledge, class consciousness, and collective action (Brecht 1991: 91; Piscator 1980: 46). These approaches to amateur performers were also to be found among the numerous Agitprop, Living Newspaper, and workers' theatres that proliferated during the interwar period, and sought to inform and mobilize audiences about pressing social issues. Notable theatres included the Proletkult and Blue Blouse Soviet Living Newspaper (1923–27) of Russia. The latter was a touring amateur troupe that provided revue-style stagings of news, topical issues, and revolutionary propaganda that were designed to inform illiterate comrades in particular. The troupe had widespread success and spawned numerous similar groups across Europe, North America, and Japan (Casson 2000: 108–12). However, while these groups engaged with contemporary people and aspects of amateur performance, they required forms of training and multiple skills similar to those of professional actors and did not centralize self-representing protagonists. Another format of the interwar period that contained some features of the Theatre of Real People mode was the reworking or re-enactment of recent events through mass spectacles. In the Russian Futurist re-enactment in 1918 of the storming of the Winter Palace in 1917, a real battalion demonstrated their expertise and equipment, as did the thousands who put their personal life experiences to good use in their roles as Petrograd citizens. The same event was dramatized by theatre director Nikolai Evreinov in 1920, and he reportedly sought out people who had been involved in the historical event and used them in the performance (Bishop 2012: 57–9).

The period in which the first surge in characteristic features of Theatre of Real People occurred has also been associated with the emergence of a culture of authenticity. In his mapping of a shift within American arts and material culture that began in the 1890s, Miles Orvell identifies a movement away from a culture that valorized the arts of imitation, illusion, and replication – and a culture that had faith in the power of the machine to create credible simulacra. The new culture of authenticity that gradually emerged, without necessarily fully replacing the old one, both established a modernist aesthetic vocabulary, and attempted to get beyond the manufacturing of illusions to restore contact with 'the real thing' – or, better still, to make contact with *new* real things (Orvell 1989: xi–xv). Aspects of Piscator and Brecht's work – particularly anti-illusionist strategies such as Piscator's integration of expository material delivered by non-actors, and Brecht's interest in revealing the actor-cum-social-demonstrator behind the character – can be read as also participating in a culture of authenticity in so far as they both, in different ways, pursued a desire to restore contact with the real thing. Piscator's case in particular displays the kind of complex relationship with technologies of imitation that is often to be found in Theatre of Real People, one that involves both appropriation (in his case through the use of slides and film) and challenge through the casting of performers who do not imitate another person (like many amateur and professional actors), but who present an aspect of their own expertise.

Many other modernist or *avant-garde* artists and theatre practitioners who have provided legacies for contemporary Theatre of Real People, including Dadaist-influenced Duchamp and Artaud, can also be regarded as contributors to a culture of authenticity. Duchamp's ready-made pieces, framing real manufactured objects as works that could possibly be art – like the infamous placement of a porcelain urinal in a piece called *Fountain* (1917) in the first Society of Independent Artists exhibition in New York – are a practice often raised in discussions of the way non-actors are framed in Theatre of Real People (Lehmann 2008: 157; Metzger 2010: 340). For Artaud, like Brecht, the real was to be located beyond bourgeois illusion, but in his case it lay in a mystical experience that was more 'authentic than the constructed social reality of the time' (Tomlin 2013: 20) and which could be accessed via a body and voice beyond representation and repetition. Artaud's vision has contributed to the development of numerous ways of performing that eschew imitation of the emotional and physical states of a character in favour of a performer who *lives* before the audience rather than acting, a state of being that non-trained performers are in certain respects well equipped to deliver.

Second wave: counter-culture and theatricalization of everyday life

The second surge in the practice of putting voluntary non-professional performers on stage in Western theatre, and in engaging with authentic performance and experience, occurred in the 1960s and was, in a number of locations, characterized by an increased emphasis on collective theatre-making, self-representation, cultural diversity, and the blurring of boundaries between art and life. Again this surge coincided with a wave of German documentary theatre born out of the social crises connected with the effects of world war. Brian Barton attributes the wave (c. 1963–70) to an understanding that the socio-political questions of the day were felt to be too pressing and overwhelming to be addressed through fictional actions or characters. Therefore, artistic truth had to be authenticated through concrete documentary evidence (Barton 1987: 2). This theatre was spearheaded by the dramatists Rolf Hochhuth, Heinar Kipphardt, and Peter Weiss, who themselves were inspired by (and enlisted) directors such as Piscator. Characterized by dramas about historical events within living memory such as the Holocaust, the Frankfurt Auschwitz Trials, and J. Robert Oppenheimer's opposition to the creation of the hydrogen bomb, this theatre presented recent or living people through methods such as slides, tapes, and film clips. Although these dramas drew on primary witness reports and transcripts of official trials and hearings, they did not simply reproduce historical figures and their texts, often working instead with devised characters and crafted language such as dramatic monologues and verse (Garde et al. 2010: 13). Unlike much contemporary Theatre of Real People, these playtexts and productions did not foreground the staging of the live bodies of the recent and contemporary protagonists upon which they were based. Rather, they were typical of much documentary theatre, which, as Carol Martin has observed, is more often than not where '"real people" are absent – unavailable, dead, disappeared – yet reenacted' (2006: 9).

In Britain in the 1970s, a similar surge in socially engaged forms with Theatre of Real People characteristics occurred – including documentary and community theatre – though in this case they were precipitated less by the repercussions of war and more by Marxist-inspired and counter-cultural responses to the capitalist status quo. New tendencies in the documentary form included the appearance of traces of real people through verbatim techniques such as the presentation by actors of transcribed text from interviews, and the use of audio-recordings of the interviewees speaking themselves. Such techniques were greatly facilitated by the advent of the portable cassette recorder. They also aligned well with the political drive to transform hierarchical theatre structures, such as the subordination of actors to playwrights and directors, through more dialogue-based and collective methods of creating text (Paget 1987: 317–18). Interviews, often conducted by the performers who would present the interviewees, and other oral history methods also suited the goal of giving culturally and socially marginalized voices a public hearing. One significant contributor to the early development of what Derek Paget would later coin 'verbatim theatre' – a form of realist theatre that centralizes interviews with people, especially recorded vernacular speech – was Peter Cheeseman, with his oral history work and community documentaries in Stoke-on-Trent. Cheeseman's work at the Victoria Theatre included shows such as *Fight for Shelton Bar* (1974), a piece about a local steelworks and resistance to its closure, which featured an actor's portrayal of Ted Smith, a member of the Shelton Works Action Committee, giving way to a recording of Ted's own voice (Favorini 1994a: xxxii). Another contributor to the verbatim form was Joint Stock, which first worked closely with the techniques in *Yesterday's News* (1976), techniques that fitted with the company's emphasis on creating new plays through processes that brought writers, directors, performers, and other company members into collaboration. During his tenure as Artistic Director of the Royal Court Theatre in London, Joint Stock co-founder Max Stafford-Clark presided over well-received verbatim theatre productions such as the 1983 staging of Louise Page's *Falkland Sound/Voces de Malinas* (Hammond and Steward 2008: 46), a form of testimonial theatre based on the letters and poems of a young lieutenant killed in action during the Falklands War.

The period after the Second World War also saw the development of geographically diverse countercultural, radical, postcolonial, educational, and liberational theatres (van Erven 2001: 1) that encouraged the involvement of real people in collective and egalitarian theatre-making, and in the representation of voices marginalized in public discourse. These included community theatres that prioritized local and personal stories, sometimes presented by the authors and protagonists themselves, and the Forum Theatre of Brazilian artist-activist Augusto Boal that formed part of a national literacy project in Peru in 1973. In Forum Theatre, whose initial participants came from social groups with low levels of literacy, so-called 'spect-actors' are encouraged to intervene in the staging of a story about a social problem by stepping into an improvised or rehearsed scene, replacing any actor, and momentarily leading the action in what she or he regarded as the most appropriate direction for resolving an oppressive situation (Boal 1998: 139). This period also witnessed the emergence of the community arts movement in the UK, which Bishop describes as 'part of an international push across Europe and North America to democratize and facilitate lay creativity, and to increase accessibility to the arts for less privileged audiences' (2012: 163). One of the striking differences between these radical theatres and more recent experimental Theatre of Real People from Germany is the radical theatres' overtly declared (and often government-sponsored) agenda for a form of social change – be it political, therapeutic or pedagogic.

Such participatory theatre has much in common with the post-1968 public and art performance forms that Martin argues were symptomatic of a broader belief that participatory democracy could provide an antidote to the discontent of a generation (Martin 2013: 24). These forms, which included marches, sit-ins, draft-card burnings, strikes, rock festivals, concerts, and Happenings, were symptomatic of a growing theatricalization of public and private life: in many of these, non-professional theatre performers staged their own personal experiences and identities in a bid to advance social justice and consciousness, and to introduce transparency as a counter to opaque systems of power (2013: 22–3, 28, 57). The theatricalization of private life was also given significant impetus by the second-wave feminist movement of the 1960s whose influential slogan 'the personal is political' drew attention to the way the problems women experienced in everyday and domestic life were not simply personal but part of a (socio-economic) system of gender oppression. Supported and inspired by this feminist movement, female artists and many others who also viewed themselves as marginalized subjectivities, including lesbian, gay, black, and transgender people, used autobiographical performance to talk back to dominant representations of their subjectivities, and to engage with pressing matters such as equality, justice, citizenship, and human rights (Heddon 2008: 2–3, 20). In the USA, female artists working on the west coast in the late 1960s and early 1970s, such as Rachel Rosenthal and Carolee Schneemann, created explicitly autobiographical material. They were influenced by other artists of importance to Theatre of Real People developments, such as Piscator, Artaud, and a major proponent of Performance Art and Happenings, the American painter Allan Kaprow. Meanwhile in Britain, performance groups such as Women's Theatre Group and Gay Sweatshop emerged in the mid-1970s, utilizing autobiographical and interview material for script building. These companies also contributed to the supplementation or replacement of the actor by the performer as auto/biographical persona. For example, in Gay Sweatshop's *Mister X* (1975), which presented the writer-performers' experiences of moving from being fearful of their sexual identity to proudly open about it, the main actor abandoned his fictional role and declared his own name and address, and 'came out' as gay (Heddon 2008: 25).

Just as activist theatre often tested the separation of the political from the personal, it questioned the art-versus-everyday life distinction, a boundary vigorously explored in the period after the Second World War by many artists who engaged with new approaches to performing and spectatorship, often in order to critique the commodification of both art and existence. These approaches challenged the norms of professional acting, especially within dramatic or illusionist theatre, and invited participation from non-trained performers, often in ways that sought to redistribute the power to create and perform. In a consideration of the ways participatory art of this period engaged with everyday life, Bishop notes two distinct directions: 'one preserving the category of art, but expanding it to include transgressive activities; the other dissolving this category to make life itself more artistically fulfilling' through 'sublating life into a more intensely lived everyday life' (2012: 101). Bishop positions Happenings as typical of the first direction. Pioneered by Kaprow in the late 1950s, the Happenings were exhibition events that often involved a sequence of scenes staged in galleries, and later in mundane settings like streets and car parks, in which both artists and spectators carried out actions or tasks, many of them quotidian in nature. Happenings were part of Kaprow's bid for 'lifelike art' that can be created by anyone, anywhere, any time (Martin 2013: 27). Some Happenings were fully fledged Theatre of Real People forms, such as the event *To Induce the Spirit of the Image* (1966) by Argentinian artist Oscar Masotta, for which he hired twenty elderly men and women from the lower middle class to dress in the class beneath them, stand in a storage room before an audience, and be subjected to fire extinguishers and a harsh high-pitched sound and white light. The work's aggressive attitude towards its participants, an approach not commonly found in Happenings, was a harsh reflection of the types of social manipulation that Masotta believed occur in real society every day (Bishop 2012: 109–10).

In his influential essay 'On Acting and Non-Acting', Michael Kirby positions the Happenings as a significant reason for a shift in American art theatre during the 1970s and early 1980s away from complex acting and towards forms of non-matrixed performing (1984: 110–11). Kirby defines complex acting as characterized by, first, feigning, simulation, representation, and/or impersonation, and second by an emphasis on projecting something (particularly a psychic or emotional component) for the benefit of an audience (1984: 103–7). He argues that participants in Happenings, by contrast, operated a non-matrixed form of performing because they 'tended to "be" nobody or nothing other than themselves' and did not 'represent, or pretend to be in, a time or place different from that of the spectator' (1984: 98). That is, the performers in the Happenings like those in Theatre of Real People forms, were not deeply embedded in matrices of represented character, situation, place, and time (1984: 99). Such non-matrixed performing was a prominent feature of many experimental types of theatre from the post-war period that have contributed to the development of the Theatre of Real People mode. These include the durational live art pieces of Marina Abramovic and her fellow European collaborator Ullay (Uwe Laysiepen), whose work with non-matrixed actions that emphasize the 'here-and-now' of the performer's authentically enduring (and often suffering) body was, as we discuss in the next chapter, influential for a number of the HAU practitioners and their preference for performing rather than acting.

Other contributors to the Theatre of Real People mode include the large number of post-war artists who have programmatically expanded the category of art to incorporate mundane aspects of everyday life. Select examples include the international Fluxus network of artists inspired by the likes of Duchamp and John Cage, who have often opposed the artificialities of market-driven art by engaging with the banal and the everyday. Early experimenters with delegated performance include Oscar Bony and his *La Familia Obrera* (*The Worker's Family*, 1968), for which he paid a real Argentinian working-class family of three to sit on an exhibition plinth where they ate, read, talked, and similarly occupied themselves for eight hours a day, and theatre director Pi Lind and his 'sociological exhibition' *Living Sculptures* (1967). During the exhibition, a diverse group of twenty Swedish citizens were placed on plinths accompanied by text panels with information about each individual for nine hours over five days in Stockholm's Moderna Museet (Bishop 2012: 113–15). In the realm of dance, important contributors include the Judson Dance Theater artists based in New York City who worked with non-trained performers and dancers to explore 'ordinary' movement, and the dance theatre of Pina Bausch and her company Tanztheater Wuppertal, who worked with quasi-autobiographical processes and gestures and later also with teenage and elderly non-professional dance performers. Relevant American companies include The Living Theatre, the Open Theatre, and The Performance Group, as well as the artists trained in these theatres such as Spalding Gray and Elizabeth Lecompte, all of whom used autobiography in their processes and performances, as well as forms of non-matrixed performing (Martin 2013: 23, 45–58).

Examples of the second approach to the art-versus-life distinction that Bishop describes can be found in the work of Polish director Jerzy Grotowski, geared towards the dissolving of the art category. In his early experiments, Grotowski pursued an interest in transcending representation, initially through mentoring performers to move beyond psycho-social conditioning (including the rules and practices of actor training) in order to achieve a revelation and sharing of their authentic or true self behind their social mask during a performance (Grotowski 1976: 212–13). In the 1970s, he particularly sought to transcend representation and facilitate self-knowledge and communion with others by removing the boundary between performer and spectator. To this end, he instigated a 'paratheatrical' or 'active culture' phase, in which he moved away from theatre institutions to events that often unfolded in outdoor pastoral settings. Here his Laboratory Theatre members joined former spectators who became co-participants in 'work on the self' through meetings, encounters, and archaic or archetypal forms of dance, songs, and chants (Schechner and Wolford 1997: 207–12). While the case studies from the HAU explored in this book expand the category of art to include transgressive activities rather than dissolving it, and are more sceptical than Grotowski about the notion of an authentic self, they share an interest in challenging the conventions and artifice of dramatic and illusionist theatre representation, particularly complex acting.

Third wave: socio-economic crises, global mobility, and cultures of artifice

The upsurge of genres such as delegated, documentary, participatory, re-enactment, and verbatim performance since the early 1990s can be attributed to a number of causal factors relating to political turbulence, economic crisis, globalization, and the revolution in digital technology. These factors include events such as: the fall of the Iron Curtain within Europe in the late 1980s, and the concomitant rise in neoliberalism (Bishop 2012: 2–3; Raddatz 2010: 140); the attacks on the United States by the Islamic terrorist group al-Qaeda on 11 September 2001 and the ensuing counter-terrorist military campaign led by the USA, UK, and their allies (Edgar 2008; Paget 2009: 234–5); the Global Financial Crisis (Karschnia 2007a: 155); an increasingly intercultural world fed by unprecedented levels of voluntary and enforced global mobility, a phenomenon addressed by this book and its HAU case study productions; and last but by no means least, the escalation of new digital technologies and media forms since the 1970s, including the exponential growth of the internet in the early 1990s (Martin 2013: 5, 175). In the remainder of this chapter, we focus on how these factors shaped Theatre of Real People, and on the nature of its forms, genres, characteristics, and concerns during what we call its third wave.

Performance in the wake of 1989

In her mapping of a genealogy for participatory art, Bishop argues that its conspicuous resurgence in the 1990s was part of a marked and now near global 'artistic orientation towards the social', which, from a Western European perspective, can be contextualized as a response to the 'collapse of a collectivist vision of society' and to the 'dismantling of welfare state and other neoliberal reforms' (2012: 2–3, 193). Within German theatre, the fall of the wall and its social effects were overtly thematized in documentary works such as *Waiting Room Germany* (*Wartesaal Deutschland*, 1995), a play by Klaus Pohl that involved actors presenting semi-poetic monologues based on interviews with people from former East and West Germany dealing with reunification, and economic and personal crises (Irmer 2006: 24). In the documentary play *The Kick* (*Der Kick*, 2005) by Andres Veiel and Gesine Schmidt, the text draws on interview material to probe the reasons for the brutal murder of a youth in 2002 by three young neo-Nazi men in the East

German village of Putzlow. One of the causes addressed is the impact of the village's collapse after reunification, even if this event is ultimately not presented as the most significant factor (Dürr 2008). In 2004, the documentary performance-maker Roland Brus created an oral-history walking tour through an allotment garden in Berlin situated along a section of the wall that used to be in the East (Irmer 2006: 25; Kranz 2004). As audiences moved from station to station, they experienced stories and dialogues presented by the gardeners themselves about topics such as their everyday lives during the Cold War.

In the 1990s, Brus had worked with a different theatre of experts when he directed pieces by RATTEN 07, a company associated at that time with Berlin's Volksbühne, and one whose key performers are homeless people. Founded in 1992, this theatre group has presented productions that have been based on the performers' life experiences (RATTEN 07 website). The company was formed following a production of *Pest*, a Volksbühne production that dealt with the impact of reunification on individuals and featured both professional performers and homeless people. In the 1990s, the Volksbühne gained a reputation for its commitment to navigating East German identity and East/West frictions, and to addressing critically the capitalist future of a united Germany, a vision influenced in particular by director Frank Castorf and his chief dramaturge at the time, Matthias Lilienthal (Baecker, Lilienthal and Müller 2012: 11–12). *Pest* was directed by Jeremy Weller, whose British company, the Grassmarket Project, became renowned for its staging of people who had experienced social marginalization or trauma. Since its inception in 1989, the company has integrated non-professional performers (homeless youngsters, prison inmates, women with mental health issues, old-age pensioners, prostitutes, football hooligans, street gang members, soldiers) as co-devisers and semi-autobiographical performers (The Grassmarket Project website). In Germany, a related artistic and social agenda was pursued not only by Brus, who founded the theatre group AufBruch in Berlin's Tegel prison in 1997 and directed inmates in semi-autobiographical performances, but also by some of his collaborators including practitioner-scholar Gudrun Herrbold. Since the late 1990s, Herrbold has often brought diverse non-professional performers together – female prison inmates and law students, for example – or featured people involved in high-risk activities, such as aerial arts, boxing and other combat sports. Many of her projects have presented individuals who transgress social and physical norms, and explored their experiences of contradiction, intensity or extremity (Gudrun Herrbold website).

Claire Bishop has characterized the impact of 1989 on artistic production as less rapid than in previous waves of *avant-garde* work, due to what she calls the 'slow burn' nature of change in Western Europe since the fall of communism (2012: 193). The extended nature of the aftermath may explain why after more than two decades since the demise of communism in Europe, both observers and makers of Theatre of Real People continue to present the collapse of a collectivist vision as an important catalyst. At times, this catalyst has triggered opposing responses, including both a shift away from (Tiedemann 2007: 7) *and* a move further towards autobiographical and micropolitical narratives about concrete individuals. With regard to the latter, in a 2007 discussion of projects that exemplify the Theatre of Real People mode, theatre-maker Lukas Matthaei explained that, from his point of view, the big models that held weight across the twentieth century had not functioned since 1989, and that it was important now to turn instead to the realm of the concrete as the appropriate resource for finding the capacities to navigate our way out of dead ends (Karschnia 2007b: 175–7). In the same discussion, Matthaei referred to the production *On the Right Life 1* (*Vom richtigen Leben 1*, 2006), which presented, recorded, and staged portraits by and of individual Düsseldorf citizens, each of whom 'offered knowledge in the mastery of personal upheaval on the other side of the Capitalist promise' (matthaei-und-konsorten website). In a commentary on the attention given to individuals and their stories in Rimini Protokoll's theatre of experts, David Barnett interprets this attention as a response to 'an age in which the individual is overshadowed by larger formations', a response informed by the arguably problematic idea that specificity and particularity offer sufficient counterpoints to generalizing discourses (Barnett 2015: 106–7). The political implications of the recurrent emphasis on the individual within recent Theatre of Real People forms and contemporaneous genres such as Reality Television remain a debated issue. While the emphasis can serve to illuminate, for example, the way people exceed collective identity categories and demographic roles (Bishop 2012: 239; Kavka 2008: 39), it can also run the risk of spectacularizing personal particulars and reinforcing neoliberal versions of individualism (Dovey 2000: 22, 95, 103, 113). Indeed, the capacity of some Theatre of Real People forms to address systemic social problems is a recurrent issue for practitioners and scholars of performance that stages contemporary individuals (Mumford 2015: 292).

The resurgence during the 1990s and 2000s of an Anglo-American theatre that foregrounds real people, such as documentary theatre and verbatim drama, was also shaped by political crisis and cross-cultural theatre transmission processes. British actor and playwright Robin Soans has credited his experience of performing *Waiting Room Germany* in 1995 at the Royal Court in London as being a defining moment in his development as a verbatim dramatist (2008: 20–3). Soans is among a group of British theatre-makers – including director Max Stafford-Clark and his company Out of Joint, playwright David Hare, playwright and journalist Nicholas Richard Norton-Taylor, and director Nicholas Kent – who, since the mid-1990s, have used a variety of verbatim methods to present contemporary people's personal experiences of national and international issues. These included the emergence of an underclass in English housing estates, privatization of the railways, institutionalized racism, conflict in the Middle East, war crimes, and terrorism. A number of these practitioners have worked with the tribunal play genre, staging the verbatim testimony of often living witnesses in dramatized public enquiries. Like Werner Kroesinger, whose significant contribution to German documentary theatre since the mid-1990s is addressed in the next chapter, these practitioners have produced theatre that uses professional actors. However, in cases such as Hare's *Via Dolorosa* (1998), where Hare performed a monologue that drew on his own 1997 journey through Israel and Palestine, the real people themselves made an appearance.

As these practitioners and other commentators have observed, one reason for this surge in documentary and verbatim work within Britain and beyond has been a desire to remedy a perceived failure of print and media journalism in an age of political 'spin' and mass-media competition (Hare and Stafford-Clark 2008: 62–3; Reinelt 2009: 12; Soans 2008: 17). The inadequate mass-media representation of political events is one of many concerns addressed in new Theatre of Real People forms such as the re-enactment piece *The Battle of Orgreave: The English Civil War Part II* (2001), orchestrated by British artist Jeremy Deller. In this partial re-staging of a violent clash during the British miners' strike in 1984, Deller drew together over 800 participants from re-enactment societies as well as former miners and police officers from the original strike. One of the goals of the re-enactment was to provide a counternarrative to the historical television news reportage, which, by reverse editing the sequence of events, presented the impression that unruly miners rather than mounted police cavalry had initiated the riot (Bishop 2012: 34; Kitamura 2010).

Spin, scepticism, and socially engaged theatre

In considering the recent prominence of verbatim strategies, Liz Tomlin notes that the prevalence of documentary methods since the new millennium seems paradoxical 'amidst the culturally dominant scepticism of the real' (2013: 14). Recent scepticism in the Western world towards representations of the real by politicians and the mass media is partly related to disillusionment with both communist and capitalist systems, and with government responses to crisis and complexity. Paget describes contemporary politics as increasingly privileging 'the figure of the *witness* as the last best hope of opposition', and partly attributes the resurgence of documentary forms in such political contexts to a perception that 'the participant in a live event and the witness of events have special claims to being something to be trusted' (2009: 234–5). The scepticism Tomlin refers to is also philosophical and ideological, influenced by postmodern ideas stemming from systems of thought – such as historical relativism and poststructuralism – that have questioned the practice of totalizing metanarratives and the possibility of absolute truth, authenticity, and unmediated experience. This is a line of questioning we ourselves address in our presentation of an aesthetics of Authenticity-Effects in Chapter 3. As Tomlin points out, such scepticism can jeopardize a political commitment to representing and intervening in social reality precisely because it places all discourses about reality and all ideological commitments in doubt (2013: 14, 120).

Both Tomlin and Carol Martin demonstrate that recent theatre artists are attempting to reconcile the fruits of philosophical and postmodern scepticism with the promotion of agendas for social knowledge and change. For example, Martin observes that while theatre of the real's strategies in the twenty-first century have often been postmodern, including its acknowledgement 'that truth is contextual, multiple and subject to manipulation' (2010: 3), it has also asserted 'that there is something to be known in addition to a dizzying kaleidoscopic array of competing truths. Scepticism and irony are still present but no longer center stage' (2010: 4). Tomlin argues that while contemporary verbatim practice has often pursued a postmodern pluralist approach, providing a multiplicity of testimonies rather than insisting on the authority of one narrative or authorial voice, it has often ensured that the testimonies as a whole contest a dominant interpretation of the event (2013: 120). According to Tomlin, the current popularity of verbatim theatre is not only due to the presence of the witness figure and capacity to accommodate a pluralist approach, but also to criticism of the shortcomings of dramatic representation that have emerged from postdramatic, anti-colonialist, and feminist theory. Whereas Western dramatic theatre has often assumed the right of political playwrights (white male authors in particular) to represent the other, usually through fictionalized characters, verbatim practice seems to open up opportunities for others to speak for themselves (2013: 117).

Such practice is one Theatre of Real People form being used today by artists who wish to counter the partial and homogenizing nature of 'manufactured' media coverage by more multi-vocal and open-ended presentations of diverse perspectives (Anderson and Wilkinson 2007: 153–4).

Representing others in our intercultural condition

A recurrent strategy within contemporary Theatre of Real People for enabling the voices of multiple and diverse others, especially marginalized or culturally unfamiliar people, has been to expose, destabilize or replace the authority of the professional actor and character-based acting. This strategy is often informed by the need to address the politics of authorship and speech. In works such as *The Laramie Project* (2000), which examined the brutal murder of a young homosexual man in Wyoming two years earlier, New York-based Tectonic Theater Project drew on techniques, including role doubling, that help separate the real-life interviewees and the actors who present them. In many of their post-millennium documentary and tribunal productions about contemporary issues – such as government scandals and treatment of asylum seekers, media frenzies, and the war on terror – Sydney-based company version 1.0 took a slightly different approach to staging contemporary people. While their texts were also delivered by professional theatre-makers who showed their separateness from the people being represented, the performers tended to use less matrixed forms of performance than complex or character-based acting, and in ways that encouraged an inquisitive attitude towards seemingly authentic witnesses and seemingly truthful representations of their words and actions (Garde and Mumford 2013: 153–8). Such an approach has been a trademark feature of much contemporary documentary performance and playwriting, including the HAU case studies presented in this book.

In solo performance work dealing with interracial trauma in America during the early 1990s, *Fires in the Mirror* (1992) and *Twilight: Los Angeles 1992* (1993), Anna Deveare Smith created a type of mimicry of testimonials that also diverged from character-acting. Rather than using editing and interpretation techniques to turn a large body of culturally diverse interviewees into consistent characters authored by artists, she carefully imitated the vocal and physical mannerisms of the recorded subjects in a kind of 'verisimilar portraiture' (Favorini 1994a: xxxvii). Smith's aim was to avoid imposing the self on the other, and instead, when performing multiple people of different gender and cultural identity, to simultaneously communicate both her difference from the other and desire to reach the other (Forsyth 2009: 142). Together with the rapid development of technologies such as radio receiver packs and supra-aural headphones (Wake 2013a: 324), Smith's monopolylogue approach has made a considerable contribution to the emergence of headphone verbatim performance. In such theatre, trained performers wear headphones during a performance and visibly listen to digitally recorded material that they recite with absolute fidelity to the text and vocal behaviour of the interviewees. It was British director Mark Wing-Davey's contact with Anna Deveare Smith that gave impetus to his own experiments with headphone verbatim, such as the 'Drama Without Paper' workshop at the Actor's Centre in London (Blythe 2008: 79–80). These experiments were further developed by workshop participants, including Alecky Blythe who went on to form the UK-based company Recorded Delivery, and the Australian director Roslyn Oades who initially worked closely with Bankstown Youth Development Service and then Urban Theatre Projects in Sydney (Roslyn Oades website). In what Wake has called the 'epic mode' of headphone verbatim (2013a: 327), the combination of recited audio scripts and a sense of verbal authenticity with, and the defamiliarizing use of, cross-casting and role doubling, encourages from performers and spectators both cross-cultural identifications and acknowledgement of cultural difference. While all verbatim productions with professional performers need to navigate the problem of partially obscuring their real subjects by the performers' authority, expertise, and perspective (Mumford 2014: 193–4), the recent strategies detailed here demonstrate a desire to attend to the labour and politics of listening to and representing other people.

An alternative response to this political issue is the supplementation or complete replacement of actors and performers with the real people themselves. One contributor to the recent explosion in this approach is the impact of a marked increase in human mobility. In a world where encounter with culturally diverse and migratory subjects is occurring on an unprecedented scale, particularly in urban contexts, such subjects are repeatedly represented on stage, and often quite literally appear there. For example, since the millennium there have been an increase in refugee theatre where contemporary asylum seekers and their supporters have themselves become the medium for representation in such genres as autobiographical monologues by former detainees, performance art where artists publicly undergo trauma in order to raise awareness about the mechanisms of refugee suffering, and a 'growing global genre of verbatim plays produced in collaboration with refugees, asylum seekers and irregular immigrants' (Wake 2013b: 102). In some of these verbatim works, interviewees perform themselves and their stories. At the HAU under Matthias Lilienthal, as the case studies in this book testify, a recurrent feature has been the literal placement on stage of migratory subjects such as refugees, members of forcibly resettled communities, immigrants, diplomats, and airport kids who have either involuntarily or willingly moved within and across countries. A commitment to engaging with diverse communities in the contemporary metropolis also informs the recent development in Germany of the *Bürgerbühne* (Citizens' Stage), a phenomenon that recalls aspects of the participatory democracy models from the 1960s and 1970s. Since the founding of a citizens' company in 2009 by the Staatsschauspiel Dresden, the *Bürgerbühne* movement has been characterized by an emphasis on involving diverse residents of a city in participatory, research-based, and experimental theatre productions that draw on state, municipal or independent professional theatre practitioners and facilities. These projects give citizens a public platform where they can stage themselves and the issues and plays of interest to them, as well as opportunities to explore and develop new theatre forms (Hintze 2014; Roselt 2015).

Figuring and disrupting economic precarity and labour norms

During the third wave, Theatre of Real People has also thematized forms of economic exploitation and precarity within a globalized and neoliberal context, and has itself been interpreted as a symptom or even perpetuation of these forms. Delegated performance works such as *250cm Line Tattooed on 6 Paid People* (1999) by Santiago Sierra have used real people situated in countries such as Central and South America as a medium to demonstrate the inequities of capitalism and globalization 'in which rich countries "outsource" or "offshore" labour to low-paid workers in developing countries' (Bishop 2012: 224). Sierra's use of recruitment agencies to source non-professional performers who are willing to be objectified and sometimes permanently marked for only the minimum wage, have been received as both a problematic repetition of the economic status quo, and a provocative consideration of the artist's own implication in such economic systems (2012: 223–4). In some Theatre of Real People, the on-stage fragilities of inexperienced performers become a compelling vehicle and metaphor for communicating the idea and experiences of bodies touched by socio-economic precarity. This is the case in Rimini Protokoll's *Sabenation* (2004), where the protagonists tell stories of personal careers broken by the collapse of a national airline industry (Festjens and Marthens 2015: 128–47). Since the global financial crisis of 2007–8, the temporary employment by artists of non-trained performers (rather than, say, a permanent ensemble of actors) has been interpreted as an expression and/or perpetuation of insecurity within a neoliberal context marked by a 'tragic fall' from a secure world of work (Karschnia 2007a: 155; Wille 2012: 35).

The use of non-professional performers in contemporary performance has provoked discussion about whether it constitutes a form of exploitative 'outsourcing' and exhibition, or offers a disruption of 'agreed ways of thinking about pleasure, labour and ethics' (Bishop 2012: 239). In a brief consideration of non-professional performers in community theatre in the United Kingdom, Nicholas Ridout suggests that the quality which allows such performers to be experienced as bearer of values associated with community, is one of the features that he seeks to account for in his discussion of resistant 'passionate amateurs' (2013: 30). Ridout defines such amateurs as a theatrical variant of the 'romantic anti-capitalist' who seeks to 'make theatre, or try to make of the theatre, a fleeting realm of freedom within the realm of necessity', and who has the 'capacity to trouble some quite fundamental assumptions about both ... the work of time and the time of work' (2013: 6). Some of Ridout's examples of passionate amateurism include: an interruption of a theatre rehearsal led by Latvian director Asja Lacis in an orphanage in Orel during the 1920s where street children literally broke into the event and took over the improvised scene about a group of robbers, replacing theatre of imitation with theatre based on specialist expertise (2013: 71–2); Oklahoma Nature Theatre's production of *No Dice* (2007), a show in which a group of actors re-performed recorded telephone conversations they had had about the struggle to do the work they need to do in order to do their work as performers, a show about actors as workers and one 'performed by real people, rather than by actors pretending to be real people' (2013: 127); and the so-called 'professional' in everyday life who in certain contexts may work for the sake of work rather than money (2013: 45). While Ridout excludes amateur and community theatre from his discussion of 'passionate amateurism' on the grounds that both tend to leave the distinction between work and leisure untroubled, he nevertheless suggests that some non-professional performers have the potential to interrupt our relation to work and time (2013: 29–30).

Addressing cultures of the archive, artifice, and simulacra

One of the most significant causal factors for the proliferation of Theatre of Real People since the early 1990s has been a concomitant surge in digital media, which has provided an unprecedented capacity to archive and recycle reality (Martin 2013: 5, 120). These developments have contributed to a fascination with recording what people do and say, and with intimate forms of self-representation, as well as a desire to explore or resist the implications of a culture of the artificial and simulated. In instances such as the theatre of Vivi Tellas from Argentina, who began in 2000 to produce a series of pieces with real people – including relatives, philosophy professors, and driving instructors – an aesthetic that draws on Duchamp's ready-made pieces is combined with a *Zeitgeist* commitment to archiving. This commitment is played out in Tellas's conceptualization of these works as archives rather than plays, and her premise that 'every person has, and is, an archive: a reserve of experiences, knowledge, texts, and images' (Pauls 2010: 247, 251). If digital technology has afforded new capacities in archiving, it has also greatly extended our capacity to publicize the personal. Not only has it ensured a proliferation of dissemination spaces – blogs, online chat rooms, live streams, Facebook, Twitter, YouTube, and other social media platforms – but it has also contributed to the diversification and deregulation of Western media industries and consequent rise in popular factual television, including Reality TV and chat shows (Hill 2005: 5). As we demonstrate in future chapters, the cultures of manufactured celebrity, confession, and intimacy that are fed by such public spaces are showcased and often challenged within Theatre of Real People, and inform the latter's deployment of Authenticity-Effects.

The contemporary 'glut of mass-mediated confessional opportunities' (Heddon 2008: 17) both respond to and further fuel what David Shields has characterized as 'reality hunger'. Shields links this hunger to the perception that we live in 'a manufactured and artificial world' wherein 'we yearn for the "real", semblances of the real. We want to pose something nonfictional against all the fabrication' (2010: 81). Many Theatre of Real People works since the early twentieth century have consciously or unconsciously engaged with the forms of fabrication regarded as influential in this period. For some people, these forms include a highly 'stage-managed' society of capitalist illusion and spectacle (Weiler 2006: 58–60). Martin Puchner has clarified that 'spectacle' denotes here 'not simply the mediatization of post-war Western capitalism but its entire ideology: television, advertising, commodity fetish, superstructure, the whole deceptive appearance of advanced capitalism' (2006: 221). In her

analysis of artist-theorists critical of capitalist ideological illusion, Liz
Tomlin argues that Brecht's attempt to expose such illusion through
theatre that interrupted mimetic representation was underpinned by an
approach to the real similar to that presented by Situationist Guy Debord
in his theoretical work *The Society of the Spectacle* (1967). According to
Debord, in modern society authentic and lived social life had been
replaced with its representation, and in particular a spectacle of unity
that masks the very class division upon which the unity of capitalist
production is dependent. While Debord initially shared with Brecht
(and Artaud) a conviction that a concealed reality could be uncovered
and fought for, Tomlin notes that when revisiting his original thesis in
1990, Debord's understanding of the spectacle moved closer to Jean
Baudrillard's theory of the simulacrum (Tomlin 2013: 20–1, 27).

In Baudrillard's eyes, our world of (mass) media and information
technology is pervaded by simulation, 'the generation by models of a
real without origin or reality: a hyperreal' (1994: 1). Simulacra today
produce the real 'from miniaturized cells, matrices, and memory banks'
and can reproduce it 'an indefinite number of times from these' (1994:
2). Simulation involves a type of feigning to have what one does not
have, comparable to a situation where a person, feigning illness,
'produces in himself some of the symptoms'. Such feigning 'threatens
the difference between the "true" and the "false," the "real" and the
"imaginary"' (1994: 23). Today, the simulated nature of reality does not
conceal truth or the true real, but the fact that neither of these exist
(Tomlin 2013: 28). Baudrillard interprets a contemporary 'plethora of
myths of origin and of signs of reality' as a nostalgic and '[p]anic-
stricken production of the real and of the referential' in the face of a real
that 'is no longer what it was' (1994: 6–7). While some Theatre of Real
People works could be described as nostalgic in this way, productions
such as the case studies analysed in this book demonstrate a willingness
to engage with the uncertainty about the true, the real, and the original
that has characterized the age of simulacra.

An instance of perceived fabrication addressed by recent Theatre of
Real People is the performative and theatrical nature of everyday life, and

the artificially constructed nature of identity. Today, the perception that humans perform their social roles and identities, and that their actions and interactions are practised, framed, and displayed just like staged events (Fischer-Lichte 2007: 18–21), is relatively common. This idea was memorably explored in Irving Goffman's sociological study *The Presentation of Self in Everyday Life* (1959) and shaped some theatre of the real in the same period (Martin 2013: 27). However, it has become decidedly more prominent in what Janelle Reinelt characterizes as our 'aggressively theatrical' times, where 'the technologies of display and artifice are typically mobilized throughout all channels of everyday life' (Reinelt 2006: 70). In an age marked by artifice and economic crisis, the ability to represent or stage one's self has been interpreted as vital for survival (Keim 2010: 129). Much contemporary experimental theatre embodies, explores or resists a current fascination with creating a successful image of a masterful or authentic self, both on and off stage. Since the 1980s in particular, such theatre has often engaged in a discourse of failure that undermines, for example, 'the perceived stability of mainstream capitalist ideology's preferred aspiration to achieve, succeed, or win', and the competitive hierarchical culture of neoliberal politics (Bailes 2011: 2, 13, 16). The refusal to pursue the types of perfection and illusion aspired to in mainstream theatre (Roselt 2006) has often taken the form of (false) amateurism and studied awkwardness, a mode perfected (ironically enough) by trained performers in companies such as the UK's Forced Entertainment (Bailes 2011: 30). Interrogations of societal and theatre norms of virtuosity and mastery have also been vividly pursued in productions by Australia's Back to Back Theatre, which predominantly feature disabled performers whose partially self-representational mode challenges many category boundaries, including that which divides the professional and the amateur. As we discuss in Chapter 3, in much recent Theatre of Real People the non-trained or differently trained performer not only engages in acts of self-representation but also, through moments of non-perfection that are clearly orchestrated, creates an impression of how both mastery and authenticity are often (or even always) the product of historically and culturally specific staging.

Across its history, Theatre of Real People has embodied a concern with theatre's capacity to represent, perpetuate or resist social reality, particularly a reality believed to be characterized by capitalist (and now digitally enhanced) illusion, spin, celebrity, and simulacra. In such a context it has both asserted and thrown doubt on the possibility of absolute truth, authentic experience, and clear dividing lines between 'the real thing' and the fake. On some occasions, it has been a paradoxical vehicle for the attempt to transcend the limits of artistic representation, or a tool for dissolving boundaries between art works and everyday life. At the heart of its operations lie artistic strategies such as putting 'real people' or aspects of them on stage, or using new technologies for archiving, imitating, and simulating reality. These Authenticity-Effects have the capacity to expose the arts of self-representation as well as the masterful appearances of actors and professional performers, or to fuel a demand for presence, immediacy, and intimacy. Theatre of Real People has simultaneously attempted to deal with how to represent or provide arenas for people who are often marginalized in dramatic theatre and public life, particularly the culturally marginalized, economically precarious, and socially transgressive, as well as those other people who have been (mis)represented within dominant narratives. As we discuss in this book, as well as attending to the politics of listening to multiple and diverse others, Theatre of Real People has also sought to enable encounters with and between culturally unfamiliar people, both on and off stage. This concern with the politics of representation also makes itself felt in the attempt to transform or highlight hierarchical theatre structures, and to operate more egalitarian and collective processes of creation. Whether the representations and multi-vocal arenas provided by such theatre effectively disrupt neoliberal individualism, economic exploitation, and/or cultures of commodification and spectacle remains a concern for makers and critics alike. In the following chapters, we explore how the HAU under Matthias Lilienthal, and selected productions during his tenure as artistic director, managed Theatre of Real People's twofold concern with the problems of representing social reality through the arts of theatre, and of representing culturally unfamiliar others within a capitalist, postmodern, and globalized world.

2

Theatre of Real People at the HAU

Under the leadership of Matthias Lilienthal (2003–12), the Hebbel am Ufer (HAU) established itself as a theatre production house committed to artistic engagement with contemporary society and pressing social issues. This emphasis was memorably signalled through a bold publicity campaign for Lilienthal's first season, which featured portraits of individuals from the torso up – mainly young men and women, but also Lilienthal himself – in sports attire reminiscent of a boxer (Pilz 2006). The individuals showed signs of facial bruising and strenuous physical effort (Figure 2.1). The placards were accompanied by the use of the production house acronym, HAU, and in some cases the use of the

Figure 2.1 The boxer publicity campaign at HAU2. Photograph by Sven Neumann, 2003, courtesy of Hebbel am Ufer.

slogan 'Go For It' ('Hau rein': Wahl 2012).[1] This invitation playfully offered options such as entry to the HAU's three theatre houses in Berlin-Kreuzberg, and to a world of encounter where you might be knocked off balance. The boxer imagery also invited comparisons with the forms of pugilism found in Brecht's version of a realist theatre. However, the documentary nature of the portraits suggested a different approach, one focused on individuals from the here and now – in this case, actual members of a boxing club in Neukölln (Lilienthal, in Visser 2012: 25), rather than fictional or historical figures played by actors. That Lilienthal regarded the photographed subjects as possibly the children of Slavic, Russian or Polish parents (Lilienthal, in Vollmer 2004: 48) suggests that he viewed the portraits also as an opportunity to demonstrate interest in the cultural diversity that marked the HAU's neighbourhood and host city. As the publicity campaign declared, the HAU would pursue an artistic agenda well suited to the development of Theatres of Real People. That is, theatre where diverse 'real people' – contemporary, self-representing, usually physically present in the performance event, and rarely trained as a professional performer – are put in the spotlight.

This artistic agenda further developed the socially engaged and experimental approach to theatre that had often characterized the three theatres that were merged to create the HAU consortium in 2003. The oldest of these, the Hebbel Theater (HAU1), is a 500-seat theatre. The HAU2 (formerly the Theater am Halleschen Ufer and before that the Schaubühne am Halleschen Ufer) has 200 seats, and the intimate, studio-style HAU3 (formerly Theater am Ufer) can accommodate 100 spectators (Yamaguchi 2009: 3). Prior to the merger, HAU1 had hosted distinguished practitioners from German theatre history, including contributors to socially critical, experimental, and documentary work such as Frank Wedekind and Erwin Piscator. Under Nele Hertling's leadership from 1989, it presented internationally recognized contemporary theatre. HAU2 was the venue where Peter Stein began to establish himself as one of Germany's leading directors of politically engaged theatre. It also played host to the political theatre of

Theatermanufaktur Berlin, which staged work by, among others, Bertolt Brecht and the documentary playwright Peter Weiss. Both HAU2 and the intimate studio-style HAU3 have not only developed the legacy of Peter Stein (Raddatz 2008: 20), but also provided particular support for experimental work from the independent theatre scene. Since the merger, the HAU has programmed a wide variety of local, national, and international performance events across an array of theatre and non-theatre spaces.

A realist credo

During the nine years of Lilienthal's leadership, the HAU gained a reputation for its commitment to interdisciplinary experimentation and its support for a wide range of performative actions in locations throughout Berlin and beyond. Across a programme of about 120 productions per year (*Theater heute* Redaktion 2012: 26), it showcased and combined numerous arts disciplines and media, often in ways that challenged conventional approaches to art and its relation to social reality. This commitment to innovation and a broad conception of what art might be was guided by a realist credo that set certain parameters. Lilienthal often took pleasure in expressing his version of that credo through blunt statements such as: 'No art shit! Only reality shit!' (Keine Kunstkacke! Nur Realitätskacke!: Emcke 2012: 7). These sorts of comments were symptomatic of his rejection of art-for-art's sake and his much quoted self-declared 'hysterical yearning for reality' (hysterische Sehnsucht nach Realität: Behrendt 2004). They were also a shorthand description of the HAU team's interest in integrating aesthetic with societal discourse (*Theater heute* Redaktion 2012: 26). One manifestation of the realist credo was the prevalence of a documentary flavour at the HAU where, according to Franz Wille, 'the normative power of the factual' (die normative Kraft des Faktischen) was pursued (Wille 2012: 35). Towards the end of his term as director, Lilienthal enthusiastically likened the HAU's theatre programme to 'a

documentary film festival' (ein Dokumentarfilm-festival: *Theater heute*
Redaktion 2012: 30).

Under Lilienthal, many ventures at the HAU, including its Theatres
of Real People, shared an insistence on 'unmistakable connections to
the reality of the original events', an insistence Janelle Reinelt, drawing
on Stella Bruzzi's film theory, describes as a characteristic feature of
documentary forms:

> This link [between a representation and the reality it refers to] sets up
> a realist epistemology where knowledge is available through sense
> perception and cognition linked to objects/documents. While this
> status as conduit is never sufficient and is often deficient, it does
> characterize the unique attributes of documentary in contradistinction
> to fiction. Spectators come to a theatrical event believing that certain
> aspects of the performance are directly linked to the reality they are
> trying to experience or understand. This does not mean they expect
> unmediated access to the truth in question, but that the documents
> have something significant to offer. (Reinelt 2009: 9)

Reinelt attributes a recent appetite for documentary to 'an increase in the
desire for contact with those "indexical traces of the presence of a real
past" in a globalized world of indecipherable uncertainties' (2009: 13). In
the case of Theatre of Real People at the HAU, we would argue that a
distinguishing feature of this mode of performance, one found in much
documentary theatre (though not necessarily documentaries concerned
with historical protagonists), is an appetite also for contact with the
indexical traces of a real *present* via living subjects, and one that, as we
demonstrate later, is relatively open to negotiating and valuing uncertainty.

Approaches to the real and Theatre
of Real People at the HAU

We now outline approaches to the real that were fostered and
disseminated at the HAU between 2003 and 2012, as well as the Theatre
of Real People it hosted. In particular, we survey approaches to

encounter and performing that provided the impulses to Theatre of Real People forms. As we demonstrate, many productions at the HAU were characterized by an interest in representing and encountering contemporary people – in making their words, narratives, bodies, and associated objects, documents, and environments present in some way in the performance space or event. In those cases of greatest relevance to our investigation, the act of representing and encountering contemporary people involved literally putting people on stage who do not usually perform their everyday activities within the theatre or performing arts world. Such people were selected through a casting process, and on some occasions performed side by side with professional theatre-makers.

Neighbourhood encounters

An appetite for contact with the indexical traces of a real *present* via living subjects informed Lilienthal's development at the HAU of his trademark *X-Apartments* (*X-Wohnungen*) and *X-Schools* (*X-Schulen*) formats. *X-Apartments*, one of the Theatre of Real People formats given close consideration in this book (see Chapter 6), was first presented in Duisburg 2002 during Lilienthal's time as programme director of the festival Theater der Welt (Theatre of the World). It was later staged in Kreuzberg, other nearby Berlin suburbs, and in overseas cities from Warsaw to São Paulo and Johannesburg. Inspired by curator Jan Hoet's *Guest Rooms* (*Chambres d'Amis*) of 1986 (Lilienthal 2003: 19), an event where artists exhibited work in private houses in Ghent, *X-Apartments* is a multi-site format where audience members are guided through a series of private apartments in a residential area. Within and between the apartments, participants experience encounters created by theatre, film, and visual artists that involve real people and/or professional performers. To date, these encounters have often played with a sense of the authentic, destabilizing the participants' sense of the line between authentic and staged, and sometimes prompting audience members to regard any aspect of the event – from a passer-by on the street to even a tree on the side of the street – as a staged element. *X-Apartments* created a frame that invited spectators to view the district neighbourhood as a ready-made (Wahl 2012).

The *X-Apartments* format is informed not only by a yearning for contact with reality, but also the idea that social reality is a performative arena where, just like theatre events, actions and interactions are practised, framed, and displayed (Fischer-Lichte 2007: 10–12). Such an idea is compatible with a conceptualization of theatre as an overarching context capable of including all possible performative actions, not only the staging of material from dramatic literature. According to Christoph Gurk, this concept underpinned the work at Berlin's Volksbühne from the early 1990s and was an artistic direction to which Lilienthal, in his role as the Volksbühne's chief dramaturge (1991–98), made a significant contribution (Meinecke and Gurk 2012: 73). Led by Frank Castorf since 1992, and lauded as an innovative socially engaged theatre, the Volksbühne's support for artists such as Christoph Schlingensief helped pave the way for the development of modes of encounter and performance relevant to recent theatres of the real (a field of theatre activity defined in our Introduction).

It was Lilienthal who first invited Schlingensief to mount a production at the Volksbühne in 1993. In a number of his works, Schlingensief developed a form of activist performance that gave its diverse participants opportunities for directly shaping opinions, policies, and events. Some of the practices of creating (and destabilizing) an impression of authentic encounter with contemporary people that Schlingensief developed in this work included: playing with documentary formats, appearing as a version of himself or making personal revelations in a theatre performance or television show, and working with non-professional theatre performers including audience-participants. In the interactive protest project *Please Love Austria: First Austrian Coalition Week* (*Bitte liebt Österreich: Erste österreichische Koalitionswoche*, June 2000), in which Lilienthal was involved as dramatic advisor, Schlingensief played with a sense of authentic encounter in a manner that has parallels with *X-Apartments*. At the

Vienna Arts Festival 2000, he launched a protest against the rise of the anti-foreigner, far-right Austrian Freedom Party through a parodic recasting of the *Big Brother* reality television show as a competition for asylum seekers. The 'game' was played out on Vienna's Herbert von Karajan Platz where a compound of disused shipping containers housing the twelve contestants was installed for six days. A large sign 'Foreigners Out' ('Ausländer Raus') was positioned prominently above the compound, and a website enabled Austrians to vote for the eviction of two asylum seekers per day from their country (Varney 2010). As in *X-Apartments*, elements such as the re-framing of an urban site and the maintenance of an ambiguity about whether the contestants were truly asylum seekers, contributed to confusion and uncertainty about the lines between the real and the staged, and the possible political implications of failing to get to know the unfamiliar foreigner.

More a community engagement than a protest, the HAU's *X-Schools* project (2010) approached the task of getting to know unfamiliar people through collaboration between diverse artists and the community of the Hektor-Peterson comprehensive school. At the time of the production, 95 per cent of the students at this secondary school had a migrant background (Schlagenwerth 2010), with the majority sharing close connections with Turkish culture. Curated by Peter Kastenmüller, Cecilie Ullerup Schmidt, and Mijke Harmsen, the works were staged in numerous spaces across the school from the cellar to the roof and involved collaborations between students and international artists. A number of these artists – including Tim Etchells, Chris Kondek, Rabih Mroué, Boris Nikitin, the theatre collective Turbo Pascal, Branca Prlic, and Tamer Yiğit – had prior experience creating theatre with or about contemporary people. Similar to forms of community-based theatre, a number of the performances included self-representational episodes mentored by the artists. These ranged from a video installation – where students spoke laconically and movingly about their feelings, dreams, and fears – to seemingly authentic moments of disintegration in an ethics class that gradually dissolved as smirking students individually made their exit (Laudenbach 2010b: 14; Wildermann 2010).

Stadtteiltheater: local and diverse people

Both of the aforementioned formats are connected with Lilienthal's interest in what he named 'city district theatre' (Stadtteiltheater: Vollmer 2004: 48), a term that playfully signals both an attentiveness to culturally diverse local communities, and a departure from the state-funded 'city theatre' (Stadttheater) system. Used half-jokingly in a discussion about the future of Berlin's theatres initiated by the Vice-President of the Bundestag at the time, member of the Greens Antje Vollmer, Lilienthal employed the term to position the HAU in relation to the other five main players of the Berlin theatre scene: the Berliner Ensemble, Deutsches Theater, the Maxim Gorki Theater, the Schaubühne, and the Volksbühne. In contrast to the artistic director of the Deutsches Theater, Bernd Wilms, who during the discussion presented this established institution with its 'conservative repertoire' as Germany's future national theatre (Laudenbach 2004), Lilienthal alluded to a shared interest with the Greens in an engagement with local political issues, including cultural diversity. Lilienthal's *Stadtteiltheater* neologism only foregrounds one of the HAU's strengths, focusing on its engagement with the local environment rather than its equally strong support of international work, probably in an attempt to clearly distinguish the HAU from the concurrent dominant German model of the *Stadttheater*.

Lilienthal's strategic use of the neologism can be related to a broader debate that continued throughout his leadership at the HAU and beyond, about the relationship of the German *Stadttheater* and the 'independent theatre scene' (Freie Szene). In this debate, municipal theatre was commonly associated with 'a tendency to be conservative, incapable of reform, professional and rich' (tendenziell konservativ, reformunfähig, professionell und reich: Roselt 2012) based on its publicly funded, long-term professional ensembles, the staging of texts by established authors played in repertoire, and audiences who tended to be from the educated elite. The *Freie Szene*, by contrast, was often presented as 'having a tendency to be progressive, innovative, experimental, semi-professional and poor' (tendenziell fortschrittlich, innovativ, experimentell, semi-professionell und arm: Roselt 2012), a division Roselt has characterized as simplistic. Annemarie Matzke claims the discourse of division was 'mainly about an ideological struggle between the classical canon and a middle-class orientation on the one hand and experimental forms and a different access to the audience on the other' (Matzke 2014). By separating the HAU from the municipal theatre, Lilienthal was free to experiment with different institutional structures and working processes, a move only taken by a small number of other German institutions at the time, such as the Forum Freies Theater in Düsseldorf and the Kampnagel in Hamburg. This flexibility at the HAU was supported by a hierarchically flat approach to teamwork (Emcke 2012: 7). For example, once Lilienthal had approved a project, his team was free to make all manner of decisions from then on, 'an extreme freedom of action' (einen extremen Handlungsspielraum: Garde 2012). This partially decentralized organizational structure could also be found within many of the theatre groups that worked at the HAU. The production house embraced the way collectives worked, an approach that hitherto had been 'a hallmark of the independent scene' (Matzke 2014).

This different way of making theatre was combined with a wealth of experimental and interdisciplinary projects, which, unlike the *Stadttheater's* traditional division of disciplines, crossed genres and art forms, an artistic diversity acknowledged abroad (Billington 2011). This programme attracted equally diverse audience members, an important factor at a time when the *Stadttheater* was struggling to retain audiences due to a societal shift away from a more homogeneous culture (Pinto 2012). In a 2010 interview, Lilienthal referred to the Berlin audience as separated into '50 ghettos' – among which he included, for example, the Latin American communities, and the trendy hipsters from Berlin-Mitte – and stated that his team endeavoured to stay in contact with about fifteen to twenty different groups (Laudenbach 2010a). The HAU's programme also drew in and catered for (culturally) diverse artists, many of whom were underrepresented in the *Stadttheater* system. In turn, these artists often utilized – or invoked a sense of – documentary and self-representational forms.

Semi-documentary theatre and cultural encounter

As part of his application for the job of artistic and managing director, Lilienthal declared his intention to invite people with migrant backgrounds to work at the HAU, including those from German-Turkish communities in Kreuzberg (Raddatz 2008: 18). One of the fruits of this approach was the 2006 premiere of *Black Virgins* (*Schwarze Jungfrauen*) written by Feridun Zaimoglu and Günter Senkel and directed by Neco Çelik, a piece that has been described as an 'Islamo-feminist docu-drama' (Cheesman and Yeşilada 2012: 6). Performed by actors, the work presented a series of monologues that Zaimoglu was to claim combined a crafted artistic language with 'authentic' content from interviews with young Muslim women in Berlin (Zaimoglu, in Ulbricht 2007). The HAU also commissioned pieces that featured contemporary people by theatre, film, and music maker, Tamer Yiğit, and by the dance company Constanza Macras/Dorky Park. A number of Yiğit's works at the HAU brought together autobiographical and documentary material with fiction, including his first full-length theatre play *My Melody* (*Meine Melodie*, 2006). In the HAU staging, described by one critic as 'a semi-documentary, movingly authentic play' (in dem halbdokumantarischen, berührend authentischen Spiel: Draeger 2006: 13), Yiğit presented his own experiences of growing up in Kreuzberg through the use of young and relatively inexperienced performers – including his teenage brother who played the figure of Yiğit – and a multimedia combination of rock, rap, breakdance, word, and film. In *Warning Poem* (*Warngedicht*, 2008), co-authored with Branka Prlic, secondary school students were involved both as performers and in the research and creation processes surrounding the text, which integrated both the style of the young people's language and anti-naturalistic elements (Müller 2008a). Choreographer Constanza Macras also worked with a similar cohort. *Scratch Neukölln* (2003) presented local children ranging from three to eleven years of age with Arabic ancestry, while *Hell on Earth* (2008) presented members of the same cast five years later (Macras 2012: 27). These dance theatre versions of Theatre of Real People explored themes such as discrimination and coping with feelings of foreignness through contemporary and popular dance forms, choreographed quotidian movement, and the protagonists' narratives about their own dreams and desires.

Freie Szene engagement with the real via 'experts' and audience-participants

Lilienthal's *Stadtteiltheater* was also a hub for the *Freie Szene* as well as its international equivalents. At the HAU, this scene was characterized by its emphasis on the freedom to develop new artistic forms, its variety of organizational structures, as well as its reliance on temporary project-based forms of funding. Lilienthal has attributed the blooming of the Berlin scene to the successful efforts of Nele Hertling, former artistic director at the Hebbel Theater (HAU1), and of the Arts Council to establish the Capital City Cultural Fund for Projects with a Connection to Berlin (Hauptstadt-kulturfonds für Projekte mit Berliner Anbindung: *Theater heute* Redaktion 2012: 29). While the independent scene enjoyed a strong presence at the three HAU theatres prior to this cultural fund, its formation considerably increased the orientation towards Berlin of graduates from innovative tertiary theatre studies programmes, such as the Institute for Applied Theatre Studies in Gießen and the Institute for Media, Theatre and Popular Culture in Hildesheim (*Theater heute* Redaktion 2012: 29). Many of these graduates – andcompany&Co, Gob Squad, Hoffman&Lindholm, Rimini Protokoll, She She Pop, Showcase Beat Le Mot, Turbo Pascal and Werner Kroesinger – would bring impulses from live art, performance, and documentary theatre (Behrendt 2012: 22) that fed directly into the development of new Theatres of Real People.

These graduates were both influenced by, and in turn shaped by, what Hans-Thies Lehmann has described as a more general shift in theatre practice:

> After the emphasis in the eighties and nineties on a search for new forms, the dialogue between theatre and society, between theatre and criticism of society increased. Mediality, forms of play with documents and thereby also with insecurity about what is authentic, became

widely spread. Theatre became more and more a publication organ for real experiences. (Nachdem in den achtziger und neunziger Jahren die neuen Formfindungen im Vordergrund standen, hat der Dialog zwischen Theater und Gesellschaft, Theater und Kritik der Gesellschaft zugenommen. Medialität, Formen des Spiels mit Dokumenten und dabei auch mit der Unsicherheit über das, was authentisch ist, haben sich verbreitet. Theater wurde mehr und mehr ein Veröffentlichungsorgan für Realerfahrungen. (Lehmann 2012: 171)

One of the lead contributors to this shift, and to Theatre of Real People, was the award-winning performance collective Rimini Protokoll led by Helgard Haug, Stefan Kaegi, and Daniel Wetzel, who became artists-in-residence at the HAU in 2003. Not only did their long-term presence there increase the attractiveness and public profile of the HAU (Raddatz 2008: 17), it also provided them with the opportunity to explore and disseminate modes of engaging with real people. Rimini Protokoll has achieved renown as the founders of a type of documentary performance that illuminated the reality of living in a world marked by late capitalism, mediatization, and globalization through techniques such as the casting of so-called 'experts of the everyday' rather than actors. These performers are experts in so far as they are specialists in a particular field or aspect of their life.

In addition to working with a diverse range of experts – including Bulgarian long-distance truck drivers and Indian call-centre workers, nursing home inhabitants and airport kids, Kurdish trash-recyclers and Egyptian Muezzins – Rimini Protokoll have explored ways of staging these real people through experimentation with space, media, and genre. For example, while their experts have appeared in theatres, they have also been presented in urban sites, vehicles, places of work, and in off-stage events framed as theatre, as occurred in *Annual Shareholder's Meeting* (*Hauptversammlung*, 2008). Some have been transported and mediated via technologies such as telephone, video, radio, and iPad. In productions involving audience participation in dialogue or action, such as *Call Cutta in a Box: An Intercontinental Phone Play* (2008), audience members became something akin to what we call 'real-people performers'. However, unlike such performers they were not pre-cast and staged. The comparatively extensive nature of Rimini Protokoll's engagement with a theatre of diverse real people, both at the HAU and internationally, is one of the reasons for the particular attention given to their work in this book.

In the *Blackmarket for Useful Knowledge and Non-Knowledge* (*Schwarzmarkt für nützliches Wissen und Nicht-Wissen*) format that was hosted on three occasions at the HAU under Lilienthal, a format conceived by curator-dramaturge Hanna Hurtzig and her Mobile Academy collaborators, real people similar to Rimini Protokoll's 'experts' present themselves and their knowledges in interactive situations (see Chapter 8). Described by Kirsten Hehmeyer, head of press at the HAU, as 'performative learning formats' (Performative Lernformate: Wenner, Regus, Hehmeyer and Pees, 2012: 61), the *Blackmarkets* are staged usually on one night only and bring together a diverse group of experts from an array of social and occupational backgrounds. Each expert presents a story-narrative to a single 'client' and dialogue partner within a short 30-minute session at one of numerous small tables. The experts' inexpensive presentations are all connected to a chosen cluster of topic areas of relevance to the *Zeitgeist* of the host city, and are primarily for the paying client, although other audience members equipped with headphones may also listen in and watch. The full title *Blackmarket for Useful Knowledge and Non-Knowledge* refers to an interest in knowledges that are – for various reasons – 'in the dark'. The pursuit of such interests is carried out through a non-exclusive approach to the casting of the numerous experts and an encouragement of multiple and heterogeneous areas of expertise. Like the *X-Apartments* format, and Rimini Protokoll's work with experts, the *Blackmarket* embodies a sustained engagement with diverse non-trained theatre performers, which is one of the reasons why we have chosen to give it further attention later in this book. Furthermore, its careful management of proximity to the experts and their expertise also offers a unique model for encountering diverse people and perceiving the (un)familiar.

Freie Szene and self-representation

One of the impulses that fed into Rimini Protokoll's work and the Theatres of Real People showcased at the HAU more broadly, was the impact of performance art and live art traditions. Lilienthal has noted that the Gießen graduates' exposure early in their undergraduate studies to the work of performance artists such as Marina Abramović, expressed itself in a move away from the playing of characters and use of disguise or pretence to being only who you were in the moment (Baecker et al. 2012: 14–15). Versions of this form of being in public are often to be found in the work of both performance-makers who eschew acting, and of people engaged in self-representation who are not trained performers. In the case of the predominantly female performance collective She She Pop, acting is usually replaced with the task-based actions of performers who present (a version of) themselves in interactive situations that allow for in-the-moment responses from performers and spectators. She She Pop draw on their own lives and experiences in order to develop perspectives on the tasks and material at hand and use autobiographical material that can metonymically represent broader phenomena. In one of their fêted productions at the HAU, *Testament: Belated Preparations for a New Generation Based on Lear* (*Verspätete Vorbereitungen zum Generationswechsel nach Lear*, 2010), members of the collective appeared on stage alongside three of their own fathers (Figure 2.2). As well as exploring territory such as negotiations between fathers and daughters, inheritance, retirement, and power (She She Pop website), this production also engaged with the nature and problems of intimate revelation within the public realm of theatre.

New forms of documentary theatre

While the HAU developed a reputation for a 'yearning for reality' played out through contact with the indexical traces of a real present via living subjects, it also embraced the more traditional documentary focus on contact with 'traces of the presence of a real past' (Reinelt 2009: 13). Hans-Werner Kroesinger has arguably been the most active

Figure 2.2 She She Pop members Ilia Papatheodorou, Sebastian Bark, and Lisa Lucassen performing with some of the fathers cast in *Testament*: Theo Papatheodorou and Manfred Matzke on the screens, and Joachim Bark on his son's shoulders. Photograph by Doro Tuch, courtesy of She She Pop.

contributor at the HAU to a documentary theatre dedicated to historical research and associated documents. Kroesinger presents his works across a variety of venues, but he produces most regularly at the HAU. During the Lilienthal period, he staged on average just over one production per year, including the award-winning work *Rwanda Revisited* (2009) on the subject of the 1994 Tutsi genocide. While Kroesinger has addressed current issues and contemporary people, such as suicide bombers and child soldiers, his goal is 'to track complex, historical trajectories in his theatrical analyses of war, genocide and political decision-making and, in this way, to delineate the relevant political or economic interests with the greatest possible precision'. The staging techniques Kroesinger uses to achieve his goal have included actors working with a Brechtian gestic approach, and installation-like arrangements of space and documents (Wahl).

Kroesinger's attention to detailed research and the use of theatre as a medium for information and political analysis are reminiscent of German documentary theatre from the 1960s and 1970s. However, as we discuss later, his self-reflexive attention to the complex and relative nature of truth, and to his own truth-making processes, mark a departure from this tradition. Many original performances of the early political plays by Peter Weiss in particular, but also authors such as Rolf Hochhuth and Heiner Kipphardt, sought to present texts as objective reportage, or to give the impression of an accurately recreated tribunal (Birkenhauer 2008: 130). In their time, these authors created a new political theatre, which directed audiences to their own stance towards Germany's history (Birkenhauer 2008: 129; Favorini 1994a: xxxi), especially on the topic of the Holocaust. However, in light of later historical developments such as increased scepticism towards the documents and information provided by the mass media, some of these playwrights moved towards viewing documents themselves as the subject of criticism (Barnett 2001).

By contrast, contemporary documentary and Theatre of Real People productions at the HAU tended to acknowledge their theatrical frame and their play with documentary and fictive elements. They no longer pursued the position of moral leaders who would guide audiences in their responses to current (and very recent) issues, offering instead multiple points of view by casting a range of experts on a given topic. Moreover, a sense of objective truth, commonly associated with the documents used in the theatre of the 1960s and 1970s, was largely replaced by the concept of the 'narrative truth' of the many autobiographical stories (Freeman and Brockmeier 2001: 75–99) that are woven into the productions. These recent trends in documentary also pervaded the work of the many international artists invited to the HAU. In Lilienthal's final season, these artists included Rabih Mroué from Beirut, a regular guest at the HAU who has also presented work there together with his partner Lina Saneh, and Milo Rau from Switzerland with *Hate Radio*, another hard-hitting treatment of the genocide in Rwanda.

During Lilienthal's nine years as artistic director, a vast number of contemporary people were represented or literally placed on the three HAU theatre stages and in a multiplicity of urban sites and vehicles, both within Berlin and abroad. As Stefan Kaegi observed in 2012, the HAU was ready to meet the needs of those practitioners who wanted to go beyond imitation to work with elements of the real. For example, if, instead of an actor, an entire choir, a school, a family or an IT programmer was required, it could just as easily be found. If instead of the theatre auditorium you needed an inflatable tent, a ship or a lorry, these too would be found (Kaegi 2012: 28). The HAU's readiness to engage with social reality through new approaches such as working with real people was an important factor in the creation of a theatre that strove for and played with authentic encounter. Its parallel and overlapping readiness to provide a *Stadtteiltheater* that explicitly worked with culturally diverse and previously under-represented artists, participants, and suburbs was an important contributor to the creation of a theatre that also strove for and interrogated encounter with diverse unfamiliar people.

Note

1   Unless otherwise stated, all translations are our own.

3

Theatre and Authenticity-Effects

Theatre of Real People is one of many theatre phenomena that offer direct connection and encounter with manifestations of past or present reality. It is our contention that such theatre, and particularly Theatre of Real People, characteristically employs what we call 'Authenticity-Effects', and that these effects vary in accordance with their socio-historical contexts. In this chapter, we introduce our definition of the paradoxical term 'Authenticity-Effects', as well as recent manifestations of such effects in Western theatre. We then clarify the polysemous nature of the term 'authenticity' and outline the way authenticity discourse surges and remoulds itself in times of social change. When explaining our use of 'authenticity' in the context of theatre analysis, we introduce our focus on two main semantic clusters. The main work of the chapter, however, is to introduce the nature and manifestations of divergent approaches to Authenticity-Effects in Theatre of Real People today, which we refer to as the idealizing and the sceptical (or destabilizing) approach. While doing so we establish our interest in the potential of the sceptical approach to generate forms of uncertainty that encourage fresh perspectives on diverse real people.

By 'Authenticity-Effects' we mean theatre techniques and modes of representation, as well as the resulting perceptual experiences. Representational techniques frequently associated with recent Authenticity-Effects include: verbatim, autobiographical, self-representational or improvised words, often delivered by the original speakers; spontaneous actions in the here and now; use of original objects and non-theatre locations like the performers' own homes; actors' careful imitation of the speech patterns and physical gestures of interviewee-characters; and a focus on the body, personality, and history of non-professional performers who transgress the norms and conventions practised by trained actors and performers.

These types of effects have the capacity to generate one or more of the following sensations: that of the sincere and genuine and therefore credible, in the sense of honest and free from pretence or counterfeit, or really originating from its reputed maker or source; that of referential truthfulness and veracity, a sense that the theatrical event accurately refers to the world beyond the staged cosmos and/or is factual; and that of unmediated and intimate contact with people who actually exist or have existed. We argue that it is these sensations and meanings that are most relevant to the Theatre of Real People because they occur most frequently in descriptions of personal behaviour, humans and objects, and social interaction, whether on stage or off. These sensations, like the term 'authentic' itself, are often related to a yearning for genuine origins. The Latin etymon of 'authentic' is *authenticus*, which refers to originals, particularly original documents. 'Authentic(ity)' has subsequently turned into a protean term, with its promise of access to an origin manifesting itself in many different, but related, strands of meaning (Knaller and Müller 2005: 40).

We propose to use 'authenticity' as an umbrella term that contains two main semantic clusters that are central to our discussion of artistic and social encounter in theatre productions at the HAU: first, a group of terms which refer to the nature and demeanour of the performers on stage and the impressions they can create as a result, such as sincerity and genuineness, which might in turn create a sense of credibility and referential truthfulness; and a second cluster of terms which describe the nature and degree of mediation involved in the access to and encounter with other people, such as a sense of unmediated and intimate contact in a theatre production. Currently, 'authenticity' is a topical issue in art and theatre circles, with some critics noting a recent 'authenticity hype' (Hype eines Authentischen) in the German postdramatic theatre scene (Raddatz 2011: 374). It is our contention that this heightened interest referred to is but one of many instances when 'authenticity' has been evoked as a 'term of crisis' (Straub 2012: 15). The polysemous nature of the term and its plasticity has allowed its users to adapt its meanings and applications in times of social and technological change which appear to threaten the promise of 'authentic' interpersonal encounters.

One relevant period of crisis was modernity, during which a range of social changes was precipitated by industrialization, urbanization, and technological progress. In the early twentieth century, Benjamin forged a new application of the term 'authenticity' when discussing the recently developed technologies of reproduction – (sound) film and photography. He argued that 'the whole sphere of authenticity eludes . . . reproduction', including technological reproduction, because '[t]he here and now of the original underlies the concept of its authenticity' (2008: 21). While Benjamin examined the role of new media of his day in shaping the modern aesthetic experience and perception, more recently media theorists such as Bolter and Grusin have shifted the focus to the present cultural context, which is governed by the contradictory imperative to both erase all traces of mediation and to multiply (old and new) media (Bolter and Grusin 2000: 5). They argue that, from an epistemological perspective, immediacy is transparency, the notion that 'a medium could erase itself and leave the viewer in the presence of the objects represented'. People experience a sense of immediacy when they feel that the medium has disappeared and that their experience is therefore authentic (2000: 70). Underpinned by the belief in some 'necessary contact point between the medium and what it represents', a belief Bolter and Grusin speculate is fuelled by a desire for union and wholeness, immediacy requires the creation of an experience that is received as very close to our daily sensory experiences (2000: 83, 22).

Similarly, the concepts associated with the first cluster of meanings connected with 'authenticity' have been shaped by social change. For example, during the period when court culture was dominant in Europe, the terms 'sincerity' and 'naturalness' were used to describe behaviour that contrasted with social role-play in public. Ernst van Alphen and Mieke Bal point to sincerity's close link to the sixteenth-century preoccupation with pretence and concealment 'during an epoch in which the theatre emerge[d] as the dominant idiom of secular representation' (2009: 2). Doris Kolesch notes how 'naturalness' was used from the sixteenth century onwards, most prominently by Jean-Jacques Rousseau, to advocate behaviour that avoided the rhetorical-theatrical etiquette expected at the French court (2005: 223). However, while Rousseau could still use the metaphor of mask because he could detect a clear contrast between the masquerade of an elaborate public persona and a natural state, contemporary cultural critic Diedrich Diederichsen regrets the loss of this difference. He attributes this loss to the wide use of strategies, invited by consumerist culture, for (re)inventing 'authentic' selves as part of self-optimization. He also observes a concurrent blurring of the boundaries between art and life in entertainment and art formats 'that work with supernumeraries, participation, competition and certain recurrent performers who are their own directors' (die mit Statisten, Partizipation, Wettbewerb und bestimmten wiederkehrenden, mit sich selbst identischen Darsteller-Regisseuren arbeiten: Diederichsen 2012).

The complexity that characterizes the aesthetic experience of authenticity, and its use as a conceptual tool in discussion, together with the term's ubiquity have contributed to it being called 'a site where postmodern quandaries are played out in all their tearing tensions' (Funk, Gross and Huber 2012: 11). In this book, we respond to some of these areas of conceptual complexity and tension in two main ways. First, we delineate and focus on the two aforementioned clusters of meaning relevant to the discourse of authenticity in the theatre we explore. And second, we outline the differences between what we characterize as idealizing and sceptical destabilizing approaches to authenticity in the theatre. While the idealizing approach usually does not interrupt or trouble a compelling *sense* of contact with the authentic, the sceptical approach involves a sense of both contact and its destabilization. One of the main aims of this book is to explore the potential such destabilization has for inviting fresh perspectives on contemporary unfamiliar people.

The idealizing approach to Authenticity-Effects and its critics

In theatre typified by the *idealizing* approach to authenticity, makers or spectators often operate under the assumption that performance can offer direct access to truthful, sincere or unmediated speech, selves or bodies. That the representational means by which this access is made possible are themselves artistic choices and techniques, and therefore forms of artifice, is rarely foregrounded and sometimes even concealed. The idealizing approach to Authenticity-Effects tends to be accompanied by the promise to provide – or the spectator's certainty that she has experienced – 'integrity', 'honesty', 'truthfulness', 'immediacy', and an alternative to the artifice and fabrication often associated with contemporary media representations. Concepts and perspectives such as these have often appeared in discussions and reviews of contemporary forms of verbatim drama (see, for example, comments by the editors and theatre-makers in Hammond and Steward 2008: 10, 17, 24, 33, 61–3). Our use of the term 'idealizing' draws on a commentary by Julie Salverson about another genre of theatre involving 'real' people, Canadian community-based popular theatre, a prominent feature of which is the telling of personal stories, often by members of targeted communities rather than actors. Writing in the mid-1990s, Salverson observed a tendency among workers in this field to be 'faithful to the integrity of the storyteller – not to interfere with her words, to make her the final arbiter of what gets shown or said', and refers to it as an 'idealization of "authenticity"' (Salverson 1996: 184). Underpinning this practice is the notion that unmediated access to personal stories (whether scripted and/ or told by the originary speaker) is the ideal, and that this may not only protect the participants from being violated, but also help ensure sincerity and honesty. The approach to storytelling described by Salverson regards unmediated autobiographical speech as an ideal route to integrity and consequently to a form of wholeness for the speaker. Salverson questions aspects of this approach when she argues that an overemphasis on a single authentic story does not adequately allow for multiple points of view: 'Such a story may remain either outside the experience of the listener, as the exotic and impenetrable but vicariously viewed "other"; or, it will be collapsed and assimilated as "just like me"' (1996: 184).

A similar version of the idealizing approach has often been observed in verbatim theatre. For example, in commenting that 'when the bricks and mortar of a play are real conversations, people use such idiosyncratic and bizarre language that it is immediately recognizable as lacking in artifice' and 'has the undeniable ring of truth about it' (Soans 2008: 24), British verbatim playwright Robin Soans makes the point explicitly. Such language, he argues, offers a truthful channel of reportage capable of countering the age of spin and 'decline in standards of honesty in public life' (2008: 17). Recent scholarship has suggested that the characterization of verbatim methods by practitioners such as Soans implies that it can give unmediated access to the words – and thereby to the authentic thoughts and feelings – of the original speakers. Both Stephen Bottoms and Stuart Young have criticized documentary drama that privileges what they refer to as 'the illusion of' direct speech, while at the same time disguising the editorial mediation or artistic invention processes involved in the creation of speech in such drama (Bottoms 2006: 59, 61, 67; Young 2009: 76). For similar reasons, Carol Martin criticizes verbatim theatre that fails to display quotation marks (Martin 2006: 4). Young links the practice of framing testimony as arriving unmediated from the sources' mouths with what Derek Paget has called the 'recording' tradition of documentary. Paget characterizes this tradition as informed by a belief that facts and information merely need to be assembled in order for truth to emerge, and that the effacement of the artistic creators and their subjectivity will produce an 'objective' account. He claims the alternative tradition is a radical 'reporting' one that declares the perspectives of the artist-creators, and recognizes facts and information as value-laden (Paget 1990: 39–40). As Martin reminds us, poststructuralist thought has insisted that such reporting on social reality is also constructed: 'There is no "really real" anywhere in the world of representation... Representation creates multiple truths for its own survival' (2006: 14).

The preference shared by Bottoms, Martin, and Young for a self-aware theatre practice that draws attention to the mediation and manipulation processes that are part of artistic and social discourse, and to the complicated relationship between representation and the real, is informed by a scepticism regarding the idea that unmediated speech and objective assemblage are either possible or ideal. Bottoms and Young each acknowledge a preference that is also partly informed by Derrida's poststructuralist critique of the privileging of direct speech.

In a concise explication of that critique, Christopher Norris argues that Derrida viewed such privileging as the result of hierarchical dualist thought that prioritizes speech as an ideal moment of pure self-presence in which an intimate link between sound and sense, signifier and signified can be experienced. By contrast, this tradition of thought demotes writing – reductively conceived as graphic or inscriptional – to the status of a lifeless transcription of speech, an alien depersonalized medium that stands between intent and meaning (Norris 1991: 28). Against this tradition Derrida redefined writing as 'the "free play" or element of undecidability within every system of communication', and as the 'endless displacement of meaning which both governs language and places it forever beyond the reach of a stable, self-authenticating knowledge' (1991: 28–9). Not only positing writing as the precondition of language, he conceived it as prior to speech. Derrida's notions of undecidability and displacement are related to his theory of the endless deferral of meaning and his critique of what he called the Western 'metaphysics of presence'. This metaphysics is clearly expressed in any idealizing treatment of speech as a moment of pure self-presence. Derrida's critique was a response to linguist Saussure's insight that language is a differential network of meaning – that is, a network where differences of sound and sense that have been agreed and made conventional by a group of language users are the markers of meaning (Norris 1991: 24). Derrida observed that within this network neither the signifier (e.g. the spoken or written word as material vehicle) nor the signified (the concept it evokes) are ever fully present, but always similar to and different from other signifiers and concepts.

Thinking about the impact of Derrida's theories on Western theatre, Elinor Fuchs argues that the idea of spontaneous and immediate speech has been questioned through practices such as showing how any spoken utterance is already infiltrated by the pre-existing linguistic system. For example, various methods have been used in what Fuchs calls 'theatre of Absence' to show the pre-written scripts and scores that actors usually hide. Through concealing memorization of words, modes of verbal delivery and gestural sequences, actors in illusionist theatre create *a sense of* spontaneous presence or immediacy (Fuchs 1985: 166). She also considers the way in which Derrida's theory of traces, like his theory of deferred meaning, challenges the idealization of the actor's 'Presence' that was especially prominent among Artaud- or Grotowski-inspired North American artists of the 1960s and 1970s. For Fuchs, this Presence is constituted by the actor's magnetism and the heightened awareness that moves between co-present actor and spectator, which sustain the 'unique self-completion of the world of the spectacle' (1985: 163). Linking this idealization to a desire for a clarified self, and a situation in which the self fully possesses the present, she states that, according to the trace-structure theory, no human can become entirely present to him/herself, because everything is inhabited by the trace of something it is not, including traces of the past and future (1985: 163–5). Among work that has challenged idealization of the actor's Presence, Fuchs counts Richard Foreman and Robert Wilson's early experiments, presenting their use of what she calls 'amateurs' as a bid to avoid contamination by 'the enlarged personal "presence" of the professional' (1985: 165). Non-professional theatre performers have the capacity to trouble idealizing approaches to presence by, for example, revealing the rehearsed rather than spontaneous nature of their words and actions. However, as the use of the non-professional performer and her autobiographical speech in the community-based theatre witnessed by Salverson (1996) testifies, any likelihood of aspects of such a performer's presentation troubling the metaphysics of presence will depend on whether they are operating in a suitable context, such as the 'theatre of Absence'.

Sceptical approaches to Authenticity-Effects: potential invitations and outcomes

In the case of the HAU productions we explore in this book, both the performance works and responses to them have been characterized by a greater scepticism regarding the possibility of authentic speech and bodies than can be found in the idealizing approach. Such scepticism is a prominent feature of the experimental productions we analyse. Reasons for this include the fact that, as already mentioned, many of the practitioners and companies who presented at the HAU during the Lilienthal era trained at the Institute for Applied Theatre Studies in Gießen, where they were exposed to practice and theory informed by poststructuralist and postdramatic thought, including 'theatre of Absence'. For example, Kroesinger met Robert Wilson and Heiner Müller in Gießen and later worked for both of them as a production assistant. He went on to become a significant contributor to what Thomas Irmer has referred to as a new form of German documentary theatre that 'explores the phenomena of the present through an elaborate understanding of media culture' as well as the poststructuralist theory of deconstruction (Irmer 2006: 20). Irmer has interpreted specific work by Kroesinger as interrogating 'the ways in which audiences relate to documents in different media'. In so doing, Kroesinger sharpens awareness of how perception becomes relative and of how 'truth is negotiated, found and lost again – bound to media' (2006: 21–2). Rather than promising truthfulness, such work allows an experience of the complexity and difficulty of truthful representation. Kroesinger's attention to the problematics of representation brings his work into contact with what Bill Nichols classifies as the 'reflexive mode' in film documentary, a vehicle for a sceptical perspective that challenges assumptions about transparent language and objectivity (Nichols 1991: 63–5).

Our use of the phrase 'Authenticity-Effects' is itself an endorsement of a sceptical approach towards the notion of direct contact with truthful, sincere or unmediated speech, selves, and bodies. It is a paradoxical term that, by referring to the artifice of theatrical techniques, points to the complex nature of authenticity both on and off stage. Jonathan Culler has noted that *aesthetic* authenticity involves a paradox because

> to be experienced as authentic it must be marked as authentic, but when it is marked as authentic it is mediated, a sign of itself, and hence lacks the authenticity of what is truly unspoiled, untouched by mediating cultural codes. (Culler 1988: 164)

The employment of Authenticity-Effects in sceptical ways has the capacity to illuminate the way staging – which includes framing or marking – is a constitutive moment of authenticity (Fischer-Lichte 2007: 24). It can also make apparent the way authenticity (both on and off stage) is 'constituted by a performative act and observation' (Knaller and Müller 2005: 45). That is, the sceptical approach can illuminate the way a sense of the authentic can be constituted by a certain mode of (re)presentation and viewing, and an agreement between performers and observers. Furthermore, it can show that the authentic is not a given and fixed entity, but rather the product of an agreement that has to be renewed for each authenticating act. For example, a performance claiming to present people who are experts or specialists in a particular field rather than professional actors might be watched by audiences presuming that it offers an authentic glimpse of the social realities that mark these people's lives. During the performance, each instance revealing the experts' seemingly genuine vulnerability, lack of theatre training, and idiosyncrasies such as speech mannerisms initiate a renewal of the authenticity contract. Manifestations of these instances include: struggles with the memorization and delivery of text and choreography, use of the performers' off-stage names, and improvised dialogue dominated by dialectics and sociolects (Garde 2013b: 184–5). What audiences perceive as genuine, untrained behaviour reflects current conventions and individual expectations of professional acting. When the conventions associated with trained actors in mainstream early twentieth-first-century theatre and film suddenly become clear in the work of non-actors – such as when the presentation appears very polished and the text unexpectedly complex – for some receivers the authenticity agreement might be challenged and the sense of authenticity disrupted. However, other viewers may see the betrayal of these conventions as an honest acknowledgment of the artifice of theatre.

A common result of the sceptical deployment of Authenticity-Effects in theatre, and one often featured in the HAU productions we investigate, is a state of uncertainty about whether one is, or ever can be, in the presence of the authentic. Such uncertainty invites such questions as: what is the ontological nature of a particular phenomenon? Are this performer's actions rehearsed? Is this element of the spoken or written text fictional? Are we being asked to respond to the text within the framework of a theatrical performance or within that of everyday life? Who authored it? Is this moment meant to appear authentic or artificial? How complete is my understanding of this person or event? The practice of generating the uncertainties exemplified by these questions recalls what Hans-Thies Lehmann has referred to as 'the postdramatic theatre of the real'. In his seminal work on the postdramatic, first published in 1999, Lehmann argues that the main point of such theatre 'is not the assertion of the real as such . . . but the unsettling that occurs through the *indecidability* whether one is dealing with reality or fiction' (2006: 101). What Lehmann calls 'an *aesthetics of indecidability*' (2006: 100) can manifest itself in different forms, such as a single moment in a performance that audiences might identify as real (or as fictive), or as an ongoing oscillation between the two.

One of our findings regarding the potential outcomes of the uncertainty created by the HAU productions we focus on is that the uncertainty can produce something like the ambiguity and openness of meaning, the incompleteness of understanding and of proximity that characterize encounters with people and their worlds, particularly culturally diverse people. As we have argued elsewhere, theatre that uses Authenticity-Effects in a way that opens up liminal states of disorientation for the spectator 'can encourage new and unstable modes of perceiving self, other and representations' (Garde and Mumford 2013: 164). In an appraisal of documentary theatre, Stephen Bottoms draws a related conclusion when he asserts that uncertainty and circumspection are necessary to 'any honest appraisal of history – which is of course the story of competing discourses, not unmediated facts' (2006: 64). As we shall demonstrate in the production-analysis chapters of this book (Chapters 5–8), Theatre of Real People at the HAU has often created moments of uncertainty by both delivering and troubling a sense of authentic contact with contemporary people. As we show in the next chapter, this frequently playful treatment of authenticity is well placed to destabilize perceptions, in particular those regarding familiar and unfamiliar people from both the past and present.

Authenticity-Effects and recent German theatre theory and practice

In recent German-language discussion of authenticity in theatre, particularly contemporary work that casts real people, terms such as *Authentizitätseffekte* (Authenticity-Effects) and *Authentizitätseindrücke* (Authenticity-Impressions) have already been employed, and associated with a sceptical approach. As well as using both terms, Annemarie Matzke, a theatre scholar and member of She She Pop, has offered one of the most extensive elaborations by a practitioner of the purpose and nature of these effects. In a 2006 essay, she argues that onstage authenticity is always the effect of a construction. She outlines how scepticism regarding the concept of authenticity has featured in various scientific discourses, including theory that has challenged the idea of authentic gender through concepts such as performativity and masquerade. Extending Helmut-Lethen's thinking about the way authenticity seems related to a criterion for differentiating between degrees of artificiality, Matzke presents stage authenticity as no longer about how authentic representation can be achieved, but about a rhetorical problem: how can the spectator be given an impression of immediacy when such an impression is the result of construction? In the context of performance work by companies such as her own that are concerned with the self-representation strategies of people both on and off stage, and with exposing how effects of authenticity are constructed, she attributes the interest in this rhetorical problem to the contemporary insistence that we be good at selling ourselves and therefore at creating an authentic self-image. Matzke interprets the attention to degrees of artifice and staging as much more than a simple de-masking of social reality as staged. In a context in which the difficulty of distinguishing between the real and the staged has become a pressing issue, it constitutes an important attempt to meet the complexity of that reality with equally complex artistic means (Matzke 2006: 41–7).

In the case of works employing non-professional performers, Matzke outlines a number of structures and devices that provide an impression of authenticity and/or show how such impressions may be constructed. These include the opposition between, on the one hand, the performer's closeness to everyday life and, on the other, the theatrical frame. The non-professional performer seems authentic because she does not fulfil the conventions of an actor conjured by the theatre frame. Instead, she wears everyday clothes, makes verbal mistakes, and seems personally committed to what is said. Another strategy is the laying bare of the (relatively small number of) staged elements utilized, such as the rationale for casting-choices and pre-arranged tasks. As well as providing a truthful acknowledgment of artifice, the performance may seem minimally artificial compared with more established forms of staging such as realist illusionism or Brecht's self-reflexive interruption of fictional figures and fables. Other techniques include orchestrating moments in which performers fail to achieve, or provide alternatives to, the usual standards of professional performance. This can occur when a non-professional performer lacks training in vocal projection and diction, or when lengthy improvization sequences lead to fatigue and loss of control. These strategies reveal that the impression of immediacy is the effect of differences that operate in a particular context, particularly between degrees of artificiality and types of theatre (Matzke 2006: 39–45).

To better illustrate how notions and senses of authenticity are culturally and historically determined, Matzke instances Grotowski, whose work, though intended as a form of authentic performance, no longer seems to her authentic. By contrast, for more recent companies and their spectators – Matzke includes She She Pop and Forced Entertainment as examples – moments of representational failure are common sources of a sense of authenticity (Gronau 2006: 22). Another representational technique that can be added to the list of recent sceptical approaches to Authenticity-Effects is the emphasis on destabilizing the dichotomous conceptual coupling of the 'real' and the 'fictional', which Erika Fischer-Lichte regards as a prominent feature of recent theatre developments in Europe (Fischer-Lichte 2008: 84). Ways of blurring the boundaries between the factual and the fictional in recent documentary theatre include the refusal to display quotation marks (Young 2009: 80), or to clearly indicate character, time, and place designations, and in such a way that deep uncertainty is created about whether a spoken text or episode is fictional, mediated or verbatim.

As Chapter 6 in particular will illustrate, this uncertainty can have an especially strong impact on audiences when they are directly addressed by performers and have to decide whether to respond to the pressure to make decisions, as is intrinsic to everyday communication, or whether to interpret the verbal address as fictional – that is, without 'having consequences relevant to action' (Habermas 1987: 195). When theatre's conventional markers of artifice have been lost or toned down – for example, through a replacement of actors by real people and of the proscenium stage with public spaces – the boundaries between real life and theatre performance can be blurred to such an extent that audiences are unable to decide whether they are being exposed to everyday language and its illocutionary force (Habermas 1987: 196), or to fiction. This inability to assess an individual performance moment is reinforced by potentially conflicting signposts of reality and fiction in different aspects of the overall performance, such as its framing, use of different modes of communication and media, and its narrative content. Some of the potential effects of the types of uncertainty discussed above include the drawing of attention to the manipulative processes of documentary representation (Young 2009: 80), and/or to our inability to fully grasp the thoughts, feelings, and actions of people (Garde and Mumford 2013: 157). This inability to grasp is an issue we return to in Chapter 8 in particular.

One reason why the outlined techniques and modes of representation have successfully created (and destabilized) a sense of authenticity is that they have broken with the more familiar conventions of contemporary Western theatre. As Shannon Jackson has observed, in an essay for the 2012 Monsters of Reality performance festival in Oslo (a festival dedicated to new 'dramaturgies of the real'): 'The deployment of a medium or technique in a zone where such a medium or technique is new or unfamiliar instigates effects that feel real' (Jackson 2013: 128).

In a discussion about approaches to authenticity that occurred in 2004 between theatre-makers and scholars at Berlin's Free University, Annemarie Matzke associated 'Authenticity-Effects' with a knowing self-representation concerned not with a true 'I' or self, but a good staging (Matzke, in Gronau 2006: 19). Our use of the term is broader in so far as we extend it also to theatre practice that *is* concerned with a sense of the true self, or which is less assertive about the impossibility of achieving the true and genuine. However, we share Matzke's appreciation of the staged nature of authenticity, relevant structures and staging devices used in recent performance, and the way that authenticity can be an agenda for not only audiences, but also some theatre-makers. The latter issue in particular has prompted a range of reactions in German-language discussions of authenticity between researchers and practitioners. For example, in his contribution to the aforementioned Monsters of Reality publication, Imanuel Schipper, who has worked with state theatres in Germany and Switzerland as well as companies such as Rimini Protokoll, proposes a thought-provoking if unresolved line of argument. He argues, on the one hand, that 'authenticity is constructed by the public' and is 'not an attribute of the performance or the story, ... rather describ[ing] a "mode of perception" within the spectator'. And on the other, that 'it is possible to construct authentic feelings for the audience' (Schipper 2013: 68). While we agree with his acknowledgment of the audience's role in perceiving and producing authenticity, we argue that performances that employ the techniques and modes of representation outlined in the present pages are more likely to invite the mode of perception he refers to. That is, we view a sense of the true, sincere, and unmediated as the result of an interaction between theatre-makers, the performance events they instigate, and the participants in those events.

In the 2004 discussion involving Matzke, Daniel Wetzel of Rimini Protokoll presented the term 'authenticity' much as Schipper does, claiming that it was used by spectators of his company's productions, by observers rather than the observed. Describing it as a form of conceptual *Torte* (a rich multi-layered cake), he stated that during audience discussions it was the term often reached for by spectators trying to describe: an effect of the genuine, a feeling of proximity, an impression that one has not only received a presentation that follows the agreed rules, but contains something that cuts through this demonstration and functions more directly (Wetzel, in Gronau 2006: 14). In a 2010 interview with Ulrike Garde, Wetzel's collaborator Helgard Haug's response to the suggestion that the group's work with experts of the everyday often created an experience of oscillation between the impression of authenticity and of staging was that this oscillation was important. While the experts, she said, initially attempt to speak about themselves 'as authentically as is possible' (möglichst authentisch), she described 'authentic' as a word Rimini Protokoll themselves tended to avoid, and then drew attention to the fabricated nature of the cast members' final narratives that are crafted knowingly for public dissemination (Haug, in Garde 2010b). While Rimini Protokoll do not themselves consciously operate a concept of Authenticity-Effects, they do use techniques that arouse a sense of the authentic. In a 2004 essay, Daniel Schreiber criticized what he described as the danger of a repetitive loop of *Authentizitätseffekte* in Rimini Protokoll's work (Schreiber 2004: 42). While we might take issue with his association of such effects with uninteresting and voyeuristic presentation of surfaces, we agree that the company's staging of everyday realities generates a play with a *sense* of authenticity.

Comparing Authenticity-Effects with reality effects and V-effects

In recent German reception of theatre that works with real-people performers, the term 'Authenticity-Effects' has on occasion been used interchangeably with 'reality effects' (Schreiber 2004: 41–2). Sometimes this use of the latter phrase consciously draws on the definition of this term by Roland Barthes in his essay 'The Reality Effect' ('L'effet de réel', 1968). While there are points of overlap between Barthes' concept and our definition of Authenticity-Effect, it is important to distinguish the two, as they refer to distinct phenomena in different media. Barthes defines reality effects as produced by details, in descriptive sections of literary and historical narratives, that he argues are 'superfluous' or 'futile' in so far as they have no structural function (Barthes 1986: 141). As an example, he cites the following description from Gustave Flaubert's 'A Simple Heart' from *Three Tales* (1877): 'on old piano supported, under a barometer, a pyramidal heap of boxes and cartons'. According to Barthes, in the context of the narrative, the piano and boxes can be read as having symbolic and atmospheric value, but 'no purpose seems to justify reference to the barometer' (1986: 142). While 'superfluous' details 'cumulatively constitute some index of character or atmosphere', at first glance and on its own, a single detail like the barometer only serves the function of signifying the real. Such a detail says nothing but 'I am the real' and thereby produces a reality effect. Barthes claims such an effect is crucial to the 'verisimilitude which forms the aesthetic of all the standard works of modernity' (1986: 148).

What our concept of Authenticity-Effect and Barthes' reality effect have in common is an artistic device that can intensify the appearance or suggestion that the art work is directly linked to the reality it refers to. However, in the theatre we discuss, the main vehicle for this sense of a direct link with reality is the real-people performers who, unlike Barthes' superfluous literary detail, can both represent and *be* that which is represented. This ontological doubling can invite various audience responses, including a sense that these performers are signifying 'I am the real', a sense that they *are* the real, or an uncertainty about their ontological nature. Moreover, the nature of these performers is important to the narrative structures and meaning-making processes of the productions they participate in, and, as Ariane de Waal has argued, 'these bodies "matter" both within and beyond the world of the play' (2015: 19). The doubling encourages the audiences to consider, for example, whether the performer and what she or he does is authentic (sincere, genuine, truthful), and/or whether the contact with the performer is unmediated and intimate. Such consideration can turn attention to the nature of the social behaviours and relations both on and off stage. While Barthes' concept of the reality effect 'is an analytical tool that throws light on how fictional narratives can promulgate a sense of the real' (Bensmaia 2010: 492), our concept of the Authenticity-Effect is an analytical tool for assessing and questioning the relation to social reality of both performers and spectators in Theatre of Real People.

Our concept and the so-called 'A-effects' of Bertolt Brecht also require differentiation, and that is why we do not abbreviate 'Authenticity-Effects' in the following pages. Unfortunately, A-effects continues to be used as an English-language shorthand for 'alienation effects', a term frequently criticized as a misleading translation of *Verfremdungseffekte* (defamiliarization or distantiation effects) (Brooker 1994: 192–3; Mumford 2003: 1404–5). While we want to avoid confusion with Brecht's *Verfremdungseffekt* (which we shall refer to as the V-effect), it is important to negotiate the points of overlap this concept has with ours. V-effects often involve a self-referential display of theatrical artifice in order to make the familiar strange. It is the case that some defamiliarization techniques, and the sense of inauthenticity they engender, can paradoxically contribute to the generation of Authenticity-Effects. For example, through a self-reflexive disruption of a fourth-wall illusion, drawing attention to how that illusion (and theatre) is made, V-effects can create a sense of being in the presence of authentic theatre-making processes.

Brecht's V-effects differ from Authenticity-Effects in a number of ways, however. For example, as we discuss in our analysis of HAU productions, Authenticity-Effects are often used not only to make the familiar unfamiliar, but also to make the strange familiar. Unlike V-effects, they are also not always intentionally created by theatre-makers, although the use of the associated techniques and modes of representation already outlined above make them a likely occurrence. Furthermore, Brecht's V-effects differ from those idealizing approaches to Authenticity-Effects that assert the possibility of direct access to the essence of social phenomena. This is because his anti-essentialist techniques draw attention to the socio-historically specific and dialectical nature of the social world, and thus its fluid and ever-changing nature. V-effects can also differ from those Authenticity-Effects informed by a sceptical attitude, because Brecht's artistic devices are utilized to show that causal laws underpin social and material reality, and that, using Marxist modes of analysis, they can be known and managed (Mumford 2000: 43–9).

Brecht's tendency to regard *certain* aspects of social reality as stable and given has been modified in the HAU productions examined in this book. Such theatre embodies a shift from a vision of the world marked by ideological coherence to an ambivalent and multi-perspectival vision of a world in which fiction and fact, everyday life and art meet. In turn, that shift can be connected to an increasingly networked and intercultural world full of encounters with people and representations whose ontological status is hard to assess. What we invite readers to consider throughout our case studies is in what ways Theatre of Real People at the Hebbel am Ufer worked with and produced Authenticity-Effects, and whether the mobilization of these effects opened up fresh perspectives on diverse and contemporary real people.

4

Encounters with Cultural Diversity at the HAU

The Hebbel am Ufer (HAU) under Matthias Lilienthal established a reputation as a production house firmly committed not only to addressing contemporary social topics, but also to encouraging an openness to artistic and cultural diversity and exchange. When asked in 2009 about his intentions as artistic director of the HAU, Lilienthal stated an interest in creating work that puts 'things out there that are unknown, or that involve issues that are still incomprehensible' (Yamaguchi 2009: 7). This chapter explores the HAU's approach to both cultural diversity and to the unfamiliar, placing the work presented under Lilienthal's leadership into the broader context of discussions about cultural diversity in theatre studies.

In the *Import Export* collection of commentaries and discussions on the HAU, Lilienthal relates that the HAU team played an important role in providing topics to which resident and guest artists would bring their aesthetics (Hehmeyer and Pees 2012: 18–19). A prominent feature of these topics was a focus on diverse cultural encounters. It is noteworthy that when Lilienthal discussed cultural and artistic identities, he frequently referred to the local (the suburb of Kreuzberg and the city of Berlin) and the global rather than to national identity. Furthermore, when discussing how people from diverse backgrounds interacted in the theatre scene in post-unification Berlin, he did not shy away from pointing out tensions arising from their differences, while at the same time emphasizing that the encounters offered an opportunity to get to know each other better (2012: 18, 22–3).

In our analysis of these cultural interactions in HAU theatre productions, we regard encounter with the unfamiliar as an important component. A significant contributor to a sense of the unfamiliar in the productions we explore is the staging of people who may be perceived by those involved as different, foreign or insufficiently known. This is because of, first, their occupational, socio-economic, and ethnic background, and second, their status as 'theatre strangers' – that is, as non-professional performers who do not usually perform their everyday activities in the theatre and thus represent a kind of 'foreign body' on stage (Roselt 2006: 34). Sources of the former's unfamiliarity include personal idiosyncrasy and social-class differences that can be expressed through elements of verbal and non-verbal expression, body language, elements of costume and clothing, as well as the actions performed as part of a show. A major source of the latter's unfamiliarity is their transgression of dominant theatre conventions.

Our use of the term 'unfamiliar' draws on the denotations of the German word *fremd* (Albrecht 2003: 234). That is, we use it to encompass the following related concepts: 'different', 'foreign', 'strange', and 'insufficiently known' (including the marginalized and not publicly visible). In this book, we sometimes use the term 'stranger' as a synonym for 'unfamiliars' in order to avoid the latter neologism's unwieldy nature. Cultural Studies scholar Sarah Ahmed has cautioned that many stranger discourses are based on the assumption 'that being a stranger is a matter of inhabiting a certain body', and that the stranger is 'a figure of the unassimilable'. She posits instead that the figure of the stranger is produced by the 'processes of expelling *or* welcoming the one who is recognized as a stranger' (Ahmed 2000: 4). Far from being something that simply exists, the stranger is the result of discourses that create a figure of the other that does not belong to a given space, one example being the marginalized figure (usually a black and/or working-class male) who, according to 'stranger danger' discourse, does not belong to the local (usually white middle class) community (Ahmed 2000: 31). By contrast, we use 'stranger' not in the sense of a given and fixed entity that does not belong, but to denote phenomena that have the potential to become better known and hence neither purely familiar nor unfamiliar.

The semantic range of the term 'unfamiliar' indicates that what is regarded as familiar and unfamiliar in and between cultures and subjects is not a stable fixed entity, but rather the result of processes of mutual positioning during encounters both in the arts (Gutjahr 2010: 26) and in everyday life (Baecker 2011: 5; Leggewie and Zifonun 2010: 12). Working from this premise of instability, we propose two versions of cultural encounter. In the first, what is unfamiliar has the potential to become better known and, in the second, something thought to be well known loses its sense of familiarity.

With regard to the first version, we argue that the performances we examine illustrate the potential for the unfamiliar to become *better* known, without suggesting to their audiences that it can or should be *fully* known. The idea of the capacity for becoming partially familiar informs our use of the terms 'strangers' and 'unfamiliar'. The word 'unfamiliar' is also useful to our discussion of the limited knowledge of and partial proximity to people that characterize the approach taken in our case studies. Its prefix 'un' serves to disrupt the intimacy suggested by 'familiar' and its Latin etymon *familiaris*, and challenges the strands of meaning that associate 'familiar' with phenomena that are 'well-known, habitual, customary' (OED 2000).

With regard to the second version of encounter with the unfamiliar, Theatre of Real People at the HAU frequently offered its audiences the opportunity to experience what they regarded as their *own* local, national or transnational space of belonging as unfamiliar. As Rimini Protokoll's Helgard Haug explained in an interview:

> [the unfamiliar] also refers to neighbours, to what is close and seems obvious, or institutions from your own country that you want to learn about. I wouldn't at all say that it [the unfamiliar] always has to be something that lies outside my own reach, but rather something I haven't previously opened up. ([das Fremde] bezieht sich tatsächlich auch auf den Nachbarn, das Naheliegende oder zum Beispiel auf Institutionen, die man kennen lernen möchte im eigenen Land. Ich

würde gar nicht immer sagen, das muss etwas sein, was außerhalb
meiner eigenen Reichweite liegt, sondern es bezieht sich auf etwas, was
sich mir vorher nicht erschlossen hat). (Haug, in Garde 2010a)

In this version of cultural encounter, what might appear initially
unremarkable to audiences can lose its sense of familiarity and
graspability as a performance develops. This version is well illustrated
by Rimini Protokoll's *100% City* (*100% Stadt*) and Lilienthal's brainchild
X-Apartments (*X-Wohnungen*). In the former production format, a
game with the representation of city inhabitants is played afresh in each
new city that hosts the show. In the latter, performances are staged in
apartments across a specific district in a city. The Berlin iterations of
these two formats challenged audiences' perceptions of local people
and environments that might have seemed generally familiar at the
outset, through an engagement with the cultural complexity and
unfamiliarity of not only the people living in the suburbs immediately
surrounding the HAU, but also those further afield within Berlin. This
engagement with cultural complexity – as evident in the cross-section
of the city's multifaceted residents present on stage in *100% Berlin* –
acknowledges cultural difference as a fact of our everyday life that
is shaped by our '*Intercultural condition*' (Leggewie and Zifonun
2010: 14).

As we employ it here, the term 'intercultural' both includes and
stretches beyond ethnicity as one possible marker of cultural identity. As
our title indicates, we generally prefer to use the term 'diverse', referring
both to encounters with diverse people and to the varied nature of these
encounters and their reception (Rancière 2009: 13). Originally a past
participle of the Latin verb *divertere* (to divert), 'diverse' suggests that
those involved in an encounter constantly position themselves with
respect to the other participants, rather than assuming fixed and
homogenized identities. Our emphasis recalls that which Rustom
Bharucha calls '*doing*' and which he presents as his preferred approach
for '*practicing* or *performing* the "intercultural"' (2014: 179). This active
approach was evident at the HAU as well as in the productions we
discuss. It was manifest, for example, in the experimentation with diverse

ways of presenting and inviting encounters between contemporary people from various backgrounds across a wide range of productions. For example, instead of presenting the Vietnamese community and artists as a single homogeneous group, the Dong Xuan Festival (2010) took a multifaceted approach to the two groups who either came as contract workers to the former German Democratic Republic (GDR), or were taken in as refugees in the former West Germany. The festival, partially located at the Vietnamese market halls in Berlin, featured work across genres by artists from different cultural backgrounds, including the visual artist Danh Vo and performance collective Rimini Protokoll. The diverse encounters that characterized this festival, as well as many other events at the HAU, reflected and contributed to a world marked by increased human mobility and global interconnectedness. These events offered alternatives to the nineteenth-century conceptualization of a (national) culture as a people's fixed, homogeneous 'island' (in Johann Gottfried Herder's sense), and as a sealed set of acts and objects. Instead, they operated with a concept of culture as a fluid complex of shared traditions, beliefs, and practices that characterize the way of living of a particular human group (Eagleton 2000: 34).

Discourses about a changing world and the HAU

When Lilienthal took the helm at the HAU in 2003, he and his team not only developed a responsiveness to its location within the ethnically diverse suburb of Kreuzberg and the cosmopolitan city of Berlin, but also fostered productions that, in their engagement with diverse 'real people', reflected the state of recent theoretical debates about key concepts of cultural identity and cultural entanglement. By 'real people' we mean here, as discussed in our Introduction, contemporary people who are usually non-professional theatre performers, and who appear in a theatre event as consensual self-representing protagonists (Figure 4.1).

At the HAU, the work with these 'real people' was informed by, for example, feminist and postcolonial theories that had challenged

Figure 4.1 Matthias Lilienthal in front of HAU 2 and the publicity campaign that demonstrated an interest in both real people and cultural diversity. Photograph by and copyright Georg Knoll.

previous stable, essentialist, and/or nation-based concepts of cultural identities. Such theories suggested instead that identity is created through repeated performative acts (Butler 1988), and argued that the 'interstitial passage between fixed identifications opens up the possibility of a cultural hybridity that entertains difference without an assumed or imposed hierarchy' (Bhabha 1994: 4). In Germany, the philosopher Wolfgang Welsch's concept of transculturality, an important contribution to the debate about cultural identity, took into account increased global mobility, migration, and networking. Like previous cultural theorists (Bhabha 1994; Said 1993), Welsch worked with the concept of hybridity, which described the '*inner differentiation and complexity of modern cultures*' and the 'multiple cultural connexions [that] are decisive in terms of our cultural formation. We are cultural hybrids' (1999: 198). He used 'the phrase "transcultural people" to refer to both what modern identities *are increasingly becoming* (a description of a condition), and to what they *should be* (a desideratum)' (Mumford 2014: 186).

The search for terms that adequately captured the social world of Germany (and other Western countries) in the first decade of the millennium also generated the neologism *zweiheimisch* to denote that many migrants, and even more so their children and grandchildren, felt at home in more than one national culture (Spohn 2006). At Berlin's House of World Cultures (Haus der Kulturen der Welt) in 2010, towards the end of Lilienthal's term at the HAU, the anthropologist Arjun Appadurai argued for intercultural dialogue that focuses on selected topics. In the same year, the journalist and migration expert Mark Terkessidis highlighted the new forms of (multiple) belongings and/or citizenships that marked Germany's diverse social reality. He also called for better access for all individuals, including migrants, to institutional frameworks, proposing that this access could generate greater diversity in the organizational structure of all institutions and result in what he defines as *Interkultur* (loosely translatable as 'inter-culture') in his programmatic book of the same title (Terkessidis 2010). Terkessidis' statements contrasted sharply with the claim by the then-prominent board member of Germany's central bank, Thilo Sarrazin, that Muslim immigrants in Germany were 'unfit and unwilling to integrate into society'.[1]

Negotiating the opportunities and pitfalls of cultural encounter

As part of their overall engagement with cultural diversity, the creative teams at the HAU responded to the challenging socio-political issues raised in such discussions by attending to questions of cultural identity and migration, on both a small and large scale. To this end they built on, for example, Lilienthal's experience as director for the 2002 Theatre of the World Festival (Theater der Welt), which had also launched the *X-Apartments* series. In 2004, as part of the HAU's larger project called Migration, *X-Apartments* were adapted to selected Berlin suburbs.

Another large production- and organizational format that dealt with cultural identity and encounter was the festival series Beyond Belonging. The first two festivals – called Migration[2] (2006) and Autoput Avrupa from Istanbul to Berlin (2007) – were hosted by the HAU and curated by Shermin Langhoff. The title of the latter festival refers to 'the transit route through former Yugoslavia which many work immigrants took to Germany from Yugoslavia, Greece and Turkey' in the 1970s and 1980s (Kulturstiftung des Bundes 2007). The festival has been described as a celebration of these migrants' contributions to cosmopolitan dispositions and experiences (Kosnick 2009: 39).

Apart from his desire to open the HAU's 'doors to this [local] community' of the Kreuzberg district by 'involving young Turkish directors, curators, stage artists and actors' (Lilienthal, in Yamaguchi 2009: 4), Lilienthal also addressed Berlin's position in Central Europe. While working with Frank Castorf at the Volksbühne, he had explored the social and artistic changes in Germany caused by the collapse of state communism. He went on to expand the scope of his social engagement by exploring the consequences of this historical change for neighbouring Poland in the festival Polski Express, which featured innovative theatre from Poland and had three iterations (2003, 2006, and 2010). This interest in social change was paired with a determination that the work at the HAU would 're-evaluate the concept of globalization in a positive way', a concept that, according to Lilienthal, was 'ostracized in the debate of the political left' ([[der Globalisierungsbegriff], der in der politisch linken Debatte verfemt ist, in der Arbeit des HAU positiv umwerte[n] ...) (Hehmeyer and Pees 2012: 18).

However, Lilienthal and his team chose a different approach to intercultural theatre, a form that is characterized by the inclusion of elements from other cultures' theatre traditions in a bid to change and renew the theatre-makers' own culture (Fischer-Lichte 2014; Knowles 2010). Instead, the HAU established a large-scale international festival hub that provided a platform for culturally and artistically diverse artists to showcase their *own* work, as well as for organized public and informal discussions. The Wirtshaus am Ufer, the bistro at HAU2 known as the WAU, played the important role of facilitator in these discussions. As Tom Sellar has pointed out, 'Lilienthal's practice is dramaturgical in the broadest sense, shaped around advocacy, research, and investigations of a political economy and culture which links across national lines'. The 'strategic institutional network he cultivated' (Sellar 2014b: 115) – and whether he did so as a dramaturge or curator (Sellar 2014a, 2014b) is a moot point – allowed for artists from the HAU and around the world to meet. Lilienthal mentions, for example, the fruitful interactions between Rimini Protokoll and Alvis Hermanis from Latvia (Hehmeyer and Pees 2012: 18). Hermanis himself has acknowledged that the production called *Latvian Stories* (*Lettische Geschichten*, 2006) was influenced by his encounter with Rimini Protokoll's use of people from everyday life (Seidler 2006).

This institutional-network approach encourages what Etienne Wenger has called 'communities of practice' (1998) – that is, communities that grow out of collaboration or interaction across national borders based on a shared practice or interest. In short, the aim was to foster diverse non-hierarchical encounters between artists, rather than invite local artists to integrate formal elements from other cultures into their work. In a manner that moved towards addressing what Bharucha calls 'the fraught dynamics of intercultural exchange', including 'the myth of an "equal" playing field in the global cultural economy' (Bharucha 2014: 180; Lo 2014: 119), most of the HAU's cultural festivals did not focus on national or ethnic origins and cultural practices. Rather, they were organized around particular themes – such as, in the case of Polski Express III, the issue of alternatives to capitalism in a post-communist world – to which everyone involved could contribute in his or her own way.

Any attempt to avoid reducing the polycultural inspirations of individual artists and their works to single origins is made more difficult when performance projects are organized under labels such as 'migration', labels which, as artists who have worked at the HAU have acknowledged, are sometimes necessary for securing additional funding (Çelik 2012: 51). Such organizational strategies and funding parameters can reinforce authenticating behaviour, which, according to sociologist Dirk Baecker, we are inclined to exhibit in our daily encounters with different cultures. Baecker observes a tendency to develop a sense of stable cultural belonging by searching for the reassurance of 'authentic' origins in everyday life, describing how people tend 'immediately to overestimate the identity and authenticity of the other culture, to search for the identity and authenticity of [their] own culture, and to reach for something that is subsequently celebrated, ideologized and ritualized' ([S]ofort überschätzt man die Identität und Authentizität der anderen Kultur, sucht nach der Identität und Authentizität der eigenen Kultur, findet auch irgend etwas, was dann zelebriert, ideologisiert und ritualisiert wird: Baecker 2011: 5). Within the framework of postcolonial studies, Gareth Griffiths describes how clinging to the myth of authenticity frequently coincides with an 'overwriting [of] the actual complexity of difference' (Griffiths 2006: 165). Neco Çelik, who in 2006 directed the premiere of Feridun Zaimoglu and Günter Senkel's provocative play *Black Virgins* (*Schwarze Jungfrauen*) at the HAU, has noted that there is a strong tendency in contemporary German theatre to turn artists whose biographies combine a socialization in Germany with experiences of (post) migration into '"top" specialists for Turkish culture' (Oberspezialisten für die türkische Herkunft: Çelik 2012: 48). This remark is an instance of the authenticating tendencies observed by Baecker (2011: 5).

It also points to the possibility that the initiative during the early years at the HAU to have artists such as Çelik, Tamer Yiğit, and other 'German-Turkish' film- and theatre-makers working there, was a double-edged sword. On the one hand, Lilienthal rightly states that, at the time, '[o]pening [the HAU's] doors to this community through our programs dealing with the issues and meaning of the immigrant situation at our theater [was] in itself quite a sensational thing' (Yamaguchi 2009: 4). These programmes were carefully supported by the provision of a professional theatre team, including the curator Shermin Langhoff, whose cultural and production expertise was greatly valued. On the other hand, reaching out to local artists and communities helped develop a new audience market, which has been received by some as motivated primarily by economic interest (Peters 2011: 170–1). Irrespective of such assessments, this new outreach represented an important stepping-stone for both artists and curators. It enhanced the artists' public profiles and prepared them for further development of their work at the Ballhaus Naunynstraße, which Langhoff re-opened in 2008 with the aim of making it a hub for what she called 'postmigrant theatre' (Langhoff 2009). This theatre acknowledged the cultural heterogeneity of German society and individual negotiations of the complexity of everyday life in a society where many people have different life stories due to migration. Looking back at his time at the HAU, Çelik acknowledges Lilienthal and Langhoff's warm support, while also requesting access to all German theatres without having to assume the role of specialist for migration issues (Çelik 2012).

Çelik was not the only artist associated with the HAU who invited further discussion about fixed and homogeneous views of (post) migrants, people he himself described as 'children of Germany' (Kinder Deutschlands: Çelik 2012: 50). Theatre-makers who were part of the 2004 version of *X-Apartments* that focused on the theme of 'migration' challenged the potential emphasis on ethnicity or national origin as the sole or predominant marker of cultural difference. For example, film-maker Fatih Akın and writer Feridun Zaimoglu chose to stage their contribution to *X-Apartments* in an anonymous space in urban Lichtenberg rather than in Kreuzberg (Akın and Zaimoglu, in Krottenthaler 2004), and Ayşe Polat's concurrent production invited audiences to explore their reactions to young people's provocative behaviour in such a way that the production drew stronger attention to socio-economic status than to ethnic background. Both theatre works are indicative of the HAU's way of uncovering and highlighting complexity and diversity when featuring cultural identities and encounters. Although, as our production analyses will demonstrate, some Theatre of Real People events did borrow and integrate elements from other cultures' performance traditions, these borrowings were the exception rather than the rule, and were often carefully self-reflexive (see, for example, Chapter 6, and Mumford 2013: 163).

Consequently, we argue a clear distinction needs to be drawn between the HAU's productions on the one hand, and what Brian Singleton calls intercultural theatre's history of 'recontextualiz[ing] and reshap[ing] culture' on the other (2014: 80). As Ric Knowles reminds us, the 'conscious practice [of intercultural performance] in the Western world began only in the twentieth century and its theorization in the Western academy in the 1970s and 1980s' (Knowles 2010: 6; Fischer-Lichte 2014: 1). It is a practice that has been criticized for failing to acknowledge an 'appropriative relationship between source and target cultures' that frequently involves the binary system of the 'west and the rest' (Knowles 2010: 26, 59). For example, Patrice Pavis has used the metaphor of the hourglass to describe a binary process whereby the source culture 'empties into' and is adapted to the target culture (1990: 57; 1992: 4–6). More recently, this type of intercultural theatre has been referred to as 'hegemonic intercultural theatre [HIT]' (Lei 2011: 571–86), and attempts have been made by institutions such as the Berlin-based Interweaving Cultures Project (Fischer-Lichte 2014) to renew the debate about theatre culture exchange in a manner that avoids past mistakes, including the essentialist notion that a return to origins is possible and should be pursued.

While the intercultural theatre we have just discussed, and the associated model of cultural appropriation, are not directly relevant to the theatre productions featured in this book, it is nevertheless important to be mindful of the challenging power relations that underpin the dynamics of all cultural exchange (Bharucha 2014: 180). Many productions at the HAU addressed the issue of power relations in provocative terms, including *X-Apartments* in 2004. For example, in a Lichtenberg apartment a real-people performer – who behaved threateningly and looked like a builder by trade – proceeded to fill the door frame of the only exit with bricks, thus slowly blocking the spectators' way out. In another apartment, staging an excerpt of Zaimoglu's short story 'God's Warriors' ('Gottes Krieger'), Akın invited spectators to explore power relations between the audience and the performers. This production sought to engage audiences with their potential prejudices towards religion, gender roles, and violence by deliberately setting up false expectations and destabilizing them by creating surprise, thus provoking them 'to examine possible tensions between participating cultures', as advocated by Jacqueline Lo and Helen Gilbert (2002: 47). In this sense, Akın and Zaimoglu's project is characteristic of the productions featured in this book, because it highlights 'the contested, unsettling, and often unequal spaces between cultures, spaces that can function in performances as sites of negotiation' (Knowles 2010: 4).

So as to highlight the importance of these spaces between cultures, we have chosen to focus on *encounters* with different people and between diverse people that destabilize perceptions of the familiar and the unfamiliar. The term 'encounter' can accommodate meetings that audiences and, to some extent, theatre-makers, neither expect nor plan, and that might result in *counter*-reactions, such as irritation, rejection, and feelings of ambivalence. A useful theoretical framework for exploring these moments of encounter involving the unfamiliar is Jens Roselt's phenomenological analysis of theatre performances as 'intermediary events' (Zwischenereignisse). Roselt directs attention to those moments during a performance when the seeming naturalness of perceptual and interpretative processes is removed (Roselt 2008: 16), and when something comes into the spotlight because it appears to be questionable (2008: 61). Roselt reports that audiences respond with (corporeal, affective, and cognitive) astonishment and heightened levels of attention (2008: 61; 71–8) when they are confronted 'with something new, unknown and unfamiliar that transgresses the categories they are used to' (Staunen verweist also auf die Konfrontation mit etwas Neuem, Unbekannten, Fremdem, das gängige Kategorien sprengt: Roselt 2008: 19). Similarly, Helena Grehan describes how, in performance, 'linguistic or representational surfaces can be disturbed or interrupted in ways that allow spectators to reflect on and ask questions about the nature of any response to that work' (2009: 2). She describes the effects of these disturbances as 'ambivalence', and as being about 'moments of self-recognition but also about the internal processes of doubt, anxiety, reflection and consideration individual spectators go through in their attempts to make sense of, or to respond to work' (2009: 23). Such disturbances invite spectators to acknowledge 'the complex, often contradictory and multi-layered questions and responses ... performance can trigger for spectators' (2009: 25).

It is our contention that a sceptical approach to Authenticity-Effects is well placed to destabilize our everyday perceptions and the underlying cognitive schemata that shape our expectations of the (un)familiar, resulting in a twofold transformative capacity. First, these Authenticity-Effects are able not only to disrupt perceptions that lock strangers into particular categories, but also to offer fresh perspectives on familiar phenomena. Second, they can make what might appear familiar to audiences lose its sense of familiarity and ability to be grasped. In both instances, audiences' cognitive schemas are challenged and the modification of these 'clusters of ideas for thinking with' can provide them with fresh perspectives on issues and people in social terms (Calcutt, Skrbis and Woodward 2009: 171; Garde 2015: 268). Audience reactions to both types of disruption might vary. In some instances, undergoing a singular disruptive moment in performance might produce a productive state of insecurity (Gutjahr 2010: 28) that prompts spectators to re-assess not only the authenticity of what they are experiencing, but also their perception of what seems to be familiar or unfamiliar, with regard to both people and cultural phenomena. Alternatively, instead of undergoing a single moment of destabilization, audiences might also continue to oscillate between the notion that, on the one hand, they have access to and can understand unfamiliar phenomena and, on the other hand, that this access and understanding are only partial or altogether impossible. In both these forms of reception, feelings of alterity are transformed into self-reflection, a state that can last beyond the performance event without necessarily leading to a sense of closure. Consequently, these destabilizations can expose audiences to the experience of failing to grasp the full meaning of a cultural encounter, a failure that emulates the productive insecurity that also characterizes the 'never-ending processes of getting to know one another' in an 'ongoing dialogue' (eine dialogische Annäherung [als] ein unendlicher Prozess: Regus 2009: 11). In these instances, theatre offers an aesthetic playground in which both habitual and new avenues of encountering unfamiliar people are put under the spotlight and tested. The creative space generated by these cultural encounters in theatre that interrupts, transgresses, and destabilizes conventional perceptions can thus offer a glimpse of the potentiality that Bharucha continues to attribute to 'the intercultural as a philosophical and creative concept' (2014: 181) despite the term's troubled history.

In our analyses of Theatre of Real People productions at the HAU, we study the potentiality and limits of a sceptical approach to Authenticity-Effects with regard to cultural encounter. As the following chapters will illustrate, these productions contain, on the one hand, Authenticity-Effects (in the sense of representational devices or elements) that carefully negotiate modes of viewing that involve a non-essentialist and non-reductive encounter with (un)familiar people. On the other hand, a number of them point to the risk that theatre-makers and audiences might relate to these strangers from the vantage point of cultural tourists and with the gaze of 'sensation-seekers and collectors of experiences ... [who] perceive the world as food for sensibility' (Baumann 1998: 94). Bharucha has coined the term 'interculturalists' as shorthand reserved for 'traveling scholars and tourists', who engage in this superficial and exoticizing touristic activity (2014: 182). This term, we argue, could be applied easily also to local audiences observing unfamiliar, non-trained performers while reducing them to their 'authentic' origins. Our analyses will engage with the risk attached to this kind of cultural encounter, while at the same time acknowledging how selected performances at the HAU explicitly addressed this issue. For example, when, in his production for *X-Apartments* 2008, director Nurkan Erpulat forced audience members to look through a keyhole at a veiled woman getting undressed, he overtly invited audiences to confront and reflect on their role, perspective, and ethical position with regard to this kind of *mise-en-scène*. Such a destabilizing approach to Authenticity-Effects aligns perfectly with Lilienthal's general insistence on audiences' critical engagement with the tensions underlying all postcolonial curatorship (and spectatorship) (Carp 2012: 97–8).

In addition to these ethical concerns, theatre scholars have also pointed out that, as with any innovative approach in theatre, putting real people on the stage is an aesthetic phenomenon that risks losing its impact 'because audiences get used to certain kinds of conventions in documentary or reality-based theatre' (Jackson 2013: 129; Raddatz 2014b). While this is an important caveat, it should be noted that, during Lilienthal's leadership, the HAU did effectively combine an innovative aesthetic and cultural agenda, so much so that theatre critic Eva Behrendt declared the HAU a 'model for the future' (2012: 33). In the forthcoming case studies, we test the capacity of Theatre of Real People at the HAU for creating a paradigmatic interplay of aesthetics and social engagement, which, in our climate of diversity, represents an ongoing challenge for theatres both within and beyond Germany.

Note

1 In her report on Sarrazin's book *Deutschland schafft sich ab* (*Germany Does Itself In*), *Guardian* reporter Kate Connolly highlights Sarrazin's statement that 'the behaviour of [Muslim immigrants] ... is putting the country under threat' and reports that it 'unleashed an impassioned debate about Germany's immigrant population' (2010).

5

Berliners with an 'Authenticity Guarantee': Cultural Complexity in *100% Berlin* and *100% City*

In 2008, for the Hebbel Theater's 100th birthday, Helgard Haug, Stefan Kaegi, and Daniel Wetzel developed *100% Berlin: A Statistical Chain Reaction* (*Eine statistische Kettenreaktion*), which presented 100 Berliners as a cross-section of society on the historical stage of HAU 1, formerly known as the Hebbel Theater. On 1 February, audiences saw this first iteration of Rimini Protokoll's game involving the representation of city inhabitants, which the theatre-makers subsequently adapted to many locations across the world. Conceived initially as a key component of the Hebbel Theater's birthday celebrations, it showcased Berlin's diverse population in an inclusive and cheerful atmosphere, and was developed later into several productions that used a sceptical approach to Authenticity-Effects in order to destabilize spectators' expectations of seemingly familiar home towns around the world.

When reviewing its first iteration, theatre critic Esther Slevogt (2008) called the 100 'ordinary' citizens performing on stage '*Berliner mit Authentizitätsgarantie*'. Slevogt employed the phrase ironically, indicating an awareness of the various interpretations that real people on stage might invite: on the one hand, the Berliners' status as non-professional theatre performers could encourage the naïve conclusion that their performances were authentic. On the other hand, their performances might illustrate that it is impossible to have unmediated access to personal authenticity within a *mise-en-scène* (Culler 1988: 164), and a spectator's potential yearning for unmediated access to personal stories cannot be fulfilled. In addition to this individual-related strand of authenticity, Slevogt likened the various urban demographic representations on stage – based on categories such as gender, age, marital status, nationality, and residential location – to a kind of large 'group portrait' (Gruppenbild), which points to another strand of 'authenticity', that of referential truth pertaining to Berlin's everyday life.

Slevogt's comments draw attention to two strands of authenticity that shape *100% Berlin*: that of sincerity and genuineness (and therefore credibility), in the sense that audiences may feel they have access to individual performers and personal stories that are honest and free from pretence or counterfeit; and that of a sense of referential truthfulness, in so far as the production title indicates a show that will mirror the city of Berlin in statistically accurate ways. It is noteworthy that *100% Berlin* tended to emphasize the latter, while subsequent iterations of the *100% City* format have moved towards creating more of a balance between the two aspects, largely due to a stronger focus on individual stories.

One of the issues foregrounded in the introduction of *100% Berlin*'s programme booklet – the only section of the booklet available in English on Rimini Protokoll's website – is the relationship between the individual and society, which is also presented as an integral part of the Hebbel Theater's history:

> For 100 years the Hebbel Theater has been a playhouse for pieces in which the individual is portrayed in relation to his surroundings. The Hebbel Theater's stage has also always been a platform for particular individual fates for the audience to examine. The audience represents society, the actor represents the individual. (Rimini Protokoll website)

This statement is followed by a critical reflection on how statistics tend to deny human individuality. At this point, the text in the programme notes differs from that on the website, drawing attention to the underlying tension between maintaining and losing the singularity of the individual performer, and representing the collective: 'What if faces were given to these statistics? What if Berlin could be represented by 100 people on stage?' (Was wäre, wenn diese Statistik Gesichter bekäme? Was, wenn Berlin sich auf einer Bühne durch 100 Menschen vertreten ließe?: Rimini Protokoll 2008).

The individual versus the collective in *100% Berlin*

The potential conflict between emphasizing the multiplicity of individual faces and identities, and aiming to provide a coherent representation of the city in a large-scale theatre performance, marks the entire theatre production from rehearsal process (Rimini Protokoll 2012b: 72) to final product. Even the show's organizational principle for recruiting the 100 participants is characterized by a tension between acknowledging the singularity of each performer, and absorbing them into a mass for the sake of statistical representation. This tension is particularly notable in the first version of the *100% City* format. *100% Berlin* placed great emphasis on telling the audience about the recruitment process via the 'statistical chain reaction' referred to in the production's subtitle. As a result of this foregrounding of the statistical criteria, the individual could almost be considered a mere number in this sequence of people.

The first person to introduce himself on HAU1's large revolve, according to the DVD recording of 1 February 2008, is Thomas Gerlach ('1%'), a home-based interviewer for the German Federal Statistical Office. He states that he represents one per cent of Berliners, or 34,000 inhabitants, and explains that the casting process relied on his triggering a 'chain reaction' in which each selected cast member had twenty-four hours to personally choose the next performer according to the statistically relevant categories of gender, age, marital status, nationality, and residential location. This casting process is then replicated on stage with each participant stepping onto the revolve and briefly introducing themselves in the order of the recruitment process. During this introductory phase, audiences are updated twice about the statistical validity of the data presented to them, particularly by Hauke Schmidt-Martens ('76%'), a 25-year-old student with specialist knowledge in statistics. About fifteen minutes into the show, and again about five minutes later, Schmidt-Martens explains the increasingly small probability of finding a suitable cast member after seventy-one people who fit the selection criteria have already been identified.

At the beginning of the introductory round, Gerlach also informs the audience about the yellow programme booklets that dedicate a two-page spread to each performer, including their photograph and signature. These pages seem to authenticate Gerlach's description of the personalized recruitment process. The portraits' indexical quality appears to be reinforced through an embedded digital display of the exact time and date when they were taken, and by the performers holding up a yellow block indicating what percentage of the 100 representatives had been found at that stage. Audience members are encouraged to consult the booklet at the beginning of the performance, and some might find their gaze alternating between the documentary evidence, which fixes each performer in the past, and the live performance with its promise of their auratic 'presence in the here and now' (Benjamin 2008: 31). However, audiences are not granted sufficient time to engage with the unique introductory self-presentations of most individual performers because several cast members cut each other off in order to comply with the tightly scheduled nature of the production's opening section. The many hasty presentations on stage, in conjunction with the photographic presentation in the booklet of performers holding their percentage numbers, can give the impression that the individual has been reduced to a mere number in order to fit into a massive theatre production that tries to create an image of Berlin's population.

The chain-reaction casting process, together with its condensed replication on stage, fits Claire Bishop's observation of a general trend that has occurred in the performance art and visual art world, particularly since 2000. She states that:

> [b]oth performance and business place a premium on recruitment ...
> and in many cases the work of finding suitable performers is delegated to
> the curator who becomes a human resources manager. Although unique
> qualities are sought in each performer, these are – paradoxically – also
> infinitely replaceable. (Bishop 2012: 231)

This paradox largely applies to the performers in *100% Berlin*, albeit with modifications. Participants can only be replaced as long as their substitutes also fit the statistically relevant categories. The fact that performers become exchangeable is apparent in the advertisement for an 'extra' (Statist) that was placed in a newspaper in order to find the second-last person ('98%') in the chain reaction. The advertisement specified that this person should be of German, Polish or Serbian background, married or widowed, over 65, and living in the suburb of Spandau, Steglitz/Zehlendorf or Pankow (Rimini Protokoll 2008). The resulting loss of individuality due to these statistical constraints could also undermine the performers' origin(ality) – a notion important for the creation of Authenticity-Effects. This potential loss is counterbalanced by the participants' active involvement in the selection process with them choosing the next participant, in conjunction with a local artist who oversees the casting process, as well as through directorial decisions that help individualize the performers on stage. For example, instead of holding the percentage number displayed in the booklet, which could create a reifying image, the performers bring along a treasured object that individualizes them on stage. These objects help embody their responses to the two questions in the booklet, which also contains their written responses: 'What distinguishes you from the others?' and 'How will you be recognized on stage?' (Was unterscheidet Sie von den anderen? und Woran wird man Sie auf der Bühne erkennen?: Rimini Protokoll 2008) (Figure 5.1).

Once all 100 performers have formed a circle along the edges of the revolve, the main part of the performance begins. The selected Berliners of various backgrounds respond to a range of personal and socio-political questions, by either congregating under the signs 'ME', 'NOT ME' ('ICH', 'ICH NICHT'), or holding up coloured signs for more

Figure 5.1 *100% Berlin*. Photograph by and copyright Barbara Braun/ MuTphoto.

nuanced responses to questions about their habits, personal values, and lifestyles. Throughout the show, several bird's-eye view shots of the performers are projected onto a large circular projection screen suspended at the rear of the playing space, providing a different perspective of the live human opinion polls on stage, and recalling the *tableaux vivants*, such as those used by the amateur agit-prop performances in Russia and Germany during the 1920s (Gardner 2014: 255–6). *100% Berlin* also shares with this tradition the aim to create broad audience interest, beyond the groups of regular theatregoers, and to actively involve the wider population in the performance. This aim is reflected in Rimini Protokoll's decision to put a large number of non-professional theatre performers on stage for this celebratory occasion, rather than evoking the 1920s, when the Hebbel Theater attracted large audiences by featuring individual star actors such as Hans Albers, Fritz Kortner, Elisabeth Bergner, and Heinrich George, or well-known directors such as Erwin Piscator.

Celebrating the Hebbel Theater with *100% Berlin*

100% Berlin brings to mind various associations with broader German theatre history but unlike most anniversary celebrations of cultural institutions, it does not create a collective identity through shared memory between artists, performers, and audiences. With the exception of the programme's references to the Hebbel Theater's history cited earlier, the production concentrates mainly on the present. As part of this focus it showcases Berlin's diverse population in a celebratory atmosphere, which, on opening night in particular, was enhanced by the many family members and friends of the performers in the audience. Several reviewers referred to *100% Berlin* as 'the key component of the "100 Years Hebbel-Theater – The Anniversary"' birthday party (das Herzstück der Geburtstagsparty '100 Jahre Hebbel-Theater – das Jubiläum': Wahl 2008a), and reviewed it in conjunction with the subsequent *Orchesterkaraoke*. This was a large karaoke party with the support of the RIAS youth orchestra that continued the celebrations at HAU1 under the direction of Jan Dvorak, following a concept by Matthias von Hartz (e.g. Hauck 2008; Wahl 2008a).

In retrospect, *100% Berlin* can be read as a memorable embodiment of the HAU's organizational structure at the time, and therefore as a particularly fitting choice as the centrepiece of the 'birthday party'. Like many productions under Lilienthal, the show was embedded in a larger festival structure based on a central theme in which numerous events complemented and challenged one another. The premiere of *100% Berlin* was preceded by a weekend of events curated by Stefanie Wenner, under the title 'Re-Education – You Too Can Be Like Us', a title taken from a post-war slogan of the Allied Forces. Two days of movies, performances, discussions, and exhibitions with a focus on past and current wars reminded audiences that the Hebbel Theater, as a building that had remained intact among the ruins of 1945, was an important site during Berlin's post-war culture, initially for anti-fascist re-education programmes, and eventually for a broader programme that included plays by Tennessee Williams, Thornton Wilder, and Jean-Paul Sartre, as well as Brecht's *The*

Threepenny Opera and Fritz Kortner's provocative interpretation of *Don Carlos*. Two weeks later, running concurrently with three evening performances of *100% Berlin* in HAU1, the production house's other venues featured the Turkish rapper CEZA, raumlabor's *Küchenmonument* (translatable as 'Kitchen's Monument') – a mobile sculpture consisting of an enormous bubble providing a space for preparing and eating meals – as well as *little red (play): herstory* by andcompany&Co.

100% City: an evolving format

The Hebbel Theater's birthday celebration did fulfil some traditional expectations of a flagship anniversary in so far as it showcased the contemporary practices of the institution, in particular the recent interdisciplinary nature and interconnectedness of its productions. *100% Berlin* also displayed, to some extent, the aesthetics of destabilization characteristic of the HAU at the time, which challenged audience expectations of what could be perceived as authentic. *100% Berlin*, beginning with its title *100%*, could suggest that audience members will be presented with truthful – in the sense of statistically accurate – representations of Berlin's citizens, with the help of 'authentic' responses by local people on stage. However, the expectations of statistical accuracy and truthful responses are only partially and momentarily fulfilled in *100% Berlin*, a fact which two reviewers commented on: Slevogt, with her ironic remark about the performers' 'authenticity', and her colleague Doris Meierhenrich, whose initial impression that the Berliners on stage form a statistically accurate whole was subverted when it became evident that the performers' individual responses were arbitrary, rather than statistically accurate (Meierhenrich 2008). While both reviewers note the processes in *100% Berlin* that destabilize a sense of authenticity, a brief survey of the format's later iterations reveals that the destabilization of the two strands of authenticity – statistical accuracy and sincere personal self (re)presentation – became a stronger element in later productions.

It is worth noting that *100% Berlin* was originally planned as a one-off performance rather than the successful 'touring [*100% City*] format' (Tourendes Format) it became. Rimini Protokoll have pointed out that it was the City of Vienna that convinced them to adapt the format to the Austrian city in 2009 (Rimini Protokoll 2012a: 125). Haug and Wetzel also decided to explore a variation of the original structure of *100% City* in 2010 by selecting 103 inhabitants for the more politically oriented *Prometheus in Athens* (2012a: 100). Together with Prodromos Tsinikoris as assistant director, Haug and Wetzel combined questions of representation with an exploration of human suffering, set against the background of Greece's austere socio-economic climate of the time, by asking the performers which aspects of and characters in the ancient tragedy *Prometheus Bound* they could relate to. Like *Prometheus in Athens*, shown initially as part of the Athens international theatre festival Promethiade, *An Enemy of the People in Oslo*, another *100% City* adaptation and opening show of the International Ibsen Festival 2012, foregrounded the ongoing relevance of a classic text for local inhabitants. This juxtaposition of classic text with present-day realities, which also shaped Rimini Protokoll's *Wallenstein: A Documentary Play* and *Karl Marx: Capital, Volume One*, resulted in several local unrepeated adaptations of the format. These included modifications of the content for both *Prometheus in Athens* and *An Enemy*, and of the casting process for *Prometheus*. The extent to which the format in general had developed by 2012, the year Lilienthal left the HAU, becomes obvious in one of the productions that maintained the overall format and its open thematic orientation: *100% Melbourne*.

Developing a playful destabilization of Authenticity-Effects in *100% Melbourne*

This Australian production, preceded by an incarnation in Vancouver and followed by one in London, is an interesting case study because the City of Melbourne, which commissioned the work, established a relationship with the original performance through its creation of English subtitles for a video excerpt of *100% Berlin*, available on the English-language version of Rimini Protokoll's website for the Berlin show. The following brief comparison of *100% Berlin* and *100% Melbourne* focuses on Authenticity-Effects and their potential destabilization of audience perceptions, in particular those regarding familiar and unfamiliar people. Both strands of authenticity discussed in relation to *100% Berlin* – referential truth and a sense of individual authenticity – are addressed in Melbourne to a much larger extent than in the Berlin original. Like *100% Berlin*, the Australian show employed sceptical Authenticity-Effects that destabilized audiences' impressions of the statistical 'truths' presented to them, but in a more developed way. The Authenticity-Effects became a stronger component of the individual presentations on stage, particularly of the short narrative segments interspersed throughout the evening, resulting in a more diversified and complex concept of personal identity.

100% Melbourne's specific use of mimicry, a concept defined by biologist Klaus Lunau as '[a] system of interpersonal communication that involves fake signals' (zwischenmenschlichen Kommunikationssystemen mit Signalfälschungen: Lunau 2011: 194), challenged audience expectations of truthful statistical representation. Such expectations were reinforced when the City of Melbourne advertised the show with the modified subtitle, 'Our City, on Stage' (City of Melbourne 2012). By contrast, in the performances we witnessed live on 4 and 5 May 2012, it became apparent right from the beginning that, by 2012, the initially quite limited play with Authenticity-Effects in Berlin had become much more developed. For example, the first person in line, Anton Griffith, declared his professional association with, and interest in, statistics, as in previous productions. However, his introduction differed from Gerlach's in Berlin because he added the fictionalized statement that he had only been on stage 'once before' in his life. On opening night, those audience members who assumed that he had rehearsed this part of the show might question whether this statement is true, and from the second of the three performances it became even more obvious he was *not* telling the truth. Through such subtle means, doubts were raised about the reliability of the numerical information that comes straight from this expert's mouth. In Berlin, Gerlach contextualized what he called 'our' – presumably Rimini Protokoll's and his – wish to generate a 'sample' of Berlin's population with factual information about the German microcensus, a sample survey covering approximately one per cent of Germany's population each year, whereas Griffith's explanation was strongly personalized. Speaking in the first person singular, he expressed his strong desire 'to meet the people behind *my* numbers' (our emphasis) in his role as statistician for the City of Melbourne, and set up two important leitmotifs: statistical representation and an interest in encountering unfamiliar people. The indications that both Griffith's personal interest and the statistical validity of the other ninety-nine Melbournians on stage are 'fake signals' are quite subtle. These early pointers are followed by other instances where what or who is on stage is almost, but not quite the same as their equivalents in everyday life, a phenomenon Bhabha views as typical of mimicry (1994: 86). By the end, this destabilization of referential truth becomes obvious as performers openly confess 'We have lied tonight' in one of the show's later survey scenes. In Melbourne, the timing of this frank confession that they have been 'inauthentic' – that is, given falsified information – made it a crucial moment in the show's comprehensive game with mimicry because the later timing foregrounded this important statement and invited the audience to retrospectively question some if not all of the previous responses given on stage. This game unsettles assumptions about the power of numerical data in two main ways: first, it invites audiences to critically assess any political cost-benefit-based decisions that rely on a claim to correct statistics (Rimini Protokoll website), and second, it can be interpreted as challenging the ideal of an effective representational democracy.

The first effect, dismantling the power of statistical information and its reliance on 'authentic' data, gave the people making *100% Melbourne* the artistic freedom to accommodate small adjustments regarding the accuracy of data presented. This leeway was used to increase the format's emphasis on socio-political issues, including cultural diversity and representation. For example, five people on stage identified themselves as Aboriginal (one of them as Dutch Aboriginal), despite Aboriginals representing less than one per cent of Melbourne's population. Vicky Guglielmo from the Arts and Participation Programme, City of Melbourne, explained that in order to portray Melbourne's diversity more comprehensively, additional so-called search filters were added to the primary categories that included age, gender, etc.:

> The additional filters, as we called them, were in fact not filters at all. They acted like a secondary storyline for us that painted a broader picture of Melbourne that was not being picked up with the five primary ABS [Australian Bureau of Statistics]/census filters. (Garde 2015: 260)

With the show taking place at the Melbourne Town Hall, the city's centre of decision-making and politics (Kaegi, in Bowen et al. 2015: 304), the performance space served as a further indicator of one of the show's key concerns – the opportunities as well as potential shortcomings and failures of democratic representation, a topic Rimini Protokoll had explored earlier in projects such as *Deutschland 2* (*Theater*) (Brandl-Risi 2010: 59). Within the framework of the *100% City* format, this interest had grown over time, often due to the political circumstances surrounding individual iterations. According to Daniel Wetzel, for example, *Prometheus in Athens* raised fundamental questions about the nature of democracy and representation, both in the political and theatrical sense (Brendel 2010).

Moreover, as far as statistical accuracy is concerned, the limits of representation according to strict numerical rules are not only evoked by the performers who had to be selected through additional search filters, but also by those individuals who missed one of the three performances and were not replaced on stage, or those who were excluded by the selection process altogether. This issue was hinted at in Berlin, for example by the question 'Who has the feeling that they fall through the cracks?' (Wer hat das Gefühl durch alle Raster zu fallen?), which plays with the meaning of *Raster* as 'statistical grid'. Faith in statistically accurate representation was challenged more strongly in the Melbourne iteration, both numerically and politically, another indication of how the *100% City* format has grown in complexity during the process of touring from one city to another across the world.

Challenging audience expectations of authenticity

Challenging audience expectations, both with respect to statistical information and to the potential authenticity of individual stories, is one of *100% City's* important characteristics, and one that was more pronounced in Melbourne than in Berlin. While only one reviewer in Berlin commented on having paid specific attention to individual performers and their responses to individual survey questions on the night (Schütt 2008), this audience mode of reception became more common in Melbourne and was associated with surprise at individual performers' behaviour:

> I was fascinated by apparent contradictions and individual complexities;
> by the woman, for example, who believed in life after death but not in
> God. By the complete lack of overlap between those who kept weapons
> in their homes and those who had fought in wars. (Boyd 2012)

In this instance, the survey scenes destabilized the schemata that underpinned the critic's expectations of an individual's consistent value system and attitudes, resulting in an invitation to appreciate their greater complexity (Figure 5.2).

In *The Living Handbook of Narratology*, Catherine Emmott and Marc Alexander define schemata as 'cognitive structures representing generic knowledge, i.e. structures which do not contain information about particular entities, instances or events, but rather about their general form' (2015). Emmott and Alexander refer to the restaurant schema as an example that would contain common knowledge about types of restaurants, what objects are to be found inside a restaurant, and so on.

Figure 5.2 *100% Melbourne*. Photograph by Carla Gottgens, copyright City of Melbourne.

Similarly, most Australians would associate the term 'boat people' with asylum seekers reaching Australia by boat, leaving their home country for humanitarian reasons. In *100% Melbourne*, this schema was destabilized because 'boat people' referred to any immigrants who had arrived by boat rather than just asylum seekers. This became evident in a scene where, of only 'a handful of boatpeople', most who responded positively to the question 'Who came to Australia on a boat?' were 'from post-World War II Europe and colonial South Africa' (Boyd 2012). As Calcutt et al. (2009: 171) have stated, '[a]s clusters of ideas for thinking with, cognitive schemas can facilitate our understanding of how social categories are conceptualized' and modifications of a cluster, such as occurs when unexpected reasons are given for coming by boat to Australia, can provide fresh perspectives on issues and people. In this case, the alteration of a schema invites audiences to historicize and question the contextually relevant, heated discussions about 'boat people' in an almost Brechtian manner.

While in *100% Berlin* such moments of subtle socio-political or socio-economic engagement are presented in isolation (such as Jürgen Pritsch ('28%') informing audiences of his recycling of left-over soap bars pieced together from soap left over in hotels due to economic hardship thirty-five years previously), in Melbourne these moments which destabilize audience expectations are part of a larger leitmotif or embedded in sections dealing with similar or related themes. For example, towards the end of the first half of *100% Melbourne*, performers are asked to congregate under lights with the signs 'ME', 'NOT ME' according to their responses to questions about violence, weapons, and war. The thematic unity of this section is underlined by subtle sounds of gunshots and alarms. It finishes with the question, 'Who thinks our military involvement in Afghanistan has been worthwhile?', which leads into the autobiographical story by Vietnam veteran Stephen Black ('49%'), introduced by Linda Baker ('48%') earlier in the show as a 'War hero'.

Black's narrative illustrates *100% Melbourne*'s complex play with self-representation and with its Authenticity-Effects, an aesthetics that draws attention to editorial work and authorship, and concepts of selfhood, as well as the effects of the performers' delivery. Black's (auto) biographical story calls into question the textual authenticity that relies on the traditional definition of autobiography, in which '[t]he author claims individual responsibility for the creation and arrangement of the text' (Bruss 1976: 10), as his and many other short narratives in *100% Melbourne* show clear signs of the editing process that the professional performance-makers undertook with the performers. Even though it is not clear to audience members to what degree Haug, Kaegi or Wetzel have served as 'ghost writers' (Kaegi, in Bowen et al. 2015: 306) for Black's text, it is obvious that his narrative on opening night contains rhetorical devices beyond those used in spontaneous 'authentic' everyday language, such as anaphora, parallelism, and contrast:

> I'm convinced: Every generation has to fight a war. If you don't – who's going to keep the know-how? The war of my generation was the Vietnam War.

I was 20 when I voluntarily left to fight in Vietnam.

I thought 'this'll be fun' – it wasn't.

I felt I was safe from being shot,

I felt invincible – I wasn't!

I thought it was my duty to fight in this war even though there were moratorium protests going on throughout Australia – what would they know?

I returned one year later and felt more like 35 and not the 21-year-old I was – I'd changed so much. [...]

If I think back, it's like it's not me who did that – it's a very different version of me!

When we came home nobody was there to welcome us, nobody had any interest in hearing about our experiences. The whole of the society disowned us.

(Rimini Protokoll 2012b)

The rhetorical devices that mark the text, together with its rhythm, are clear indicators that the verbatim text that Black had originally produced in one of the pre-production interviews with Rimini Protokoll had been edited beyond what Kaegi refers to as 'the requirements of tellability' (Bowen et al. 2015: 306), either by Black himself or in collaboration with the artists: it had been fictionalized through acts of selection, combination, and aesthetic reframing (Garde 2015: 267; Iser 1993: 222–87). The resulting narrative contains many 'blanks' (Iser 2006: 64) that audiences need to fill with meaning, using their own imagination to do so. For example, an audience member could imagine Black's traumatic experience as a young soldier. Through this individual 'concretization' of meaning ('Konkretisation': Lehmann 1999: 191), the fictionalized text gains a surplus of meaning because it offers a glimpse of the account's underlying traumatic dimension, in line with Slavoj Žižek's observation that we are only able to bear this dimension 'if we fictionalize it' (2002: 19). Audiences are thus allowed to infer, in however brief and fragile a manner, the unbearable, unspeakable, and unrepresentable dimension of Black's experiences as a young soldier in Vietnam. At this point, the question of whether his story is authentic, in the sense that a single true version of it exists, ceases to be important, as each audience member fills in the blanks with his or her own version of the storyline, thus generating multiple personalized narratives. The show therefore destabilizes the assumption that a performer's self-representational narrative gives direct, complete, and objective access to that individual's true self.

100% Melbourne disrupts and challenges the notion that we can have complete knowledge about a society and its individual members. Black's story serves as an example of a fractured selfhood, recalling the debate

> about the extent to which personal narrative is self-expression of a unified and authentic self discovering the truth of experience; or is self-de(con)struction that frustrates unity, essence, origins, and truth. (Langellier 2001)

In Black's text, selfhood is presented as an interrupted line of development marked by traumatic experiences, referring to the past as featuring 'a very different version of [him]', and lacking the 'retrospective teleology' that characterizes most autobiographical narratives (Brockmeier 2001: 252). Instead of his narrated life moving towards a *telos*, its protagonist seems to escape death by sheer luck. The randomness with which fate strikes recurs as a leitmotif in other stories told in *100% Melbourne* (Garde 2015: 265–70), a motif in stark contrast to the cliché of the happy-go-lucky food-, sport-, and shopping-loving Melbournian that is described by many passers-by interviewed outside the Melbourne Town Hall during the production process (Rimini Protokoll website). In summary, the show presents Melbourne's citizens as a diverse group and challenges the concept of an uninterrupted and authentic selfhood.

Vulnerability and authenticity

Despite the many indications that the individual narratives in *100% Melbourne* form part of a meticulously prepared artistic work (Croggon 2012), not a single review dismisses Black's (or any other) story as inauthentic, in the sense that it is no longer his own, original account. This could be because of how performers tell their stories: like Black's, each story's delivery oscillates between an apparently authentic statement and a rehearsed and mediated story, particularly since the performers rely on a prompt script that is projected in large print on the screen at the back of the audience seating. As Mumford has observed,

> [t]his script functioned both as a hypermedial layer, pointing to mediation, and as a contributor to immediacy whenever, for example, the narrators revealed they were dependent on this digital prompter and were thus genuine experts of their everyday life rather than professional actors. (2015: 289)

As many performers cannot rely on professional experience to cope with the anxiety of performing in a show, their '[i]nsecurity and fragility' on stage can also be 'understood by many to be authenticity' (Malzacher 2008: 27). This potential impression is further reinforced when personal suffering is involved (Lethen 1996: 221) – for example when, on opening night, Black was momentarily overwhelmed, possibly by traumatic memories and a stressful public performance situation, until another cast member comforted him. In general, Rimini Protokoll set out to avoid these moments of exposure by looking after the performers through what Malzacher has called 'a dramaturgy of care' (2008: 28). However, while all live performance offers a potentially unstable situation, the comparative unpredictability of the real-people performers means that the outcome of these moments when the performance-makers have relinquished their power 'cannot be foreseen' (Bishop 2012: 237). Bishop describes similar mechanisms in delegated performance – works where the artist uses people as their medium. Here the artist 'both relinquishes and reclaims power: he or she agrees to temporarily lose control over the situation before returning to select, define and circulate its representation' (2012: 237). With regard to audience reception, it remains largely unclear if and when the artists' relinquishing of control might generate the fleeting impression of unrehearsed – and hence authentic in the sense of genuine and intimate – self-representation. For example, in the DVD of *100% Melbourne*, there is no explanation as to why Black switches from the first person singular to the first person plural for a large part of his story.

In *100% Melbourne*, the playful use of a sceptical approach to Authenticity-Effects invites the audience to engage with a more diversified concept of personal identity, and destabilizes their expectations of the seemingly familiar city, resulting in the transformative capacity to notice (a potentially unfamiliar) complexity at the level of the individual and of society. This transformation encompasses the people involved in making the performance – for example, Rochelle Humphrey ('55%') acknowledged that '[t]he personal stories were striking [...] People aren't what they seem, and that show managed to portray this very well' (Garde 2015: 269) – as well as Rimini Protokoll themselves. For the artists, with regard to societal complexity, the use of a small set of 'fixed' questions that remain unchanged in each city can lead to 'surprising results', such as the unexpectedly high number of positive responses in Melbourne to the question 'Who is in favour of the death penalty?' (Haug, in Bowen et al. 2015: 308) compared with other cities. While Rimini Protokoll discover some unfamiliar aspects of cities through this touring format, audience members might find that their seemingly well-known city becomes less familiar. Melbourne writer and critic Alison Croggon summarizes this experience as follows: 'As the show evolves, you begin to have a movingly complex and often surprising sense of where you live. It's both familiar and unfamiliar, surprising and unsurprising' (Croggon 2012). She attributes this effect in part to *100% Melbourne* extending beyond 'the usual demographics encompassed by the arts' (Croggon, in Garde 2015: 269). In short, the later incarnations of *100% City* illustrate Lilienthal's description of Rimini Protokoll's work, that 'reality surprises and is often quite different from what you imagine it to be. To show this while repeatedly pointing out the constructed nature of their theatre, this is their great art' ([D]ass die Realität überraschend und oft ganz anders ist, als man sie sich vorstellt. Dies zu zeigen, gleichzeitig aber auch immer wieder auf die Gemachtheit ihres Theaters zu verweisen, das ist ihre große Kunst: Baecker et al. 2012: 17).

6

Meeting Unfamiliar Residents in Berlin: Playing with Frames of Reference in *X-Apartments*

In 2004, Lilienthal invited theatre, film, and visual artists to leave the black box of the theatre (HAU 2004) and create five- to ten-minute site-specific performances in private homes, located in the suburbs of Kreuzberg and Lichtenberg, which audiences could access in pairs. Under the dramaturgy of Shermin Langhoff and Arved Schultze with Sven Heier as producer, the two tours through a selected residential area offered participants seven or eight short scenes that involved encounters with real people and/or professional performers in and close to the featured apartments. An exception occurred during an extra tour that featured Richard Maxwell's project *Showcase* with the New York City Players, which was performed in a Relexa Hotel room. *X-Apartments*' innovative aesthetic approach was inspired by curator Jan Hoet's 1986 Ghent exhibition of work in private houses titled *Guest Rooms* (*Chambres d'Amis*: Lilienthal 2003: 19). Lilienthal first experimented with this format in 2002 in Duisburg, with Arved Schultze as dramaturge, when he served as programme director of the Theatre of the World festival (Theater der Welt). Since then, *X-Apartments: Theatre in Private Spaces* (*X-Wohnungen: Theater in privaten Räumen*) has been adapted to more than ten cities around the world, in Europe as well as in Beirut, Caracas, Istanbul, Johannesburg, and São Paulo, and has also been further developed into the formats *X-Schools* (*X-Schulen*) and *X-Companies* or *X-Enterprises* (*X-Firmen*).

The first adaptation of *X-Apartments* in Berlin drew heavily on the original Duisburg experience, as is apparent in the HAU's 2004 advertisement that reiterates an excerpt of Schultze's 2003 essay on theatre and reality. In that essay, *X-Apartments* (Duisburg) is described as a project 'which demands new artistic questions of and approaches to the medium of theatre: can theatre in new performance spaces gain a different relationship with reality?' (ein Projekt, das ... neue künstlerische Fragen und Herangehensweisen an das Medium Theater fordert: Kann Theater an neuen Spielorten einen anderen Realitätsbezug gewinnen?: Schultze 2003: 13; HAU 2004).

Schulze's question perfectly aligns with Lilienthal's self-declared 'hysterical yearning for reality' (hysterische Sehnsucht nach Realität: Behrendt 2004), which, as explained in Chapter 2, sums up both Lilienthal's rejection of art-for-art's sake and the HAU team's endeavour to integrate aesthetic with societal discourse. *X-Apartments'* pivotal role in this enterprise is demonstrated by the fact that according to Kirsten Hehmeyer, head of press at the HAU, it was one of the first projects that Lilienthal planned and sought funding for when he took over artistic leadership of the HAU in 2003 (Garde 2012). Theatre critics equally acknowledged *X-Apartments* as emblematic of Lilienthal's artistic credo and as 'characteristic of the HAU and the theatre's desire to observe and comment on the real' (Das Projekt ist programmatisch für das HAU und den Wunsch, als Theater eine neue Relevanz als Beobachter und Kommentator des Realen zu finden: Müller 2004). In each of its many national and international adaptations between 2002 and today, Lilienthal's brainchild has featured artistic projects that play with a sense of authentic people and actions. Authentic here means genuine, or honest in the sense of free from pretence or counterfeit. This particular sensation of the authentic is closely related to the use of people's homes as the performance settings (HAU 2004), and the encounters with the people who appear to inhabit them. The ambiguous nature of these inhabitants repeatedly destabilizes the participants' sense of who or what is authentic and what is staged. Unlike in *100% City* discussed in the previous chapter, where notions of authenticity in the sense of referential truthfulness depend on an everyday reality that clearly exists outside of the theatre's aesthetic realm, in *X-Apartments* impressions of authenticity and reality are frequently intertwined in performances that have left the clearly designated theatre space behind and where performative spaces overlap with the spaces of everyday reality. This is because the boundaries between everyday life and artistic projects become blurred due to the absence of a clear frame of reference that audiences can use to interpret their experiences.

Right from his involvement in the format's first version, Lilienthal expressed a keen interest in exploring the relationship between authenticity and the theatricality inherent in many aspects of everyday life, asking himself the question: 'What does authenticity look like?' (Wie sieht Authentizität aus?: Lilienthal 2003: 9), both in and beyond the confines of the designated theatre space. In an attempt to create 'a different truth' (eine andere Wahrheit: Lilienthal 2003: 9) beyond the limits of conventional *mise-en-scène* of dramatic texts, he decided to explore the private home as a biographical place, a place able to set different artistic parameters for 'the creation of reality, disguise, language and the claim to be somebody else' (Herstellung von Realität, mit Verstellung, mit Sprache, mit der Behauptung, ein anderer zu sein, Ort der Biographie: Lilienthal 2003: 9). Many projects carried out under the umbrella title of *X-Apartments* have engaged playfully with authenticity and theatricality. They have invited the audience to ask whether they are witnessing 'everyday life portrayals of self that have been put in a theatre frame, or heightened performances of self lifted from everyday life' (Garde and Mumford 2013: 151). Many have also worked with an aesthetics of destabilization that provides participants with neither definite nor stable answers. Using a sceptical approach to Authenticity-Effects, the artists in *X-Apartments* both create and undermine a sense of contact with authentic residents, while confronting audiences with their own attitudes, including prejudices and voyeuristic behaviour.

The three-hour discovery tours, or *parcours*, in Berlin in 2004 illustrated the potential of this sceptical approach to Authenticity-Effects to put participants in contact with the local residents, while also revealing and undermining audience members' expectations of the ethnically diverse districts of Kreuzberg and former East German satellite town Lichtenberg. Both the walks from one apartment to the next as well as the performances in and around the apartments uncovered and/or challenged hidden socio-economic, ethnically- and historically-based prejudices towards the unfamiliar residents, thus offering fresh perspectives on the areas and their inhabitants. The works' invitation to experience such a change of perception was part of the broader thematic framework of the Migration project at the HAU, a project conducted in conjunction with the Cologne Art Association (Kölnischer Kunstverein) as part of a large transdisciplinary initiative funded by the German Federal Cultural Foundation.

Removing clear frames of reference for the audience

Unlike *100% Berlin*, the title of which plays with the promise of comprehensive access to and familiarity with a city and its citizens, the name *X-Wohnungen* – which can also be translated as *X-Homes* – creates a tension between the notion of privacy and potential familiarity associated with the home, and a strong sense of curiosity or insecurity *vis-à-vis* the variable X that evokes a sense of the unfamiliar: 'The factor X indicates a secret. X is a threat, a promise. Or both. X signifies: the unknown' (Der Faktor X steht für Geheimnis. X ist eine Drohung, ein Versprechen. Oder beides. X bedeutet: das Unbekannte: Schaper 2004). Many participants would have shared the sense of excitement and insecurity expressed by a reviewer of the 2004 Berlin iteration who commented on having to leave the relative security of the designated theatre space in order to undertake a kind of 'scavenger hunt' (Schnitzeljagd: Behrendt 2004). A sense of unpredictability was also generated for non-local participants, who made up the majority of the audiences (Schultze, in Garde 2013c), by having to negotiate their way through an unfamiliar part of Berlin. Instead of being provided with precise maps, they had to make their way through mostly unknown suburbs with the help of written directions, large HAU advertising posters that displayed images of young bruised boxers, and arrows marking the way on the pavement. This orientation in an unfamiliar environment was simultaneously a hands-on activity, where the participants' decisions and actions impacted the practical challenge of locating the next *X-Apartment*, and part of their immersion in a larger artistic framework in which an entire 'district becomes a ready-made that can be accessed by foot, a reality ready-made: reality is experienced as an art object' (Das . . . Viertel wird zu einem begehbaren Readymade, zu einem Reality Ready Made: Die Wirklichkeit wird als Kunstobjekt [. . .] erfahren: Schultze 2005: 34).

Theatre critics' responses to this kind of immersion in everyday life, transformed into an all-encompassing aesthetic experience, varied. While reviewer Katja Oskamp (2004) reported a sense of boredom and disengagement with the 2004 project – largely due to long waiting times before being admitted to a particular performance – most critical responses indicated that participants had modified their everyday mode of perception and perceived everything and everyone in Kreuzberg and Lichtenberg as a potential element of an artistic performance (Behrendt 2004; Müller 2004). For example, Tomas Fitzel commented:

> This long night confused all our senses and our sense of orientation . . . [We asked ourselves:] 'What is real and what is still theatre?' (In dieser langen Nacht wurden uns alle Sinne und Orientierung verwirrt . . . [Wir fragten uns:] 'Was ist real und was ist noch Theater?': Fitzel, Radio SWR2, 4 June 2004)

As this response indicates, participants were exposed to the '*indecidability* [*sic*] whether one is dealing with reality or fiction' characteristic of much postdramatic theatre (Lehmann 2006: 101).

In *X-Apartments*, this 'indecidability' is largely due to the absence of a clear frame of reference that would allow audiences of conventional theatre productions to differentiate between a theatre performance and everyday actions (Kolesch 2012: 27). As Schultze has observed:

> [t]he person who is supposed to be a spectator is suddenly himself right in the middle of it, he experiences himself as part of this reality or

fiction/drama, there is no other reality (s)he can withdraw to. (Der vermeintliche Zuschauer steckt plötzlich selbst mittendrin, er erlebt sich als Bestandteil dieser Realität bzw. Fiktion/Dramatik, es gibt keine andere, auf die er sich zurückziehen kann: Schultze 2005: 34)

This lack of an exterior aesthetic frame of reference has an impact on both how participants perceive the district they are exploring by foot and on how they interpret individual productions. For example, in an interview Schultze reports an incident where most participants did not stop to assist an injured person in the street because they interpreted this as a theatre performance (Garde 2013c).

Ayşe Polat's production: Frau Barthelmess's flat in Reichenbergerstraße, Lichtenberg

Ayşe Polat's production in and outside Frau Barthelmess's flat (Reichenbergerstraße), a two-part event that deliberately fails to frame the main performance in a clear manner, serves as an excellent example of carefully planned destabilizing Authenticity-Effects. Due to the ambiguous framing, participants are uncertain when and where everyday life ends and the artistic performance begins, which in turn affects their reactions. When spectators enter the Reichenbergerstraße concrete high-rise building (Plattenbau) in Lichtenberg, they had to pass through dark stairwells and long corridors where they found themselves confronted by a group of two or three young people who gave the impression of thugs (Schouten 2011: 2) and asked passers-by for money. When the young people collected a 'toll' in Polat's project, according to audience reaction further discussed below, they created a sense of unease, largely due to their behaviour, language, and appearance. This prelude to the apartment performance was contrasted with participants listening to Frau Barthelmess reading sentimental poetry about her deceased cat in her meticulously decorated home dominated by pink and pastel colours.

Although actors perform the prelude, its fictional nature is not necessarily obvious to the audience members who are on their way to an *X-Apartments* performance that they expect to commence only in Frau Barthelmess's flat. According to Schultze, some audience members were quite scared, despite the actors' wigs and beanies and their deliberately exaggerated display of rude and loutish behaviour (Garde 2013c) that included them mimicking the sociolect that could be associated with their appearance when asking 'You got a dollar?' (Haste mal 'nen Euro, eh?). Kathrin Krottenthaler's rough-cut video documentation of *X-Apartments* (2004) shows Ayşe Polat discussing with the actors how to find the right amount of shock effect without scaring away the audience, and is thus indicative of how the director carefully considered how the Authenticity-Effects in this performance segment would affect audiences. While Polat and the actors were able to control the scene's impact to some extent, the ultimate impact of the uncertainty of whether this prelude was staged or authentic was unpredictable. This is largely due to the fact that, rather than remaining anonymous in a large, often physically removed group of onlookers in a designated theatre space, pairs of audience members in Polat's production were directly confronted by the actors and had to decide whether to respond verbally or physically to the actors' demands as a genuine everyday speech act with potentially dangerous consequences, or whether to interpret the actors' demand for money as fictional – that is, without 'having consequences relevant to action' (Habermas 1987: 195). In this first part of Polat's project, theatre's conventional markers of artifice were hidden and the boundaries between life outside and inside the theatre performance blurred to such an extent that the audience was unable to decide whether they were being exposed to everyday language and its illocutionary force (Habermas 1987: 196), or to fiction. This uncertainty is likely to have been particularly marked in the case of theatregoers accustomed to more conventional theatre performances, who potentially would have been exposed to a *mundus inversus* because the aesthetic signals did not signify what they conventionally suggest. Frau Barthelmess's poetry reading in her carefully decorated flat – suggesting artifice – in fact offered an encounter with its true inhabitant, and could thus be perceived as authentic – while the verbal threat in the seemingly unaltered rough-looking environment of the previous scene was delivered by professionally trained actors.

The structural ambiguity of this two-part performance further reinforced participants' difficulties with assessing correctly the fictional nature of the scene in the corridor. In this context, Derrida's interpretation of parerga as '*hors d'œuvres*, adjuncts, which are neither internal nor external' (1979: 20) provides a useful explanation. The philosopher refers to the columns around a building, the frames of paintings, and the drapery on statues as manifestations of a parergon. In the case of all of these examples, one can ask oneself '[w]here a parergon begins, and where it ends', as the parergon challenges conventional definitions 'of the centre and the integrity of representation, of its inside and outside' (1979: 22). Polat's prelude provokes similar questions regarding the parergon and the main performance. The scene with the young people belongs to the liminal phase in which audience members make their way from the entrance door to the private apartment, via dark stairwells and long corridors. From this point of view, this scene remains on the outside of the main, poetry-reading performance, yet it is intrinsically linked to the main performance because of the contrasts it evokes in environment, language use, personal demeanour, and atmosphere. As Sabine Schouten informs us, audiences have compared the poetry reading in the flat, which is decorated with a strong emphasis on harmony, to 'the feeling of being in a soap bubble'; this response is largely due to the contrasting atmosphere of fear generated by the short performance that precedes it. Schouten (2011: 13) argues that these alternating atmospheres and emotions, the lack of control, and the ensuing feeling of insecurity, ultimately encourage participants to take a critical stance towards their own perceptions and associated prejudices. This change of perception also applies to some extent to the people involved in the performance making, as explained below.

On a cognitive level, the participants' confusion (and subsequent reflection) can be explained by the conflicting cognitive scripts suggested by this production. While a schema tends to be a static structure representing generic knowledge (as explained with respect to the restaurant schema in the previous chapter), a cognitive script is a dynamic, 'temporally-ordered schema' that describes an audience member's 'knowledge of stereotypical goal-oriented event sequences' that are typical of common situations (Emmott and Alexander 2015). In many *X-Apartments* performances, two overarching scripts compete: that of the spectator accessing a theatre production space and that of the guest visiting the resident of a private apartment. Both Krottenthaler's (2004) video documentation of the events and Tomas Fitzel's (2004) audio recordings for Radio SWR2 reveal that most participants conformed to the guest script. For example, they thanked their hosts at the end of a performance segment or wished them a 'good night'. By contrast, their behaviour tended to switch to that of a spectator during productions with a clearly performative character, such as the step dance by three elderly ladies under the direction of Constanza Macras (Bleckmannweg, Lichtenberg) where participants expressed their appreciation with applause, in line with the script of attending a theatre performance.

The liminal phase of transitioning between the public space and the private space where audience members expected the theatre performances to take place, were particularly marked by the conflict between different scripts. For example, when participants reached one of the multi-story apartment houses, they had to press the button with Frau Barthelmess's name at the building's intercom. In the context of *X-Apartments*, this simple pragmatic act fulfilled a double function in the sense that it provided participants simultaneously with access to Frau Barthelmess' flat and to the performance. Unlike many conventional dramatic performances, buying a theatre ticket for *X-Apartments* did not ensure easy access or exit from performances. In another production, Carsten Kieslich, a builder by trade, started sealing the door of his own flat with bricks, while audience members were eating sausages that he had prepared for them on the barbecue. Once again, it was unclear whether the visitor script applies – which would make such an absurd and unfriendly action by a host unlikely – or whether the spectator script was relevant in this context, suggesting an unconventional and provocative theatre production. Some audience members realized too late that the latter was the case and had to exit via the window, assisted by a stool conveniently placed in front of it (Deutschlandradio 2008). Due to a conflict of scripts, audience members who originally thought they were attending a series of theatre performances might be unable to assess the genuineness of the actions and words presented to them, and be unsure whether to act as a theatregoer or as a citizen in everyday life.

Interpreting Polat's project in terms of cognitive scripts provides a further explanation for audience responses to the first scene. Given that, once admitted to the building in Reichenbergerstraße, audiences needed to pass through dark stairwells and long corridors, some audience members might have been inclined to interpret the threatening behaviour of the young people as part of the script of the highwayman collecting a 'toll' from passers-by, or a contemporary variation thereof, that of people in need asking for money from strangers. This script is embedded in the performance's play with the negative stereotypes attached to the suburb of Lichtenberg, which has been frequently associated with 'Neo-Nazis, the former Headquarters of the East German Secret Police, GDR *Tristesse*, and prefabricated multi-story *Plattenbau* buildings' (Wer an Lichtenberg denkt, der denkt meist an Neonazis und an die Stasi-Zentrale, an DDR-Tristesse und Plattenbau: Geisler 2010). As a result, many participants from Berlin are likely to have approached the unfamiliar suburb with a feeling of unease, guided by schemata encouraging them to be cautious in this environment, an expectation that Polat successfully exploited and challenged in both parts of her project. For example, Schultze reported with regard to Frau Barthelmess's decorated flat:

> For people with prejudices, just like me, it was the very opposite to the block of flats where she lives [...], full of affection and colourful, decorated with attention to detail, many flowers and cushions; it was not particularly 'staged'. (Für den Vorurteilsbelasteten, genau wie ich, war es ein kompletter Gegenentwurf zu dem Wohnblock, in dem sie

lebte [...], extrem liebevoll und bunt, detailreich eingerichtet mit Blümchen und vielen Kissen [...]; es gab keine große Rauminszenierung: Garde 2013c)

By creating a productive friction between cultural differences, Polat's theatre production aligned perfectly with what Lilienthal set out to do in much of his work at the HAU (*Theater heute* Redaktion 2012: 29). Like many other projects that were part of *X-Apartments*, Polat's used a sceptical approach to Authenticity-Effects to destabilize her audience's preconceptions, creating a productive state of insecurity (Gutjahr 2010: 28) that prompted spectators and artists to re-assess not only the authenticity of what they were experiencing, but also their own assumptions of cultural differences and of what seemed to be familiar or unfamiliar in this district of Berlin.

'Authentic' encounters with diverse unfamiliar people in Lichtenberg

X-Apartments in Lichtenberg invited participants to engage with a range of unfamiliar people who could be perceived for many reasons as different, foreign or insufficiently known. Like in Polat's project, the 'new narrative contexts' (neue Erzählkontexte: Lilienthal 2003: 9) created by the private performance settings encouraged a range of artists to explore Authenticity-Effects when inviting audience members to encounter the unfamiliar people in their work. For example, Neco Çelik's project featured Frau Reich, an avid collector of autographs from popular German stars, who was connected to a lie detector. Ivana Sajevic's, Bobo Jelčić's, and Nataša Rajković's project involved Frau Jagotzky, who recalled her experience of winning the national lottery in the former German Democratic Republic of the 1970s (in Schulze-Boysen-Straße). Frau Jagotzky provided documentary evidence in the form of the worn official confirmation of her win, together with the closing comment, 'This was the true story. I hope you liked it' (Es war die wahre Geschichte. Ich hoffe, sie hat Ihnen gefallen: Krottenthaler

2004). Other projects explored cultural differences that might be associated with ethnicity and religion, such as a quarrelling Vietnamese couple who invited participants to lie down on a massage table (in Wönnichstraße) and Nevin and Züli Aladağ's project *Condolence 2036* (*Kondolenz 2036*) in which a coffin with the soldier Anton-Achmed was carried into the flat of the Görgülü family and participants were informed that he had died in the future (in 2034) fighting 'for the German people in the mountains of Peshawar' (für das deutsche Volk in den Bergen vor Peshavar gefallen: Behrendt 2004).

Züli Aladağ and Ayşe Polat were not the only young filmmakers with both German and Turkish/Kurdish migrant backgrounds to be invited by Lilienthal and Shermin Langhoff to create pieces for *X-Apartments*. Fatih Akın had just been awarded several prizes, including at the Berlinale, for his movie *Head On* (*Gegen die Wand*), and his collaboration with equally famous writer Feridun Zaimoglu 'came at the right time' for the project (Lilienthal, in Baecker et al. 2012: 13). The two artists adapted Zaimoglu's story 'God's Warriors' from the collection *Twelve Grams of Happiness* (*Zwölf Gramm Glück*) for a *mise-en-scène* in an empty flat on the tenth floor of a Lichtenberg multi-storey building (Frankfurter Allee) because they preferred its urban feel and anonymity to the highly interconnected neighbourhood of Kreuzberg (Krottenthaler 2004).

Fatih Akın and Feridun Zaimoglu's *God's Warriors* (*Gottes Krieger*)

In his *mise-en-scène* of Zaimoglu's text, Akın has an actor who is cross-gender cast perform confronting excerpts of the original short story within an ambiguous frame that initially creates similar Authenticity-Effects to those described for the first part of Polat's project. However, while Polat's project offers a sense of closure to the audience – the young actors hand back the coin to participants upon leaving Frau Barthelmess's flat – Akın and Zaimoglu maintain a sense of aggressive disturbance throughout the performance and the unfamiliar becomes an ongoing threat. It starts with participants being greeted with an unfriendly 'Shoes off' when reaching the flat – possibly by one of its residents – and ends with a loud closing of the door behind the two participants/guests at the end of the performance. In between they observe a man performing what seems like a religious cleansing ritual, followed by an aggressive sermon delivered by an actor in a black suit who appears to be one of four males and who initially stands with 'his' back to the audience. When 'he' turns around to deliver the hate speech by the 'heart-preacher' (Herzprediger), an Islamist sect leader (Yeşilada 2012: 153), the actor's female gender is revealed and the three other performers kneel in front of her on a green carpet with their back to the audience, who have been asked to sit down on a mattress at the other end of the room.

Unlike their immersion in most other *X-Apartment* projects, spectators now observe the scene in a position that recalls the more conventional theatre performance setting with a fourth wall, in which the audience become discrete witnesses who have to avoid attracting attention to themselves (Roselt 2008: 94). This position, together with the unfriendly treatment of the audience, reinforces the hostile atmosphere created by the emphatically delivered text, in which Zaimoglu combines what sounds like exaggerated snippets of Islamic critiques of capitalism, summed up by the leitmotif of the alliteration, 'Partying and fucking and being free' (feiern, ficken und frei sein: Zaimoglu 2008: 139), with expressions of violent fundamentalist beliefs bearing 'fascist elements in terms of race and faith' in a sermon that frequently borders on the 'linguistically grotesque' (Yeşilada 2012: 153). Once again, audiences are put in a position where they have good reason to be uncertain about the 'correct' frame for assessing the performance. The nature of the speech remains ambiguous because, even in the original short story, the extensive use of rhetorical devices is characteristic of both fiction and of impassioned religious sermons, which employ them to persuade their listeners.

This ambiguity inherent to the text is transferred to the playing space and reinforced because it is not evident where and when this fictional performance element finishes. As participants are not provided with a programme, they can neither gain definite clarity about the role of the three male people listening to the hate speech, nor whether it is being endorsed by them. The effect is that the speech assumes a more prominent role in performance than in the original story, where it is contextualized as memories of a 'renegade Jihadist' (Cheesman 2012: 122). For some audience members, the way excerpts from Zaimoglu's short story were framed in *X-Apartments* clearly shaped their perception, which one critic describes as follows:

> It is that simple. You enter into a flat that appears to be conspiratorial and in no time you believe that you are in the middle of an Islamist conspiracy. (So einfach ist das. Man kommt in eine Wohnung, die konspirativ wirkt, und schon glaubt man sich inmitten einer islamistischen Verschwörung: Schaper 2004)

In short, this brief performance in an almost empty flat confronts audiences with their own, potentially unacknowledged, and thus unfamiliar 'resentments' (Ressentiments: Behrendt 2004). Almost three years after the World Trade Centre attacks, the production invited moments of self-recognition and a critical reflection on attitudes towards religion that included the 'internal processes of doubt, anxiety, reflection and consideration individual spectators go through in their attempts to make sense of, or to respond to work' that Grehan has described with regard to other theatre productions (Grehan 2009: 23).

Voyeurism and the unfamiliar close-by in *X-Apartments* 2004 and 2008

In line with Lilienthal's principle of making excessive demands on everyone involved in productions at the HAU (*Theater heute* Redaktion 2012: 26), *X-Apartments*, which originally was to incorporate 100 apartments in its 2002 version (Schultze, in Garde 2013c), stretched audiences' capacity to cope with the cognitive, affective, and physical demands of the three- to four-hour long *parcours* through Berlin neighbourhoods (Oskamp 2004). The fact that several reviews explicitly mention their companion and/or call them a Sparringpartner (Behrendt 2004), highlights how the walks between performances provided an opportunity for post-performance discussions and a release of the pressure that this performative format put on audiences.

Reviewers encountered multifaceted cultural diversity as a reward for this strenuous exercise, and expressed their surprise at the unfamiliar nature of Berlin's neighbourhoods:

> The mystery, the attraction of this game, its exotic touch is not associated with any festival strangeness, neither is it situated on continents far away – the unknown is already hiding in Kreuzberg or Lichtenberg. (Das Geheimnis, der Witz des Spiels, die Exotik liegt hier nicht in irgendeiner Festival-Fremde, auf fernen Kontinenten – das Unbekannte verbirgt sich in Kreuzberg oder Lichtenberg: Schaper 2004)

As well as expressing Schaper's appreciation of people and environments that appear different or foreign, his comment points to the problematic mode of reception in which the participant consumes the exotic unfamiliar as a voyeur. As director of the 2002 Theatre of the World festival, from the outset Lilienthal was critically aware of the 'colonial' factor that can mark this type of festival and the projects developed under this format (2003: 9). In his article 'Das voyeuristische Erschrecken' (which could be translated as 'The Voyeuristic Shock'), part of a collection of essays and documents about the first *X-Apartments* in Duisburg, he explains how in order to avoid a neo-colonialist approach to the unfamiliar, he decided to shift the focus to unfamiliar people and phenomena in local neighbourhoods instead of importing folkloristic productions to Europe (2003: 10). Inspired by Richard Sennett's *Civitas*, he invited spectators to break out of the social isolation that marked their everyday lives and to engage with entirely different worlds, confronting the prejudices they might associate with them (2003: 11).

However, Lilienthal was aware that geographical closeness does not completely prevent the voyeurism that is founded in 'curiosity and the search for foreign, exotic realities' and which can at times 'easily become unpleasant' (eine Art Voyeurismus [. . .], der zum Teil ins Unangenehme umschlagen kann und sich aus Neugier und der Suche nach einer fremden, exotischen Wirklichkeit zusammensetzt: 2003: 12). In response to this problem, he and his team developed a twofold strategy. First, they relied on the fact that in the projects selected for *X-Apartments*,

> [v]oyeurism is only the entry ticket which lures spectators into participating because the project very quickly throws spectators back towards the structure of their own prejudices. (Voyeurismus ist nur die Eintrittskarte, denn sehr schnell wirft das Projekt den Zuschauer auf die Struktur der eigenen Vorurteile zurück: Lilienthal 2003: 12)

Critics have confirmed this redirection of focus, stating that in the intimate performance spaces 'the audience finds itself as much in a goldfish bowl as the performers' (Das Publikum sitzt genauso auf dem Präsentierteller wie die Agierenden: Mansmann 2004). Second, aware of the recent increased interest in homes and private spaces, including for voyeuristic purposes, Shermin Langhoff stated that several directors in *X-Apartments* were addressing this issue explicitly in their projects (Müller 2004).

The most provocative of these artistic explorations was Nurkan Erpulat's 2008 project for the *parcours* through the Reuterkiez (in Friedelstraße), where he explicitly confronted audiences with their own voyeurism. The project took place in Neukölln, an area 'known to many Berliners only in the form of prejudices' (vielen Berlinern nur in Form von Vorurteilen bekannte Region: HAU 2008) because it had been subject to ethnic stereotyping in the media (Figure 6.1). For example, it had been referred to frequently through catchwords such as 'parallel societies' (Parallelgesellschaften) and 'No-Go Areas' (HAU 2008), as well as many sensationalist reports about the ethnically diverse local secondary school (Rütli-Schule), where students' violence had led in 2006 to calls from teachers at the school to close it down.

In his project, located in a carefully restored old building, Erpulat forced audience members to kneel on cushions in front of a door

Figure 6.1 'Please wait here until you are invited to enter.' *X-Apartments* 2008 Neukölln. Photograph by and copyright Sebastian Bolesch.

separating two rooms and to look through keyholes at a veiled woman getting undressed and posing naked on a sofa smoking a cigarette. The director challenged the schema of the secret, forbidden and unauthorized observation of a potentially sexually exciting activity through a keyhole by inserting this act of watching into a performance where it becomes an overt, permissible, and authorized part of a theatre project. During this voyeuristic act, the spectators themselves were observed by another female, who wore a black headscarf together with 'westernized' clothing. She looked after the entry and exit, and interrupted the observation process by offering a glass of water just at the moment when the naked woman had put herself into position on the sofa. This position evoked the odalisque motif, which, particularly in the nineteenth century, depicted a female, sexually attractive figure associated with a harem as part of an artwork that conveyed an orientalist image of the sensual female other.

However, rather than replicating orientalist fantasies, Erpulat mimics the original scene by altering the context, in particular the background, by utilizing pictures of Ernesto 'Che' Guevara de la Serna and landscapes. In the flat, Schubert's Fantasia in F minor can be heard, which evokes a nineteenth-century bourgeois domestic image of four-hand piano playing rather than an exotic setting. In addition to the setting there is an important structural difference, because the framing performance with the second woman creates a *mise-en-abyme* for the scene of undressing. It is the woman wearing the headscarf who replaces the authorities of the past, who provide or prohibit access to the desired figure – that is, the colonial artist, or, at the narrative level, the imaginary figure of the sultan. The woman with the headscarf in Erpulat's production has the authority to disturb the process of objectifying the naked female through her firm request 'Drink a glass of water', followed by 'Leave now' (Trinken Sie ein Glas Wasser. Gehen Sie jetzt: HAU 2008). This re-distribution of power also applies to the spectators who have to take up a subordinate viewing position in front of the keyhole together with another, potentially unfamiliar participant. In response to this provocative invitation to audiences to confront and reflect on their role, perspective, and ethical position, participants described themselves as 'reluctant voyeurs' (Voyeure wider Willen: Schmidt 2008).

This performance strategy invited participants to reflect on their potentially latent cultural stereotyping, not only with respect to the odalisque motive, but also regarding the figure of the woman wearing a veil or headscarf. In the case of the latter, diverse women are often reduced to one homogeneous orientalist image (Wetzel 2006). Erpulat's use of the figure of the woman authoritatively dispensing glasses of water and controlling the participants' gaze disrupts so-called 'kitchen table ethnologies'. This shorthand expression for descriptions of cultural differences that are superficial and homogenizing, originally coined by Feridun Zaimoglu (2001: 9), reflects the focus of critical engagement in Erpulat's work (Beyond Belonging Translokal 2009). In his 2008 project for *X-Apartments*, Erpulat invited participants to engage with multifaceted cultural markers that cross a potential divide between East and West, as displayed by the two women who combine clothing that could be interpreted as traditionally religious with 'westernized' outfits. Participants are asked to remove their shoes, like in many Muslim homes, before entering an apartment featuring classical Western music and decoration sourced from various cultures.

While the undressing of the veiled woman is marked by rehearsed performativity – thus disrupting the schema of secretly observing another person through a keyhole – the status of the woman with the headscarf remains ambiguous. The arranged nature of the voyeur-scene provides a contrast to the behaviour of the woman with the headscarf, who moves comfortably through several rooms and could easily be taken for the resident of what appears to be a genuine lived-in apartment. As Annemarie Matzke (2006: 41) has observed in the context of other theatre productions, Authenticity-Effects can be generated through different degrees of artificiality with the least artificial phenomenon appearing to be authentic. In Erpulat's project, this could mean that participants ultimately are left without an answer regarding the apartment's true resident(s). Through its ambiguity and encouragement of self-reflection, this project allows for a complex engagement with intercultural power and gender relations in the context of sexuality, topics that were also addressed in his play *On the Other Side: Are you Gay or are you Turkish?* (*Jenseits – Bist du schwul oder bist du Türke?*), co-authored with Tunçay Kulaoğlu, which Erpulat had directed for the Beyond Belonging Festival curated by Shermin Langhoff at the HAU in May 2008. Like this play, Erpulat's later *X-Apartments* project invited critical engagement with taboo subjects, to which some audience members responded with a feeling of shame (Schmidt 2008). Lilienthal himself valued Erpulat's project so much that he wrote:

> It is the HAU in a nutshell. Irritations that are generated when the voyeuristic gazing at the naked woman intersects with our ideas of Islam – and [the play with the idea] that everything can be turned into theatre. ('Für mich bringt sie das HAU auf den Punkt. [. . .] Irritationen, die entstehen, wenn die voyeuristischen Blicke auf die nackte Frau unsere Vorstellungen vom Islam kreuzen – und damit, dass alles Theater sein kann: Laudenbach 2012)

The last part of Lilienthal's statement speaks of the artistic freedom to stage any subject matter while also referring to an ability to turn all elements of everyday life into a theatre performance.

The power of framing as an aesthetic strategy was also explored in later projects that were born out of *X-Apartments* in Berlin, including a striking installation for Gropiusstadt (2008), in which Heiner Goebbels worked with an 'aesthetics of absence', as explained in a publication with the same title (*Ästhetik der Abwesenheit*, 2012). In *Genko-An 12353*, the local residents were no longer physically present, except for the traces that they had left in the form of graffiti on the walls of two top-floor balconies of a skyscraper. Goebbels selected the location to present participants with two different positions for observing the local environment in this modernist large-scale housing commission: one that afforded a view of the opposite apartment blocks and the horizon beyond, and another that offered a view of the open sky. While Goebbels' project did not use Authenticity-Effects routed through seemingly real-people performers, because if offered 'minute changes of perspective with an enormous effect' (winzigen Perspektivwechsel mit enormer Wirkung: Behrendt 2008), it worked with an important aspect of *X-Apartments'* transformative potential.

The projects analysed in this chapter all invite a change of perspective by confronting the audience with cultural stereotypes (Erpulat) or destabilizing frames of reference (Polat and other directors in 2004). This framing strategy, particularly when used in projects suggesting and playing with the presence of real people, can lead to a productive state of insecurity (Gutjahr 2010: 28) that prompts spectators to continue re-assessing not only the potential authenticity of what they are experiencing, but also their perception of what seems familiar or unfamiliar, with regard to both people and cultural phenomena. The transformative power of this repetitive re-adjustment and re-positioning during individual performances and within the framework of an entire *parcours* is significant in two respects. First, it replicates the 'never-ending processes of getting to know one another' in an 'ongoing dialogue' during encounters with unfamiliar people (eine dialogische Annäherung [als] ein unendlicher Prozess: Regus 2009: 11). This open-ended dialogue with 'little bites of [information] makes you hungry to find out more about the people behind the stories' (Die kleinen Häppchen [Information] machen Lust, mehr über die Menschen zu erfahren, die hinter den Geschichten stehen: Mansmann 2004). Second, an aesthetics that challenges schemata and cognitive scripts as forms of implicit knowledge might offer the opportunity to transcend pre-existing conditions and to create new realities (Singer 2014). The versions of *X-Apartments* discussed in this chapter impacted both on the perceptions of the participants who had been 'lured' into 'unfamiliar worlds [situated] in close vicinity to one's own [world]' (die Besucher in fremde Welten gleich neben der eigenen zu locken: Behrendt 2008), as well as those of some local residents who were 'delighted [...] to see their own district in a new light' (beglückt, ihn [den Kiez] mit neuen Augen zu sehen: Behrendt 2008). Most projects analysed here invited fresh perspectives on residents who are unfamiliar, due to differences in age, socio-economic, ethnic and religious background, while showing most people as an individual rather than as part of a homogeneous group. Ideally, this mode of engagement with unfamiliar people and characters in Berlin neighbourhoods provides the '[s]mall changes of location [necessary to] change our experiences of reality' (Kleine Standortwechsel verändern die Wirklichkeitserfahrung: Behrendt 2008).

7

Unsettling Journey into the Unfamiliar: Ambiguous Guides to the City in *Call Cutta*: *Mobile Phone Theatre*

Unlike *X-Apartments* and *100% City*, which encourage engagement with between a dozen and a 100 unfamiliar people, *Call Cutta: Mobile Phone Theatre* (*Call Cutta. Mobiles Telefontheater*) enables an intensive one-on-one encounter with an individual. In its second and final version in Berlin in 2005, each participant was able to spend about an hour talking on the phone to an unfamiliar person situated in an Indian call centre, who became his or her personal guide and directed them on a city tour – from the Hallesches Ufer via Kreuzberg to Potsdamer Platz – through the lesser known areas of the district surrounding the Hebbel am Ufer (HAU) consortium of theatres. This tour followed an earlier version of the format developed by Helgard Haug, Stefan Kaegi, and Daniel Wetzel in Kolkata (formerly Calcutta), in association with the local Goethe-Institut Max Mueller Bhavan Kolkata. The project is characteristic both of Rimini Protokoll's ongoing international work and collaboration with Germany's worldwide cultural institute, and of the internationally mobile work undertaken by many artists associated with the HAU, the production house where Rimini Protokoll has had a permanent base since 2004. As discussed in Chapter 4, under the leadership of Matthias Lilienthal (2003–12), the HAU came to resemble a large-scale international festival hub that provided a platform for both incoming and outgoing artists who frequently combined different sources and partners to fund their work. According to Florian Malzacher (2005), *Call Cutta*'s audience included participants who had become disinterested in established dramatic theatre and were interested in the aesthetic thrill of experiencing a *parcours*. *Call Cutta* can thus be considered as characteristic of the HAU's 2004 performance programme because it contributed to Lilienthal and his team's plan to draw in new audiences. These also included those participants who were not regular theatregoers and people living in and interested in the neighbourhood.

Like Lilienthal's brainchild *X-Apartments*, Rimini Protokoll's *Call Cutta* was a format that could be adapted to different international contexts. However, *Call Cutta: Mobile Phone Theatre* was only produced in its original format twice before the artists developed it into the smaller-scale *Call Cutta in a Box*, where the phone conversation takes place in a room rather than the city streets. This might be at least partially due to the considerable work needed to ensure that the directions the call-centre performers could give to the local participants were correct and effective, despite them not knowing the route first hand (Wetzel 2008: 71).

In a similar way to *X-Apartments*, *Call Cutta*'s original version in Hatibagan, a Kolkata suburb, set out to change perspectives of an urban environment by shifting the frames of reference – this time through using a mobile phone, thereby combining the walkers' visual perception of the everyday environment with auditory input. The archival website of the Goethe-Institut Kolkata refers to Rimini Protokoll's *parcours* as '[t]he world's first mobile phone theatre. Theatre that transforms the city into a stage. A mobile stage' (Goethe-Institut Max Mueller Bhavan Kolkata website). For the audience-participants, this mobile stage in a selected city district activated schemata, cognitive structures that contain information about the general form of an entity, like a role one repeatedly plays, rather than specific information about that entity, such as the nature, place, and duration of a specific role during a particular event (Emmott and Alexander 2015). In this production, the schemata were associated with the distribution of key roles for the audience member: first, that of a receiver of (personal) information from an adviser in a call centre; and second, that of someone on a tour who is guided through an unknown or only partially familiar part of town. Whereas in *X-Apartments*, discussed in the previous chapter, the roles of theatregoer and house guest are in many cases ultimately separated and clarified for the audience member, this is not the case in *Call Cutta*.

Participants in Berlin's version of *Call Cutta* assumed the role of a walker who discovers the city in the footsteps of the earlier local *flâneurs*, such as Franz Hessel, as well as that of a tourist who undertakes a tour for pleasure or culture, and, at times, the role of a street performer who acts out or says certain words aloud in a public space, as prompted by their interlocutors (sometimes in front of local interested onlookers, including residents) – all while having a conversation with their partner on a mobile phone. The people in the Indian call centre had the role of the 'everyday experts' and real-people performers, sharing snippets of information about their occupation at the call centre and their everyday life in India, telling stories, and also functioning as tour guides and expert communicators on the phone. Unlike in *X-Apartments*, however, where participants were sometimes caught between the role of spectator or house guest, these roles do not conflict with each other. In *Call Cutta*, they fluctuate, with one or more roles applying concurrently to an individual situation, making it difficult for participants to assess overall situations, the information provided by their interlocutor, and the nature of their relationship with their dialogue partners. Usually a change of roles is instigated and controlled by the call-centre performers, resulting in them having the upper hand in a dialogue that plays with notions of authenticity and trustworthiness. Madhusree Mukerjee, who has collaborated on the various *Call Cutta* projects since 2005, observes a shift between staged behaviour (which is also part of her daily work), the rehearsed behaviour for the tour in Berlin, and spontaneous, authentic-seeming reactions:

> The sharp changeover from intimacy to an almost dry instructive mode [e.g. when giving directions] is deliberate and part of the script. It is a kind of an emotional roller-coaster ride where information and intimacy merge smoothly creating a canvas of various shades. (Mukerjee, in Garde 2010b)

As the majority of the performers were experienced call-centre operators, they were able to build on their performative practice in the everyday (Glauner 2005) and use their expertise at winning over their conversational partners, playing effectively with the intimacy that can be generated by a phone conversation and gaining participants' attention and trust. *Call Cutta* adopts the theatrical traits of dissimulation that call-centre operators use every day: giving false names, being informed about the caller's local conditions like weather and time, and quickly adjusting to their interlocutor so as to give their customers in England, America or Germany the impression that they are just around the corner (Rimini Protokoll 2005: 3). In short, the real people in this theatre project are individuals whose profession already requires a sound knowledge of the kind of theatricality that is part of the global call-centre economy, and who are very capable of applying some of these skills to Rimini Protokoll's *parcours*.

The performers' skills, in conjunction with the intimate set-up of this walk, during which the call-centre performers give the walker in Berlin their undivided attention, generate ephemeral sensations of authenticity. Many reviewers report how they experienced a sense of intimate contact with a person who appeared to be sincere and genuine and therefore credible, impressions that were repeatedly unsettled and re-created during the course of the walk, and resulted in participants reflecting on the nature of the person they were in dialogue with (e.g. Glauner 2005; Ruesch 2007a). These deliberations led to a deep engagement on the phone with an unfamiliar person about 20,000 kilometres away who most participants would usually only come in contact with as part of the global service industry, or whom they might avoid contact with altogether.

The following analysis explores how and whether participants' fleeting impressions of genuineness could function as potential 'authenticity-promising baits' (authentizitätsversprechende Köder; Eiermann 2012: 259). Focusing on the *parcours* in Berlin, it analyses the capacity of these Authenticity-Effects to lure audiences into a complex engagement with the unfamiliar on two levels. First, participants engage with performers who many participants in Berlin would perceive as unfamiliar (in the sense of foreign) and insufficiently known because of their location and, potentially, occupational background. Second, the performers' stories, which involve both historical facts as well as elements of fiction, invite participants to discover unfamiliar aspects of 'their own' culture. The project ultimately reveals that the encounter with the foreign 'from outside', often entails a confrontation with what could be termed 'the unfamiliar within'. Consequently, the analysis highlights the aesthetic processes that the theatre-makers deploy to expose their audience to the fault lines of the familiar, through, for example, the interrogation of communicative memory as the building block of one's own cultural identity, and through Authenticity-Effects generated by an unreliable communication partner whose 'true' nature remains ambiguous.

Encounters with unfamiliar call-centre performers in India

As the following analysis demonstrates, this production uses encounters between people from different cultures to create cracks in the images of the local (Berlin) culture, and in a manner that is simultaneously playful and provocative. In so doing, it tightly interweaves the critical confrontation with the unfamiliar outside, and the unfamiliar within one's own culture. In *Call Cutta*, the encounter with people who might appear unfamiliar due to their cultural and professional backgrounds is a variation of the topos of the journey. Ideally, participants not only complete the city tour, but also consider the interplay of aesthetics and socio-politics in a way that brings them to shift – or at least reflect on – their attitude towards unfamiliar people. This reflection potentially leads participants to the realization that notions of authenticity and of unfamiliarity share an important characteristic: neither is a stable, predetermined characteristic, and both are individually and culturally specific products of ascription.

In concrete terms, this transformative journey takes on the form of a tour through the 'social construction landscape of Kreuzberg West' (Sozialbaulandschaft Kreuzberg West: Rimini Protokoll website) and bears the appropriate subtitle 'Mobile Phone Theatre', since it is not just the medium of communication that is mobile, but also the audience members. The tour's theatrical framework is highlighted in the script that the call-centre performers use, where each of the journey's stations are labelled as 'acts' and the following information on titles and durations is provided: 'Strategies' (0–18 min), 'The Enemy of my Enemy' (19–26 min), 'Personal Attitude' (26–55 min), 'Underground' (55–60 min), 'You and Me' (60–66 min). On their way, participants rely entirely on the auditory input from the call-centre performers in Kolkata, both for receiving directions and for the delivery of the narrative. As the walkers only get a visual impression of their conversation partner at the very end of the tour, the performer's voice assumes great significance in this project.

Rimini Protokoll and the call-centre performers use voice as a medium to establish an illusion of intimacy and familiarity – as a counterpart to the foreign – by way of the word being spoken and sung directly into the ear. About twelve minutes into the tour, the performers share with the participant the information that: 'My voice has changed quite a bit since I started calling people every day' (Rimini Protokoll 2005: 22). Not only is this a seemingly intimate comment, but it also makes the voice into a marker of occupational identity. Apart from alerting the listener to the important role of the voice, this statement also appears to identify its speaker as a genuine call-centre operator rather than as a professional actor, and it hints at the physical impact of the call-centre economy. There are also moments when the use of the voice creates and destabilizes a sense of an intimate encounter with the strange, such as when the call-centre performers sing a song for the participants (during which the latter are supposed to close their eyes). This imagery of the strange that is conjured up by the singing is clichéd because it seems to provoke naïve stereotypical cultural associations according to which India is a mythical and magical land (Garde 2010b). Similarly, stereotypes seem to re-surface when the performers ask the person in Berlin to sing a song for them. To take one example, in the Rimini Protokoll video (2013) depicting selected scenes from *Call Cutta*, a young German woman is strongly encouraged to join in singing a traditional German hiking song (Wanderlied). The notion that the intimate voice gives unmediated access to the essence of another culture is troubled in both instances.

The voice of the interlocutor from India, which, despite the distance, seems so close and intimate to the participant in Berlin, also alludes to the significance of the media in bridging great distances – and in doing so, to the increased possibilities of communication in a globalized world where space seems to have been condensed. An impression of proximity and intimacy is fostered through flirting, compliments, and personal questions, including: 'Are there many people in the world who would recognize your voice when you are on the phone?' (Gibt es viele Leute, die Deine Stimme am Telefon wieder erkennen?; Rimini Protokoll 2005: 11). In this respect, the 'phone theatre' of *Call Cutta* builds on ideas that Stefan Kaegi developed in his project in the late 1990s, entitled *156 60 18 (1.49,-/Min.). A Scenic Sound Attack (Ein szenischer Lauschangriff)*. In the volume *Experts of the Everyday*, his work is described as a '[s]cenic installation based on the telephone as a confessional box, medium for flirtation and imaginative space' (Dreysse and Malzacher 2008: 221). Similarly, the phone in *Call Cutta* functions as a medium that can accommodate both imagination and fiction, as well as sensations of authenticity. The fact that in a conventional phone conversation the caller and his or her counterpart remain invisible stimulates the fantasy – a key element of erotic phone calls – as well as encouraging the 'truthful' admissions made in some calls to counselling hotlines. Florian Malzacher (2005) points to the ambiguity resulting from these mixed impressions, summing up his own experience as participant thus: 'Everything remains up in the air; the slightly flirtatious undertone might just be a projection' (Alles bleibt in der Schwebe; der leicht flirtende Unterton mag eine Projektion sein).

At times, this ambiguity surrounding experiences of intimacy and familiarity might make it difficult for the walkers to trust their guides.

However, as they are the only source of directional information available to participants, the majority of the latter are likely to accept that they have to rely on their interlocutors' knowledge. Indeed, some reviewers have noted that they were relieved when the phone connection was re-established after having dropped out in a large underground car park (Ruesch 2007a: 182). This sort of trust is one-sided, since it is based on the competence and reliability of the Indian tour guide. It has practical consequences because it is the experts who know the route and everything that goes with it. The potential power factor of this knowledge discrepancy is carefully balanced out by Rimini Protokoll's characteristic 'dramaturgy of care' (Malzacher 2007: 14–23). For example, the performers warn the participants to take care in crossing the road. The trust in the other person, which has practical implications, needs to be mutual, as the dialogue partners have to navigate a route that is in various ways unknown to both parties, similar to a scavenger hunt. For a short time, the participants in Berlin share the social world of the call-centre operators through their common activity without having access to the same knowledge that is the information about the route. However, both types of trust and the notions of access to first-hand, correct, and unmediated knowledge and information are frequently destabilized in a playful way, creating another source of unsettlement in addition to the unstable roles the participants and performers play. For example, the real-people performers do not volunteer information about how they have knowledge of the routes and they conceal the fact that they know about the clothing worn by their dialogue partners in Berlin, because they were secretly briefed by the people handing out the phones at the HAU.

The people in India, in turn, cannot verify whether participants follow their instructions, such as to take the pose of the Indian independence fighter Netaji, pointing to the left with the left arm towards India. As this instruction asks participants to perform in a public space, exposing them potentially to the ridicule of onlookers, some walkers chose not to carry out these directives, without their guide noticing (Ruesch 2007a: 184). All in all, the tour oscillates between playing with the possibility of deceiving one another, and the genuine need to believe in the authentic nature of the other person's information. As Orvell has explained, authenticity begins to matter when the possibility of fraud has a real-life impact (1989: xvii).

One decisive performance element for the development of trust and the feeling of intimacy that grows out of it are the photographic documents spread out along the tour as a kind of scavenger hunt, which consist of historical photos that recount the story of Netaji, the so-called 'Respected Leader' Subhas Chandra Bose, who came to Berlin in 1941 to seek military support. In his discussion of media and their meanings, a discussion that references Marshall Mcluhan's thinking on the subject, Wolfgang Ernst points out that 'the message of each new medium is the aura of its predecessor' (2000: 161). In this case, the black-and-white photos constitute a predecessor that could easily appear auratic when compared with the technically advanced mobile phones used in *Call Cutta*. The photos exemplify aura as defined by Walter Benjamin (2008: 23) because they evoke closeness and (historical) distance, the presence of the photo and the absence of the person depicted. All of this could result in elevating the photos' status to that of a special object (Figure 7.1).

The photos highlight Netaji's story as a key element of the tour, one that is presented in a personal and private tone. When they begin to tell the story, the call-centre performers draw the gaze of their interlocutors towards a supposed family member, depicted in a photo next to a man who is later identified by the call-centre performers as Netaji, by saying: 'The [man] on the right is my grandfather Samir Singh (father of [the performer's] mother, born in 1920)'. Here and elsewhere the brackets in the script indicate instructions and prompts for the performers. The second photo, which the viewer retrieves from under a bin lid five minutes later, supposedly shows Netaji by Ghandi's side, perhaps giving an impression of authenticity through featuring a well-known historical figure. However, doubt seems to be appropriate when the audience member is asked: 'You know the one on the left? (Ghandi, we call him Bapuji, father of the Nation) ... But who is on the right? – Recognize

Figure 7.1 Audience participant with photo in *Call Cutta: Mobile Phone Theatre.* Photograph by Helgard Haug, copyright Rimini Protokoll.

him? ... It's the guy who drank coffee with my grandpa' (Rimini Protokoll 2005: 25). Although it is suggested to the participants in Berlin that they have the capacity to recognize Netaji, they are not allowed to decide for themselves whether the visual information is reliable or not, since the power to ascribe meaning and the possibility of checking the authenticity of the documents lies exclusively with the call-centre performers. Even the information about the grandfather figure cannot be verified, since the participants saw the first photo – in which both men were wearing glasses – through a window. Participants are probably unable to call upon general knowledge about Netaji, and may suspect that all of the (many) call-centre performers are referring to one and the same person as their grandfather (Siegmund 2008: 199). Susanne Knaller and Harro Müller (2005: 47) observe that the impression of authenticity is not generated by the stable quality of an object or a person, but rather is the result of a process of verification that takes place at a specific time and place, which must always be applied anew and without guarantee. When this observation is applied to *Call Cutta*, it becomes clear that this verification cannot take place. Instead, the production allows doubts about the nature and function of the photos to arise in the mind of the participant, particularly since they would not expect to stumble upon 'relics of German-Indian history in Kreuzberg' (Relikte deutsch-indischer Geschichte in Kreuzberg; Meierhenrich 2005).

The hesitation and wavering of the audience is increased by the uncertainty created with regard to the narrator's reliability. The way the performance is structured in time also contributes to this uncertainty, since the call-centre operators ask 'Do you recognize him?' about five minutes after they have (supposedly) told the participants their real name, thus apparently switching from a professional role into that of a trusted tour guide or personal companion, along the lines of the tag line on Rimini Protokoll's German website: 'A voice with an Indian accent, if it's foreign, soon it will become your ally' (Eine Stimme mit indischem Akzent, noch ist sie fremd, bald wird sie zu deinem Verbündeten). This movement between trust and doubt, intimacy and distance, has much in common with the multi-stable perception that Erika Fischer-Lichte (2006) has described in relation to the reception of visual patterns, such as occurs in the case of figures with figure-ground reversal, where different interpretations are possible and no single interpretation can be final. The difference is that in *Call Cutta* it is not a matter of the process of perception and the categorization of signification as such, but rather of the classification of information into the categories 'authentic, true and reliable' or 'fake and unreliable'. This oscillation with regard to reliability applies both to assessing the information – that is, fixing a meaning to the photos – as well as to how the information is transferred, and therefore to the informant.

This oscillation situation automatically influences the semi-virtual relation of the interlocutors in Berlin and Kolkata; in the end, their relationship is based only on the spoken word and its reliability. For this reason, blind trust in the tour guide from India – participants are asked to be their 'eyes' – can quickly turn to scepticism, or to a swaying back and forth between these perspectives, as exemplified in reviewer Max Glauner's (2005) question: 'Or was the intimacy that was sought after just a hoax?' (Oder war die gesuchte Nähe nur ein Fake?). Glauner's remark is also indicative of the production's refusal to offer access to a genuine self and what Stegemann has called the 'true essence of an other' (das wahre Wesen des Anderen: 2015: 95). This experience of failing to grasp the full meaning of an unfamiliar person and of the related cultural encounter in the theatre can lead to the insight that a complete understanding of the unfamiliar is neither possible nor desirable (Regus 2009: 11). In the course of the *parcours*, this unsettling relationship is further amplified fifteen minutes later, because the third photo, in which Netaji purportedly can be seen shaking Hitler's hand, is not there. It supposedly 'always goes missing, because the residents here don't like it' (Rimini Protokoll 2005: 59). However, no time is allowed to decide whether this is a production trick or the truth, since the tour of the city keeps moving.

Encountering the unfamiliar within one's own culture through a German-Indian story

Call Cutta offers a complex engagement with the unfamiliar because it carefully interweaves notions of the unfamiliar *beyond* one's culture, with the unfamiliar *within* one's culture. When the performers' tale about the fake grandfather is introduced as part of the play with intimacy and sincerity in relation to the foreign, it also provides personalized access to Netaji's 1941 journey to Berlin and thereby puts the participants in contact with unfamiliar aspects of Berlin's history. The contact comes both through the figure of the Indian freedom fighter Netaji and through a fresh perspective on seemingly familiar locations and the people they feature.

So, with the second photo of Ghandi and Netaji, the unfamiliar as the forgotten familiar is produced out of the dustbin of history, so to speak (Assmann 2003: 114–29). The bizarre true story of the Indian freedom fighter connected to the photo, who was in Berlin in the early 1940s to seek military support from the National Socialists for the struggle for independence from the British colonial rulers, is likely to strengthen the participants' pre-existing mistrust of the authenticity of the grandfather figure, and seems to confirm that they are dealing with an unreliable informant. In addition, participants may well start to doubt their own historical knowledge about the city of Berlin. Ultimately, this could lead to the insight that beyond the mainstream view of Berlin as a city full of memorial sites pointing to its well-known turbulent history, many other unfamiliar pathways and dimensions are to be found. The foreign and unknown within the familiar becomes visible once the walker leaves the well-beaten path.

This fresh insight could add a further layer to an already multi-layered experience. Participants might feel that every time they try to classify the tour and its processes of creating impressions of intimacy and of (de)familiarization, a new unsettling element arrives that is often subtly connected to various preceding elements, and which modifies their original meaning. Helgard Haug speaks of a continual, self-reflexive play with regard to the different roles the experts seem to take on, and the audience's unstable impressions of whether something is theatrical (Garde 2010a). The tour through an everyday neighbourhood thus becomes a kind of hall of mirrors, in which the individual elements of the production mutually reflect one another such that conclusions can never be drawn as to what is truly familiar, intimate, unfamiliar or distant.

This instability perpetuates itself through yet another disruption of expectations as the tour reaches the old platforms of the Anhalter train station. Instead of overtly drawing attention to the importance of the station for transportation to the concentration camps by way of the stelae in front of the portico, the Indian tour guides take the interlocutors in Berlin on a path that approaches this historically important site from the forest, declaring: 'the three grey trees have sad eyes [...] These eyes are still waiting for a train [...] [r]ight under the bushes you can see platform 8, a junction to Auschwitz' (Rimini Protokoll 2005: 32). As Mukerjee confirms, this is a moment of surprise and of rupture even for informed locals (Garde 2010b). As discussed in Chapter 5 in the analysis of the Vietnam veteran Stephen Black's story in *100% Melbourne*, Rimini Protokoll use rhetorical devices to allow audience members to imagine what is unimaginable and to become moved by it. The trees are anthropomorphized and, due to their age, can thus take the place of the human witnesses who were murdered at the time or have since died. When the performers suggest that the walker 'can see platform 8', they are inviting audiences to use their imagination to conjure up an image of track eight, as vegetation has overgrown the historical evidence. Through claiming that the platform can still be seen, the performers highlight that what was once true has been replaced by a gap. By using these literary strategies, Rimini Protokoll and the performers avoid direct verbal or documentary reference to the horror, only hinting at 'that "which cannot be experienced otherwise"' (das 'Nicht-Anders-Erlebbare'; Assmann 2003: 247). By leading participants to the tracks used by the former German State Railroad (Reichsbahn), this passage of *Call Cutta* not only points to the underlying infrastructure which supported the systematic murder of people, but also gives personal and fresh access via individual imagination to a traumatic past.

Such an invitation to become personally moved and engaged is not always effective. For example, it loses its transformative capacity if something in the present overwrites participants' imaginative involvement, in a manner similar to what David Barnett has described as happening in Rimini Protokoll's city tour *50 Aktenkilometer* (2015: 100). In this piece, a mobile audience listen to audio files related to the surveillance files created by the East German Stasi while walking through the streets of Berlin-Mitte in 2011, and there are instances where a tension between what participants see and hear 'can cement the distance between what once took place under a malign regime and what now takes place in a more open society' (2015: 100). In summary, Rimini Protokoll frequently use narratives that add an additional layer to the facts that can be grasped intellectually, and to the everyday world that can be perceived by the senses. In a manner similar to how fiction is processed, each audience participant can fill the gap in his or her own way between what seems to exist and be visible and what the tour guides say. This invitation for individual involvement in creating meaning offers opportunities for engaging with the complexity of the unfamiliar in a personalized and hence fresh manner. This sense of unique and personal access to an actual and unfamiliar past is reinforced through the Authenticity-Effect created by the combination of documentary traces, such as the overgrown tracks, with fictional processes, as evident in the anthropomorphized trees.

In *Call Cutta*, the script returns subsequently to Nejati's story and participants are informed that he arrived on track four in 1941. Unsettlingly, the password for this act in the tour is 'I'm in!' As soon as the audience participant has confirmed this out loud, the corresponding sentence from the 'Grandfather Story' follows: 'In order to be accepted into the Wehrmacht, my Grandpa changed his name from Samir Singh to "Martin Heynold"' (Rimini Protokoll 2005: 39). In the words of Gerald Siegmund (2008: 199), the audience members here become 'followers, in the truest sense of the word' (im wahrsten Sinne des Wortes Mitläufer). In the German script that the call-centre workers use, they speak about 'fake names, which sound English instead of Indian', and which allow them to more 'easily slip into another role on the telephone' (sprich über falsche Namen, die englisch klingen statt indisch; mit einem falschen Namen kannst Du leichter in eine Rolle schlüpfen am Telefon: Rimini Protokoll 2005: 40). The overarching concept of dissimulation and role-play is in full effect, transcending temporal and spatial boundaries, from the performer in India via the unstable history of the grandfather to the listener in Berlin. Siegmund refers to a 'complex chronotope', which

> comes into being through the lining up of stories and places in the form of metaphors, allegories and comparisons, in which the synchronous and diachronous lines between Berlin and Calcutta, as well as those between the Second World War and today, coincide. A continuity between yesterday and today is at least conceivable in this

way, a continuity that lies nearby, that the chapter of colonialism, the struggle that grandfather was involved in, continues today in another de-territorialised form (Siegmund 2008: 198).

The performers set the chronotope in motion through the narrative strategy of intertwining the now, (partially) shared by the participants and performers, with stories involving people who have died but who continue to have a presence in the stories told. These people of the past are made present through documents and placeholders in the city landscape that the participants walk through. As the call-centre performers provide an individualized access to this chronotope via the grandfather-story, which they pretend to personally share with their interlocutors in Berlin, they contribute to a fleeting sense of the genuine, of having access to original stories told by real people.

However, this impression of authenticity is repeatedly disrupted and challenged during the *parcours* through, for example, the unreliability of the call-centre narrators. These interruptions alert participants to the performative and constructed nature of the present and past. In the invisible house of mirrors of the performance, the audience member is basically torn between various versions of identity and memory, 'foreign' and 'familiar'. On the one hand, this increases the production's fascination as a 'seductive tour through one's own urban jungle' (Rimini Protokoll website); on the other hand, the oscillation between the familiar and unfamiliar, produced by the deployment of real-people performers and historic photos, creates an aesthetically mediated unsettling of meaning, which frees up space for a critical confrontation with communicative memory, with variations of historiography, and with corresponding consequences for the conception of the self and for one's own cultural identity.

This play with ambivalences, routed through the unreliable real-people performers, is retained right to the last act, which leads participants to the car park of the Daimler Chrysler Areal, constructed in 1998 on the former 'death strip' where the Berlin Wall had separated East and West Berlin. For those participants aware of Daimler Benz's use of forced labour in its automobile and munitions factories under the Nazis, '[a] continuity between yesterday and today [was] at least conceivable'. Siegmund traces this continuity from 'the chapter of colonialism, the struggle that grandfather was involved in, [to] today in another de-territorialised form' (2008: 198), and argues:

> What binds the forced labourers of the Second World War, whom we are told about in the Daimler-Chrysler car park, the migrant workers of the economic miracle, the call-centre workers and the unemployed who have lost their jobs through the outsourcing [...] is the logic of capitalist profit maximisation, unbroken and historically uninterrupted even under National Socialism. (Siegmund 2008: 198–9)

Unlike in Brecht's theatre where the ever-changing world is governed by deducible social laws, *Call Cutta* does not offer an understanding of a socio-political world where clear power structures allow for an identification of potential causes and instigators. For example, Matthew Cornish observes for the later project *Call Cutta in a Box* that 'Rimini Protokoll has created an intercontinental phone play that [...] forces you to *participate* in global capitalism' by using outsourced labour as your guide, but also makes you aware that the call-centre operator in turn 'helped his employer to exploit' you, to participate in this economy (Cornish 2013: 173). While this observation holds true also for the earlier *Call Cutta*, the reasons for this exploitation are complex because the outsourcing of labour to call centres also depends on demand by (frequently internationally owned) companies for outside service suppliers and the acceptance of this process by their customers.

Within this socio-political and economic background, the Authenticity-Effects linked to the call-centre performers' everyday dissimulation game can also be aligned with the wider use of strategies for (re)inventing 'authentic' selves as part of self-marketing. Eight years after the performance of *Call Cutta*, cultural critic Diedrich Diederichsen (2012) attributes the wide use of strategies for (re)inventing 'authentic' selves as part of an ongoing self-optimization process, strategies originally used by freelance workers accepting outsourced work, to an economic imperative and a consumerist culture. He also points out that, unlike in earlier discussions of role-play, such as Irving Goffman's, there is now a widespread inability and/or unwillingness to make a stable distinction between a continuously evolving kind of role-play, which has been internalized as 'authentic', and a performer's 'original' self. The result is that any potential distinction between roles and selves remains unmarked. Diederichsen (2012) encourages the arts 'to interrupt the power of this unmarkedness' (Die Macht dieser Unmarkiertheit zu brechen), in particular those art forms – including theatre – 'which work with extras, participation, competition and certain recurrent performers who are their own performer-directors' (die mit Statisten, Partizipation, Wettbewerb und bestimmten wiederkehrenden, mit sich selbst identischen Darsteller-Regisseuren arbeiten: Diederichsen 2012) (Figure 7.2).

   In *Call Cutta*, the performers can only flag their inability to clearly distinguish between their performed and 'authentic' selves by explicitly referring to the dissimulation game that is both part of their professional life and of their performance in Rimini Protokoll's project. They do so by stating about seven minutes into the show, 'I can tell you my real name now' (Rimini Protokoll 2005: 17). This declaration invites doubts about whether any of the given names are correct, including this one, and thereby contributes to the production's continuous unsettling of any notion of authenticity (e.g. Glauner 2005; Ruesch 2007a) and engagement with the performative nature of identity construction. This declaration points to 'unmarkedness' rather than, as Diederichsen prefers, interruption. In this production, it is ultimately impossible to break 'unmarkedness'. This is because the theatre-makers cannot distinguish clearly between the game of authenticity and dissimulation, which the performers play in *Call Cutta*, from their performances in their everyday work life and from their everyday selves for two reasons: first, some of them use their false call-centre name beyond their workplace (Rimini Protokoll website); and second, the production relied on a seductive ambiguity as a way of drawing audiences into encounters with both the unfamiliar outside of and within one's 'own' culture. The only way to create an opportunity for a less performative

Figure 7.2 *Call Cutta: Mobile Phone Theatre* call-centre performers in Kolkata. Photograph by Helgard Haug, copyright Rimini Protokoll.

encounter was for participants to withdraw from the pre-planned *parcours* and to continue a more personal conversation with the person in the call centre.

It is a sign of the artists' openness that they considered this decision, taken by some participants, as an additional option of the project rather than as a failure (Kaegi, in Ruesch 2007b: 333). This open-mindedness also applied to Rimini Protokoll's willingness to leave the personal interpretation of the minimal script to each performer, which resulted in many individual, personalized dialogues and tours. For example, one performer tended to elaborate the narrative about Netaji, a second liked to flirt, and Madhusree 'preferred to sing and to experiment with noises. Each tour is unique' (hat lieber gesungen und mit Geräuschen experimentiert. Jede Tour ist anders: Kaegi, in Ruesch 2007b: 332). A structural openness also applied to the tour's ending. For the majority of participants who completed the entire *parcours*, multiple endings followed one after another, until the telephone exchange ended with a laconic 'was nice talking to you. Bye' (Rimini Protokoll 2005: 110).

As a result, for some participants the relation between simultaneously familiar and unfamiliar interlocutors was left hanging; others exchanged contact details and remained in contact with individual participants even after the conclusion of the tour (Garde 2010b). In one case, the conversation partners met in Germany and realized that they had fallen for the impressions of authenticity generated in *Call Cutta* rather than for 'the real person', which ultimately resulted in 'disappointment' when meeting each other (Kaegi, in Ruesch 2007b: 333). Other walkers might have experienced 'authenticity as an effect created by staging' (Erfahrung von Authentizität als Inszenierungseffekt: Eiermann 2012: 261).

Regarding the socio-political dimension of the work, some reviewers felt that issues of globalization had become tangible. It was 'as if Nike had inserted into its sneakers a photo of the person who had sewn them' (als würde Nike in jedes Paar Turnschuhe ein Foto des Nähers legen: Krampnitz 2005). However, it is also possible that some 'well-educated' participants felt uneasy about simply having taken part in a production that addresses some of the issues of globalization, as a way of alleviating their 'bad conscience' and of compensating for their 'limited horizon' and 'abstract knowledge' (das schlechte Gewissen einer Bildungselite, die um zu große Abstraktheit ihres Wissens und die Beschränktheit des eigenen Horizontes weiß: Müller 2008b).

In summary, *Call Cutta* encouraged a variety of audience reactions. These multifaceted responses can be largely attributed to the project's use of one-on-one, rather than collective, encounters with unfamiliar call-centre performers. During the *parcours*, which required audience members and their guides to jointly master an unknown route through selected areas of Berlin, audience participants were exposed to the unstable Authenticity-Effects created by the unreliable narratives and documents of the distant real-people performers, and had to keep re-adjusting their positions and attitudes in line with their personal impressions of information presented as truthful and reliable. Concurrently, this continuously shifting relationship between interlocutors also illustrated the processes of mutual positioning that characterize intercultural encounter in general (Gutjahr 2010: 26). Consequently, *Call Cutta* not only featured mobile phones and a mobile stage, but its subtitle, *Mobile Phone Theatre*, could in addition be interpreted as capturing the mutual flexibility and adjustments that characterized the encounters with the unfamiliar that it invited.

8

Getting Closer to the Subjects of Migration: Partial Proximity in *Blackmarket* No. 7 and *Mr Dağaçar and the Golden Tectonics of Trash*

In our analysis of Hebbel am Ufer (HAU) performance formats and productions to this point, we have paid particular attention to cultural encounters that provide opportunities for audience members to experience what they regard as their own familiar self and spaces of belonging as unfamiliar. In this chapter, we continue the shift begun in the previous chapter by attending a little more to cultural encounters in which what is deemed both foreign and insufficiently familiar has the potential to become better (if never fully) known. To this end, we explore two productions that focus on the subjects and subject matter of migration and other forms of mobility, as well as individuals who are unfamiliar owing to such factors as their expertise and their distant geographical location. In the production to which we shall pay particular attention, Mobile Academy's seventh version of the format *Blackmarket for Useful and Non-Useful Knowledge and Non-Knowledge* (*Schwarzmarkt für nützliches Wissen und Nicht-Wissen*), audience members spent the evening of 10 March 2007 at HAU2 in dialogue with or listening to a number of real people who presented their expertise in areas such as migration, new forms of nomadism, and/ or culturally hybrid ways of living. In the second production, *Mr Dağaçar and the Golden Tectonics of Trash* (*Herr Dağaçar und die goldene Tektonik des Mülls*, 2010–) by Rimini Protokoll, spectators seated in a conventional end-on theatre configuration experienced self-representational and meta-textual presentations by migratory subjects who have moved, or continue to move, their places of work and living within and across countries. Here the protagonists were predominantly men of Kurdish and Greek gypsy background who had travelled from various parts of Turkey to Istanbul in order to gain work as trash recyclers. Our analysis of the seventh version of the *Blackmarket* format, and of Rimini Protokoll's production – which develops further an earlier investigation of *Mr Dağaçar* undertaken by Mumford in 2013 – places emphasis on the creation and destabilization of Authenticity-Effects that impact on the audience members' sense of unmediated and intimate access to genuine people and their narratives. It attends, therefore, to the nature of the proximity to strangers that is generated by these works, typifying it as partial – that is, as incomplete, flawed, and/or biased – and assessing its effectiveness in creating ethical modes of encountering unfamiliar people.

Blackmarket encounter with the (culturally) unfamiliar and an alternate economy

Conceived by German freelance dramaturge, curator, and festival organizer Hannah Hurtzig, together with colleagues working on the interdisciplinary art project Mobile Academy, the first *Blackmarket* event took place in Hamburg in 2005. Matthias Lilienthal, the HAU's artistic director, and his team recognized its relevance to their artistic programme and arranged for three versions of the format to be presented at the HAU between 2005 and 2007. Usually staged in a single day, and in public venues such as theatres, cultural institutions, and similar places of congregation, each *Blackmarket* brings together a diverse group of what Mobile Academy refers to as 'experts'. The 'experts' are a subset of what we call unfamiliar real people, in so far as they came from an array of social and occupational backgrounds, and were for the most part not trained for the stage or else did not appear in their capacity as theatre professionals. In the *Blackmarket* format, each expert presents a story-narrative to a single 'client' and dialogue partner in a short thirty-minute session at one of numerous small tables. As will soon become clear, the *Blackmarket* format encourages encounter with culturally diverse people and their knowledges, a situation that can be related to its roots in an installation entitled *The Refugee: Services Rendered to Undesirables* that Hurtzig, together with Anselm Franke, curated and presented at the Volksbühne in Berlin in 2002. Responding to a protest march through Germany undertaken by the Sinti and Romani people who had fled from the former Yugoslavia and who were being threatened with forceful return, the project sought a new platform for discussion of the refugees' 'state of emergency' and of civil society's 'obsolete politics of exclusion' (Mobile Academy website). In her interview with us, Hurtzig stated that because they had contact with migrants, rather than convene a panel of eminent scholars, the production team 'wanted instead to work with people who had long been professionally active in the field: that is, social workers, lawyers, translators, refugee activists' (Weil wir damals auch Kontakte zu Migranten hatten, wollten wir lieber mit Leuten arbeiten, die professionell schon seit Jahren in diesem Gebiet tätig sind: Das heißt Sozialarbeiter, Anwälte, Übersetzer, Flüchtlingshelfer: Garde and Mumford 2010). Other key *Blackmarket* format features developed during this project were: the use of 'experts' rather than actors, and of dialogue between the performers and audience members; and circulating participants who listen via headphones to one-on-one discussions as well as to films with commentary from various authors.

While only a small number of experts were involved in the first *Blackmarket* in Hamburg, in the second version staged at HAU 2 (2005), the numbers had swelled to 100. By the time of the fifth version, which was staged at HAU 1 in 2006, 150 experts addressed a topic area that had clearly been tailored to contemporary social concerns, in this case the manifold nature and perceptions of American society and culture. In the seventh version, which was given the subtitle *Routes and Sites of Mobility Pioneers and Functionaries* (*Routen und Orte der Mobilitätspioniere und-funktionäre*), over the course of four hours in the evening a group of 100 local experts took turns to operate forty tables arranged in four rows. During the event, audience members journeyed through the space like travellers at a market of knowledge (Figure 8.1).

In each *Blackmarket*, the experts' inexpensive presentations are primarily for the paying client-cum-traveller, although in many versions of the format other audience members, equipped with headphones, are given the opportunity to listen in and watch. These 'spectAuditors', as we shall call them, are often located on tiered seating that surrounds the table (or game) floor. They listen mainly to dialogue transmitted live by the so-called *Schwarzradio* (Black/Illegal Radio), but on some occasions also to audio-visually recorded historical conversations. For example, according to the theatre programme for our case study – which we will refer to as *Blackmarket* No. 7 in order to convey a sense both of the format and the seventh iteration – they could experience a projection of a filmed 2005 narration by Hans-Ulrich Obrist, the prominent Swiss art

Figure 8.1 *Blackmarket for Useful Knowledge and Non-Knowledge No. 7: Routes and Sites of Mobility Pioneers and Functionaries*, March 2007, HAU2, Berlin. Photograph by Fabian Larsson, courtesy of Mobile Academy.

curator known for his research interest in the form and concept of the interview. In this four-hour recording, Obrist told his life story to the conversation partner of his choice, German art historian Professor Michael Diers.

When it comes to the experts' stories, these are often connected to a topic area of relevance to the *Zeitgeist* of the host city. In *Blackmarket* No. 7, they were linked to the theme heralded by the work's subtitle, which resonated with the context in which Mobile Academy's event took place, the festival called Autoput Avrupa from Istanbul to Berlin. This was the second festival in the Beyond Belonging series hosted by the HAU and curated by Shermin Langhoff (see Chapter 4), one that has been described as celebrating the contribution to cosmopolitan life in Europe of those labour migrants who have journeyed to and fro between Turkey and Berlin, many of them along the Autoput Avrupa transit route (Kosnick 2009: 39). Both the seating plan and the course of events at the *Blackmarket* have to date been defined by an encyclopaedic organization of catchwords from A to Z that relate in some way to the theme. In *Blackmarket* No. 7, the encyclopaedia began with 'Aids' and ended with '*Zeitzeuge*', the German for 'Contemporary Witness'. One of the declared goals of this production's organizational structure was to make 'recognizable various migration and immigration systems, new nomadism and hybrid metropolitan ways of life' (Mobile Academy website).

The *Blackmarket* format both embodies and generates an interest in encounter with the unfamiliar in the sense of that which is not known, insufficiently known, or not ever fully knowable. In our interview with her, Hurtzig spoke of how Mobile Academy valued a complex form of research that attended to the 'unfamiliar, invisible, or even ghostly' (unbekannt, unsichtbar oder auch gespenstisch: Garde and Mumford 2010), and stated that rather than the shockingly unfamiliar, what existed in our countries and cities was 'a non-knowledge, a not-wanting-to-know, and an invisibility' (ein Unwissen, und ein Nicht-Wissen-Wollen und eine Unsichtbarkeit: Garde and Mumford 2010). In the same interview, she also noted that while *Blackmarket* No. 7 foregrounded encounter with the unfamiliar in the sense of ethnically different and/or culturally complex people and phenomena, each *Blackmarket* had offered the opportunity for encounter with people of migrant backgrounds. We attribute the structural openness to this form of encounter to factors such as Mobile Academy's attempt to pursue a non-exclusive approach to the casting of the experts and to embrace multiple and heterogeneous areas of expertise. The process of selecting experts is characterized by a curatorial openness to diversity on many fronts. For example, in many of the format's versions it is simply the sheer number of experts that encourages the possibility of diversity. Furthermore, rather than inviting only well-known intellectuals to speak on issues already recognized as important, the artistic group seek to bring different types of experts together and uncover themes not yet made visible (Hurtzig, in Graton 2007b). Hurtzig believes it to be important that experts come from all areas, including that of the neighbour and professor, and from different social classes and age groups (Gronau, Hochleichter and Hurtzig 2006: 9–10). Indeed, in the programme for the sixth *Blackmarket*, which was dedicated to a panoramic exploration of America at a time of heightened anti-American sentiment in the wake of the invasion of Iraq, experts listed included: an American football umpire and customs officer in Berlin, who spoke on the topic of the drug squad in that sport; and an assistant professor of drama at Stanford University, who addressed New York Downtown Theatre.

Encounter with culturally diverse people and knowledges is also often introduced through the approach to the theme. Rather than assigning a single overarching topic, Mobile Academy arrives at a cluster of issues based on research into the concerns of the host city (Cvejić 2006: 17). A significant length of time is committed to finding people who can address these topics (Hurtzig, in Schuller 2009: 130). This thematic approach has much in common with features of the 'communities of practice' fostered at the HAU, such as the encouragement of non-hierarchical collaborations based on a shared practice or interest (see Chapter 4). In the case of the *Blackmarket* format, in a manner similar to Rimini Protokoll's *100% City* (*100% Stadt*), the search is conducted through an evolving network of contacts, with the researchers moving out beyond the realm of the art world and working serendipitously. As a result, a participant such as French journalist and immigrant to Germany, Elise Graton, who has written about her experience in *Blackmarket* No. 7, could in one night participate in dialogues with a wide variety of people: Esra Erdem, an author and social worker with a doctorate in economics, who was working at TIO in Berlin – a meeting and information centre for female migrants – who spoke on the topic of 'Praxis and Politics in the Migrant Women's Movement'; and Peyé Psimenou, a middle-aged Greek air stewardess whose topic area was 'The Different Smells of the 40 International Airports I Know' (Graton 2007a).

With regard to the client participants, while Hurtzig acknowledges that approximately forty per cent of the audience participants, or guests, do belong to a less socially diverse scene – one characterized by well-educated adults in their twenties and thirties – the majority are usually unknown to her and that the nature of the audience varies in accordance with the theme. In the case of *Blackmarket* No. 7, she has noted that the guests included elderly participants and social workers as well as a number of illegal refugees (Graton 2007b). At this event, as in many, a commitment to creating an intercultural environment attractive to diverse participants was characterized by the use of multiple languages. According to the programme, at *Blackmarket* No. 7 the experts collectively spoke twenty-one languages, mainly from across Europe, but also the Middle East and Asia. As the *Blackmarket* sound archive on Mobile Academy's website makes clear, some experts presented, or offered to present, in more than one language depending on the preference of their audience members. At each *Blackmarket*, clients are also encouraged to engage with the culturally unfamiliar, not only through casting and treatment of the theme, but also through the booking system. Bookings are organized in such a way that it is often difficult to book for all of one's preferred sessions and impossible to book two consecutive sessions (Rule 2009). The host figures are primed to persuade clients to attend a different slot when their preferred expert is already booked, a mechanism that encourages both expert and client to step outside their own comfort zones.

The *Blackmarket* format is a participatory performance, which, like much contemporary Theatre of Real People, also asks its key players to extend or step beyond their familiar social world. In this case, it is the realm of institutionalized education in a neoliberal context that can be interpreted as a targeted zone. In her recent analysis of the surge in participatory art since the 1990s, Claire Bishop notes how 'the 2000s saw a marked rise of pedagogic projects undertaken by contemporary artists and curators' that 'appropriate the tropes of education as both a method and a form: lectures, seminars, libraries, reading-rooms, publications, workshops and even full-blown schools' (2012: 241). She attributes this rise to, first, 'a desire to augment the intellectual content of relational conviviality' – a reference to the relational art that art critic Nicolas Bourriaud has defined as taking 'the whole of human relations and social context, rather than an independent and private space' as its point of departure (Bourriaud 2002: 113) – and second, as a response to the rise of academic capitalism (Bishop 2012: 241). Pedagogic projects along the lines of *Blackmarket* are not an entirely new phenomenon, especially within German culture. For example, in 1977 artist Joseph Beuys created a project entitled *100 Days of the Free International University* for the Kassel art exhibition Documenta 6, in which real people, such as trade unionists, economists and politicians to community workers, educationalists and artists, shared the stage in a series of interdisciplinary workshops (Bishop 2012: 244). Co-founded by Beuys in 1973, the Free International University was a non-profit educational organization committed to issues such as the future of society that operated until 1988, two years after the artist's death. Given that *Blackmarket* retains traces of some of Beuys's socially engaged art, and given Lilienthal's interest in Beuys's interventionist concept and practice of social sculpture (Raddatz 2008: 19), it is perhaps not surprising that the HAU embraced Hurtzig's format.

Already the title *Blackmarket* aptly describes the format's emphasis on generating a knowledge economy and public space that offers an alternative to those authorized and controlled by marketplace consumerism (Cvejić 2006: 14) and state-regulated systems. Hurtzig has commented that the *Blackmarket* plays with the neoliberal model of the ideal learner of the future, 'an entrepreneurial individual who manages himself, grasps himself as capital, voluntarily invests in knowledge and initiative' who 'trains self-administration, self-control, and self-realization'. However, 'it is above all an image of the masses and of collective learning' (Hurtzig, in Kaup-Hasler and Philipp 2007). The title of the format also refers to an interest in knowledges that are, for various reasons, 'in the dark'. For Hurtzig, non-knowledges include not only those that are not yet on the agenda or that have not yet been expressed through language, but also those that cannot be expressed because they are open secrets or otherwise inexpressible, such as faiths or phenomena beyond language (Hurtzig, in Kaup-Hasler and Philipp 2007). In many iterations, naked light bulbs are placed on, or else hang over the tables, suggesting the illegal backroom spaces of these knowledges and of the people who create them, while simultaneously allowing partial access.

Like many forms of adult education today, Mobile Academy's *Blackmarket* is a service industry. This is made clear right from the start of the participants' journey as they queue outside the arena area at a site that recalls numerous places of financial and social exchange such as a box office, an airport check-in, and a reception counter. Here figures referred to by Hurtzig as hosts and hostesses engage in service activities: selling consultation sessions for a small fee (usually a few Euros); taking bribes from canny barterers who wish to secure their preferred experts; and managing a chart-board that displays the booking system (Figure 8.2).

While these workers engage in the highly regulated behaviours and systems typical of service industries, they are also assistants in an *irregular* affair that for Hurtzig is a correction of the official learning situation (Hurtzig, in Graton 2007b). And while replacing actors and educationalists with real people experts may be an example of a form of 'outsourcing' (Bishop 2012: 144) that in other service industries in

Figure 8.2 Client check-in staff at *Blackmarket for Useful Knowledge and Non-Knowledge No. 7*, March 2007. Photograph by Fabian Larsson, courtesy of Mobile Academy.

contemporary capitalism has caused problematic disappearances and diminutions (see Chapter 1), here it contributes to the assertion of alternative and marginalized knowledge practices.

Hurtzig has likened Mobile Academy's correction of the official public spaces of learning and communication to both those spaces offered by the German adult education system known as the *Volkshochschule* (VHS) and the ancient agora (Graton 2007b; Schuller 2009: 128). An important vehicle for further education and one funded by multiple state bodies, the VHS offers adult learners across the social spectrum a broad variety of reasonably priced vocational and non-vocational events. The *Blackmarket* imitates the affordable and diversified nature of the offerings that cater for both utilitarian and non-utilitarian learning. It supplements not only the VHS model, but also those of the university, library, and archive by means, for example, of a public display of multiple, simultaneous, and live learning encounters. Hurtzig likens its very public negotiation of themes to the space of debate in the ancient Greek agora, a gathering and marketplace central to the artistic, political, and commercial life of the city. The *Blackmarket* also supplements the official institutions of learning mentioned earlier through its emphasis on narrative and dialogue as the preferred formats of knowledge transfer. While the grid of tables may recall a reading room, Mobile Academy provides instead a talking and listening room that offers opportunities for repressed or non-official spaces of learning. For the 'spectAuditors' in particular, the bedtime story-reading experiences of childhood, and associated drowsy rapture, may enter the frame as they drift in and out of the *Schwarzradio* conversations, and absorb the extraordinary beehive-like hum and buzz emanating from the mass of conversationalists. One of the effects of experts being requested to 'narrate their knowledge, not deliver it as a lecture' (Hurtzig, in Kaup-Hasler and Philipp 2007) is that an academic and journalistic pursuit of objective knowledge is supplemented by or replaced with a firm acknowledgment of the subjective and partial nature of knowledge. And the various forms of dialogue that ensue between the expert and client threaten to dissolve the more rigid encyclopaedic structure of the *Blackmarket* (Schuller 2009: 129), presenting knowledge as the ever-changing product of negotiation and inter-human encounter that always bursts the boxes of a fixed taxonomy.

Rimini Protokoll's encounter with the precarious stranger

While *Blackmarket* No. 7 engages with the social reality of mobility and education in a capitalist and globalized context, *Mr Dağaçar and the Golden Tectonics of Trash*, by Helgard Haug and Daniel Wetzel of Rimini Protokoll, explores on-going and contemporary forms of human precarity, particularly through its focus on people whose lives are touched by geological instability, labour mobility, ethnic conflict, and/or shifts in state systems of regulation. At the very opening of the production, the theme of precarity is sounded through an audio-recording of Bayram Renklihava's voice, one of the trash recycler protagonists, who tells the tale of a nightmare he had in which his own and his relatives' children all succumbed to a deadly virus. In this dream, Bayram undertakes the unenviable task of transporting all their bodies in his paper-recycling cart to the cemetery, and, is finally made to face his eldest son who, with his dying breath, begs his father not to throw him into the grave.

In another early episode in the March 2011 performance at HAU2, recorded on DVD, all five of the main protagonists, four trash-recyclers and one Karagöz-Puppetteer, introduce the work of seismographs located across areas of Turkey that are vulnerable to earthquakes. This episode conjures up a world underpinned by a powerful trembling subterranean force. On an otherwise darkened stage, the narrator-protagonists stand in separate spotlit areas. Most of them hold lit torches towards the ground. Their comments are accompanied by such phenomena as an illuminated map of Turkey that appears to indicate the locations of the seismographs or earthquake risk zones; the rumbling sound of supposedly live tectonic activity from a seismograph; and a quivering visual representation of a seismograph's recordings. In the performance witnessed by Mumford in Essen on 27 November 2010, each narrator also shone his torch on a loudspeaker that was presented as offering live connection to a seismograph. Later in the production, Bayram, the only trash recycler of Greek gypsy heritage in the show, and the Turkish puppeteer and theatre practitioner Hasan Hüseyin Karabağ, speak of their personal experiences of earthquakes. When referring to the devastating İzmit event of 1999, Hasan tells how he abandoned play rehearsals at Istanbul's municipal theatre in order to assist with the rescue efforts, and of the signs of local quake activity he continues to experience (when, for example, he takes the ferry to Üsküdar (Rimini Protokoll 2010: 6)). In a conversation with Mumford after one of the rehearsals in Berlin, dramaturge Sebastian Brünger referred to Rimini Protokoll's interest in the earthquakes as a metaphor for the mobile nature of the earth, and in the invisible nature of the moving tectonic plates. According to Brünger, the quakes offered a suggestive metaphor for many things, including the movement from East Anatolia to Istanbul of Kurdish people in search of work, and the unofficial actions of the trash recyclers (Mumford 2010b). Both of these movements involve forms of (political) invisibility or concealment.

Throughout the production, and particularly towards its end, the trash collectors refer to their experiences and dread of economic precarity. Early in the performance, the eponymous Abdullah Dağaçar (referred to both on and off stage as Apo) explains that his ancestors used to say that the streets of Istanbul were lined with gold. However, after making the long journey from their East Anatolian village in order to secure work in Istanbul, he and his Kurdish relatives and fellow stage performers – Aziz İdikurt and Mithat İçten – have found only dust and dirt from which to try and create an economic advantage (Rimini Protokoll 2010: 4). By the end of the performance, all four of the recyclers have expressed the fear that they will lose their source of income due to their unofficial status, their lack of capital, and the state's desire to have large authorized companies enforce new EU regulations about waste management. Of the real people in the show, these three are arguably touched most by forms of precarity, in large measure due to their ethnic status within a Turkish state that has instituted measures such as the suppression of the Kurdish language, the enforcement of re-settlement, and the ban until recently of Kurds from the Turkish stage, a ban referred to by Brünger (Mumford 2010b). Of all the unfamiliar (or insufficiently known) performers in this production, particularly during its Istanbul run, it is they who could be interpreted as the participants who were most resistant to being figured as invisible strangers.

In a manner typical of the institutional network approach fostered at the HAU under Lilienthal (see Chapter 4), *Mr Dağaçar* was a co-production between partners based in Istanbul and Berlin: garajistanbul, a contemporary arts cooperative and cultural organization – who for this production were working in the context of the ISTANPOLI programme – and the HAU, Rimini Apparat. One of the garajistanbul members, the multilingual Turkish directorial assistant Pınar Başoğlu, appears momentarily in the production as herself when she comes out from the audience onto the stage to help translate improvised conversation. The work was also produced by the two cultural programmes associated with the designation of Istanbul and Essen as European Capital of Culture (ECC) for 2010: ISTANBUL.10 (co-producer for ISTANPOLI) and RUHR.2010. That is, it was created within the context of a European Commission initiative designed, among other things, to highlight the diversity of cultures in Europe as well as enhance European citizens' sense of belonging to a common cultural area (European Commission website). Since its premiere, the production has to date toured a number of cities in France, Germany, and the Netherlands. As is typical of Rimini Protokoll's theatre of experts approach, the preparatory process was lengthy, with members of the collective making research trips to Istanbul as early as 2008. Even more so than the chain-reaction approach in *100% City*, the casting method was based largely on chance, as is illustrated by the encounter on the streets of Istanbul between Başoğlu, Brünger, and Apo (Mumford 2010b). This encounter and a later meeting are presented to the audience by Apo during two of the many sections labelled 'META' in the English-language script dated 14 October 2010 that formed the basis for the November performances in Essen. Here 'META' indicates meta-textual sections devoted to commentary on the making of the work. During the delivery of the first meta-text about encounter with the theatre-makers, Apo notes how he met the theatre team members at night in Kadiköy, and while other trash collectors had run off because they were unused to the attention and focused on their work, he stopped because he thought the artists were tourists. Later, the theatre-makers visited Apo and the other members of the depot (the collective of trash recyclers who are housed together and their makeshift lodgings). Afterwards, the theatre artists admitted they had wondered at the time: 'Will we get out of this place alive?' (Rimini Protokoll 2010: 5). This acknowledgment of the division and tension that can come with cultural difference is very much in keeping with Lilienthal's emphasis on critical engagement with the tensions underlying postcolonial curatorship and spectatorship (see Chapter 1).

Partial proximity, distance, and a destabilizing approach to Authenticity-Effects

As the description has begun to suggest, partial access to real people and the unfamiliar is a characteristic of both *Blackmarket* No. 7 and *Mr Dağaçar*. In the former, the use of short subjective narratives to convey expertise openly acknowledges the partial or biased nature of the imparted knowledge, as well as the incomplete nature of the access to the narrator. In *Mr Dağaçar*, Rimini Protokoll's use of strategies such as the meta-text makes clear that the theatre-makers' access to trash collectors in Istanbul was partial in the sense of being both incomplete and prejudiced. The production presents a small window and by no means a complete picture of the situation of these workers, both as a group and as individuals. In addition, it is shaped by the main participants' socio-cultural differences and, in the initial stages in particular, by mutual uncertainty. In this analysis, we argue that such incomplete proximity can generate a sense of being unable to fully grasp something or someone, and that this state in turn has the potential to encourage ethical encounter and communication.

Our approach draws on the work of Sarah Ahmed, who in *Strange Encounters: Embodied Others in Postcoloniality*, when describing the preferred approach to ethical encounter of Emmanuel Levinas, declares her interest in the ethical potential of ungraspability. Levinas, she says, seeks 'a better way of encountering the other which allows the other to live as that which is beyond "my" grasp, and as that which cannot be assimilated or digested into the ego or into the body of a community' (Ahmed 2000: 139). While Ahmed is critical of what she perceives to be Levinas's conception of 'the other' as the weak, poor, and marginal, arguing that it fixes the other as an alien being that exists prior to encounter, she welcomes the acknowledgment of 'a sense of that which can't be grasped in the present' (2000: 148). Considering how contemporary Western subjects encounter others they configure as strangers, Ahmed also puts forward her own preferred approach to encounter:

> An ethical communication is about a certain way of holding proximity
> and distance together: one gets close enough to others to be touched by
> that which cannot be simply got across. In such an encounter, 'one' does
> not stay in place, or one does not stay safely at a distance [...] It is
> through getting closer, rather than remaining at a distance, that the
> impossibility of pure proximity can be put to work, or made to work.
> (Ahmed 2000: 157)

In the following section of our analysis, we draw attention to the way in
which both productions, in their bid to create proximity for their
audience members to unfamiliar real people, generate Authenticity-
Effects. We then go on to show how not only a sense of authenticity that
is destabilized, but also a sense of authenticity that is maintained, draw
attention to the impossibility of total proximity, and suggest the ethical
and educational value of creating perceptual distance and acknowledging
cultural difference during encounters with the unfamiliar. To this end,
our analysis focuses mainly on the nature, presentation, and reception
of verbal and written texts, a key artistic component and source of
Authenticity-Effects in both productions, and on the encounters and
social relations encouraged or made possible by the approaches to these
texts. It concludes with a brief consideration of the contribution of
overt (including self-reflexive) artistry to encounter with the unfamiliar.

Inviting alternative encounters with the unfamiliar through (un)mediated dialogue, partially genuine texts, and semi-graspable language

In *Blackmarket*, the numerous types of text include the everyday service-
industry texts of the hosts with their illocutionary force, and the recorded
life story told by the art curator to the art historian. Here our analysis
focuses on the text types that are often put, literally, under a light bulb:
unplanned (or semi-planned) dialogue and the experts' pre-prepared
narratives. The dialogue occurs while the expert imparts his or her
knowledge, and varies according to the nature of both parties' attitude

towards the subject matter and situation, and the relationship that develops over each thirty-minute slot. This dialogue is an Authenticity-Effect in so far as it is well placed to generate a sense of the unmediated and intimate, due to factors such as spatio-temporal co-presence and the one-on-one exchange that recalls aspects of speed dating. The dialogue also has the potential to create a sense of the genuine and real due to numerous unplanned features such as spontaneous and improvised responses. In our interview with her, Hurtzig described with approval the dialogues as characterized by 'an evenly hovering attention to both speaking and listening, and to letting-the-other-be' (eine gleich schwebende Aufmerksamkeit von Sprechen und Hören, und Den-Andern-Lassen: Garde and Mumford 2010) (Figure 8.3).

In her review of the Mannheim 2009 event, commenting on her consultation with an expert on Identity Games, Alix Rule suggests that she experienced a shift from a classificatory rationalizing approach to this state of 'letting-the-other-be'. After discussing her struggle to relate the expert's explanation of one of her art projects to the theme of her

Figure 8.3 Dialogue partners and 'spectAuditors' at *Blackmarket for Useful Knowledge and Non-Knowledge No. 7*. Photograph by Fabian Larsson, courtesy of Mobile Academy.

talk, and Rule's doubts about the strength of the project, she says that it was hard not to warm to the expert's engagement and that 'gladly enough' she gave up attempting to figure out why she was an expert on identity (Rule 2009). Rule's 'giving up' seems a step in the direction of what Sarah Ahmed calls coming '*to know how not to know*' in order 'to overcome the relations of force implicated in "knowing" itself' (2000: 72). Rule's commentary also addresses the experience of partiality that occurs for the spectAuditors when they hear parts of conversations and when they are not always able to match voices to speaking bodies. Furthermore, as every participant can only briefly catch a handful of the multiple fragments being performed simultaneously, everyone must deal with a sense of incompleteness and ungraspability.

One further feature of the live dialogue important to Hurtzig was the way in which it enabled access not only to content, but also to close-up narrated portraits (Hurtzig, in Garde and Mumford 2010), and an experience of '"how" this content is communicated, in which form it is narrated' (Hurtzig, in Schuller 2009: 128). Such sensations, as well as the client's first-hand witnessing of the effort of the planned, performed and repeated narrative, and of his or her own concentrated listening and responding, also draw attention to the labour that creates the knowledge required for approaching unfamiliar people and their expertise. Sometimes that effort is openly acknowledged by the experts, as is the case in one of the archived dialogues from *Blackmarket* No. 7 involving the political science doctorate Manuela Bojadžijev. Introduced in the programme as a member of Kanak Attak, a group committed to the elimination of racism in Germany and whose founding members include Feridun Zaimoglu (Kanak Attak website), this expert expresses her slight disappointment to a client when he picks from her group of offerings the one topic that she has already spoken about on two occasions. Nevertheless, she proceeds to plough on steadfastly with his preferred narrative (Bojadžijev 2007a). By making the dialogue accessible to the spectAuditors, and in some cases also to listeners who did not attend the evening but later visit the online sound archive, the production not only harnesses the potential for encounter with the unfamiliar that is made increasingly available through new forms of technology, but also supplements such forms during the performance evening with the live experience of the time and effort required for inter-human dialogue.

Acknowledging that it contains features in common with the internet and the knowledge portal Wikipedia, Hurtzig has observed that the *Blackmarket* format allows for the experience of speed and of becoming involved that digital media have offered, with zapping as 'one possibility of reflecting on a theme' (Hurtzig, in Schuller 2009: 133). The spectAuditors' channel-hopping is a form of zapping and, as in the case of a collective learning forum such as a wiki space, clients help build knowledge through their questions and comments to the experts, some of which are made public immediately via live-radio transmission, and some of which can be accessed later through the sound archive. However, Hurtzig has stated that zapping 'is best combined with moments of "standing still"' (Schuller 2009: 133). We interpret one layer of this stillness as being those moments of attentive listening that open up the possibility of dwelling with others and the unknown for a more sustained period – in this case admittedly, no more than a brief half hour. However, sometimes the dialogue partners seek to extend the conversation beyond the performance event. For example, in a commentary on *Blackmarket* No. 7, Elise Graton states that during her discussion with Esra Erdem, she raised her own experiences as a migrant in the German workforce, learned from Erdem how to employ recent anti-discrimination legislation, and took Erdem's business card with every intention of meeting with her again (Graton 2007a).

If the dialogue in *Blackmarket* operates as an Authenticity-Effect that uses a sense of the unmediated and the intimate in order to facilitate encounter with the unfamiliar, and draws attention to the necessary labour involved in such an exchange, the presentation of expertise through personalized narratives encourages a sense of the genuine in a way that draws attention to the partial (subjective and hence biased) nature of knowledge and encounter. In the case of the narratives, Mobile Academy instructs the experts to offer their knowledge in the form of a short story. Thanks to the framing work of elements such as marketing, the programme, and the hosts, the narratives told by each expert appear genuine in the sense of really originating from the speaker. This sense is enforced when the speakers personalize their information and skills by, for example, explaining the reasons for and nature of their interest in them, and by clarifying their opinions and perspectives on the material they share. However, as Hurtzig has pointed out, the listeners can be '[s]educed by the encyclopaedic form, the belief in lists and catalogizations [*sic*]' and 'be taken in by liars and inventors' who make up knowledge on the spot. Similarly, experts might find themselves with clients who are looking for jobs or seeking advice rather than a sharing of knowledge on the given topic. For example, in one of director Neco Çelik's expert sessions during *Blackmarket* No. 7, an actress spent much of the dialogue seeking feedback on her own idea for a film project (Çelik 2007). Both truthfulness and credibility are up for negotiation between expert and client (Hurtzig, in Kaup-Hasler and Philipp 2007). While at times the Authenticity-Effect of the genuine may diminish the sense of other types of authenticity, such as a sense of truth if the subjective or invented quality of the narrative makes it appear potentially lacking in veracity, in this production a sense of the genuine and of the truthful often co-exist. For example, in the case of Graton's encounter with Erdem, a sense of referential truthfulness is encouraged by the gifting of a business card that provides a seemingly accurate reference to a world beyond the *Blackmarket* event.

According to Hurtzig, one dramaturgical feature and political effect of the story approach is that it allows more room for the narrator to be present in the telling than often occurs in the lecture format. This space is created by 'the pause, reflection, forgetting, searching for words, asking the other for help, [...] a joint wrestling for understanding' (die Pause, das Nachdenken, das Vergessen, das Suchen nach Worten, den anderen um Hilfe bitten, [...] gemeinsames Ringen um Verständnis: Garde and Mumford 2010). In our interview with her, Hurtzig also argued that the form inhibits receivers from making a judgement about the speaker, as it clarifies that only a limited amount of the narrator's expertise is being made available. By way of illustration, she referred to the 2008 *Blackmarket* in Vienna. Here an Austrian woman who had converted to Islam and become a contentious hard-core Muslim appeared as an expert. Rather than providing a platform for a polemical rant, the story form gave her the chance to speak simply about her knowledge of where it is written that God forgives, and for this portion of her self to be taken seriously.

Bringing storytelling together with dialogue further generates a sense of genuine grappling for understanding. Unlike a tightly scripted and fully memorized script, the expert's narrations and the improvised text of the dialogue partners often reveal uncertainty about all manner of things: the subject matter, how it can be communicated, the relationship between the interlocutors, the public situation they both find themselves in. Interrupting the story with dialogue creates additional moments in which the participants struggle to recall, articulate or express. Confining both dialogue and narration to a thirty-minute time-slot also encourages a situation in which much is left unsaid or inadequately communicated. This issue is raised by one of Bojadžijev's dialogue partners at the point when the booming gong signalling the end of their half-hour interrupts an intense discussion in which they are expressing differences of opinion. At this point, the client-listener indicates that the topic may require further discussion, and that he thinks they may have misunderstood one another (Bojadžijev 2007b). Many of the Authenticity-Effects associated with the key texts in *Blackmarket* No. 7 create an alternative performance to the presentation of mastery that is often the goal of actors in mainstream illusionist theatre, one that thereby recalls the discourse of failure often explored by experimental contemporary theatre. This discourse has been interpreted as resisting aspects of capitalist ideology such as the competitive aspiration to succeed and win (Bailes 2011: 2). In *Blackmarket* No. 7, the emphasis on partial (or incomplete, flawed, and/ or biased) knowledge and knowing can be read as resisting a totalitarian desire to master knowledge and non-knowledge, as well as unfamiliar people.

In *Mr Dağaçar*, some of the text-based Authenticity-Effects that create a sense of the genuine are not only used but also destabilized, and in ways that critically reveal and sometimes disperse the masterful authority of the artist-ethnographer and/or the spectator over the unfamiliar real-people performers. *Mr Dağaçar* presents a variety of written and spoken texts with the potential to produce various Authenticity-Effects. Some are well placed to generate a sense of the intimate and sincere, for example, the self-representational statements and stories created by the experts in collaboration with the artists, delivered in Turkish and Kurdish and/or in translation as projected surtitles, as well as occasional improvised dialogue (Figure 8.4).

Other texts have the capacity to generate a sense of honesty, such as the meta-text commentary on the theatre-making process and power relations, or a sense of veracity, such as the texts conveying statistical

Figure 8.4 Bayram Renklihava, Mithat İçten, Abdullah Dağaçar, and Aziz İdikurt (seated at the front of the cart-cum-bus) tell the story of the Kurdish trash-recyclers' bus journey from East Anatolia to Istanbul. Photograph by and copyright Rimini Protokoll.

information. As occurs in the *Blackmarket* dialogues in particular, many of the texts in Rimini Protokoll's production are the result of collaboration. And in both works the artists move away from the pursuit of objectivity towards an 'informed intersubjectivity' predicated on listening and collaboration, an approach Sally McBeth associates with much recent ethnographic writing (McBeth 1993: 145–6). However, while the *Blackmarket* dialogue unambiguously presents the expert and client as the collaborators, with the expert as the more authoritative creator, in Rimini Protokoll's production it is not always clear who has authored what, or who has what type of authority. Furthermore, unlike the approach to the narrator and story in the *Blackmarket* format, Rimini Protokoll's work destabilizes a sense of the genuine by removing authorship signposts in a way that sometimes makes the relation of the speaker to the spoken unclear. As discussed in Chapter 3, documentary and verbatim drama have been criticized for simultaneously privileging 'the illusion of' direct speech, while at the same time disguising the editorial mediation or artistic invention processes involved in the creation of such speech (Bottoms 2006; Martin 2006; Young 2009). Most of the texts in *Mr Dağaçar* do not serve the purpose of creating an illusion of direct speech, since they are instead framed as constructed for the theatre event rather than as verbatim testimony. However, it is the case that the editorial processes and authors are often not made clear, with the result that all the contributors to the production risk being considered equal co-authors in a way that conceals the social and material privilege that allows the theatre-makers to have proximity to the real people, as well as 'the relations of force and authorization embedded in the desire to know (more) about strangers' (Ahmed 2000: 63). However, as Mumford has argued elsewhere, rather than failing to signpost authorship, we suggest that *Mr Dağaçar* often generates 'uncertainty about who has created what, a strategy that draws attention to (if not resolving) the power relations involved in theatre production' (2013: 159).

One source of this uncertainty is those meta-text sections in which the trash recyclers speak of the theatre-makers' attitudes towards them. It is often here that the production process, the inequities and other differences between the unfamiliar real people and Rimini Protokoll, as well as the artists' implication in the exploitation of their protagonists, may be seen most clearly. For example, the meta-text used in the Essen performance contained statements about the doubts each party initially entertained about the other. These included the warning Aziz received from a market seller that Germany was the Mafia and that he would end up having his kidneys stolen during surgery there, and Rimini Protokoll's fear that a cast member would vanish in Germany during the week set aside for rehearsal in Berlin (Rimini Protokoll 2010: 20–1). Other meta-text outlined how the show thus far had had both a creative and destructive impact on the recyclers. For instance, it informed the spectator that by working in the theatre production, Bayram, head of his own unauthorized waste business, had earned enough money for his wife to take classes in English and become a hotel receptionist instead of a cleaner. However, as Rimini Protokoll feared, the removal of the Kurdish recyclers from their workplace did lead to the dissolution of their collective, with most of their colleagues moving to another depot (Rimini Protokoll 2010: 23–4). By means of texts such as these, Rimini Protokoll revealed their interest in replacing centralized authority, and what director Daniel Wetzel has referred to as 'imperialistic help' (Hilfsimperialismus) (Wahl 2008b), with a mutually empowering social exchange, while simultaneously acknowledging those moments in which the playing field remained unequal.

In those sections where the trash collectors speak of the theatre artists in the third person plural as 'they' and describe the artists' thoughts and attitudes towards their cast members, they appear as capable observers of the directorial team. However, while the performers deliver the text with confidence, as if the words are genuinely their own, the content suggests it is the result of some form of discussion and collaboration with Rimini Protokoll, the nature of which is unclear. And, indeed, at one point during the rehearsal period this meta-text was *not* owned and delivered by the trash recyclers, but by the directorial assistant Pınar Başoğlu instead (Mumford 2010a). One of the potential effects of this re-allocation of text, and consequent play with a sense of the genuine, is that the artist-ethnographers' rights to the dominant viewing position are challenged through a reversal of positions whereby the observed subjects become the observers. Another potential effect is the destabilization for some viewers of the sense that the insights communicated by this meta-text, if not the words as well, belong to the recyclers. Do they communicate the men's thoughts and words? Or those of the artists? Or both? Such uncertainty may prompt further questions about self and others: for example, what sort of prejudices inform the doubt that the socially marginalized trash collectors would or could create such a meta-text? Can we ever fully grasp the stranger we are facing in an encounter, either on or off stage? What might the advantages be of relinquishing the desire to fully grasp, differentiate, and categorize the unfamiliar?

In *Mr Dağaçar*, an awareness of the incomplete and flawed nature of proximity to people was also encouraged during an episode involving improvised text that re-invoked the rehearsal environment of linguistic polyphony and partial communication. Rimini Protokoll's approach to linguistic competency during this production was characterized by a readiness to work with people who do not share their languages, and in situations therefore in which neither verbal nor textual exactitude is possible. Moreover, they placed the audience in a similar environment at one point – this was when all the male performers played a game from the Kurdish men's village involving the concealment of a ring underneath upturned cups. During the HAU2 performance, recorded on DVD, Başoğlu steps from the audience onto the stage and, for the benefit of the predominantly German-speaking audience, paraphrases much of the Turkish dialogue in English. Hasan having called, in English, for a ring from the audience, Bayram makes brief humorous remarks in light of the audience's response (or failure to respond!) in both German and English. Hasan and Bayram also briefly talk to one another, a dialogue that Başoğlu does not translate. Even for those audience members proficient in all three languages involved, the gains and failures of cross-cultural communication and understanding were playfully evoked.

Overt artistry and partial proximity

Another playful refusal of a desire to master and control the object being viewed occurred in a later episode in the Essen and Berlin performances when Bayram comments on having been told by municipal authorities that, if he wanted to continue working in the Beyoglu area, he should wear an official uniform. While the purpose of the uniform, he says, was to make him 'look a bit more official for the tourists' (Rimini Protokoll 2010: 17), in reality it offered him no protection against having his goods and carts taken away. For this reason, and others such as his desire to live as a free man, Bayram did not invest in the uniform. Rimini Protokoll, however, he points out, had provided him with a uniform, and later he enters wearing it: a complete head-to-feet theatrical costume that denoted officialdom both on the stage and outside on the streets of Istanbul. In a cheeky and fun-loving dance to striptease-style music, he flings off the belt, the jacket, and shirt and teases the audience with the possibility he is going to remove much more. However, neither he nor the show go 'all the way', both allowing only partial proximity and thereby frustrating the desire to fix strangers as objects that can be mastered, often for exclusive forms of pleasure.

The light-hearted episode with the Beyoglu costume is also one of the many moments at which attention is drawn to processes of staging and artifice within both theatre production and everyday life. Similar moments include Hasan's demonstration of how he constructs his shadow-play booth, characters, and narratives. In addition, there is the interweaving of Apo, Aziz, and Mithat's representation of the arduous bus journey they took from their village to Istanbul, with Hasan's semi-factual depiction of parts of that journey through his Karagöz puppets. One potential effect of this interweaving is an awareness of how the self-representations of the seemingly originary speakers are also the product of artifice. As Rimini Protokoll commentator Gerald Siegmund puts it, the frame of theatre 'affords an undeniable distancing. It turns the trusted into something foreign: as "real" as something seems, as "real" as it might sound, it is here closely related to the possibility of fiction' (2008: 190). In other words, the foregrounding of artifice and the theatre frame in *Mr Dağaçar* reminds us of the impossibility of pure proximity given the performative nature of both stage and everyday life.

The uniform episode also demonstrates how in this production different types of Authenticity-Effect are combined with overt staging, and how the resulting sense of both authenticity and artifice contributes to an interplay of proximity and distance during encounter with strangers. For example, the impression that Bayram's autobiographical narrative about the uniform contains elements of the sincere, genuine, and truthful – an impression that is reinforced not only by the recurrent presentation of similar comments from the other trash recyclers about the municipal government's attitude towards them, but also by the presence of the uniform itself – is combined with the reference to Rimini Protokoll's purchase of the costume. This self-reflexivity, in a manner similar to that of the meta-texts, is an Authenticity-Effect in so far as it creates a sense of honesty about the theatre-making process, the socio-economic relations between the artists and experts, and about the fact that what we are observing is the product of staging. But the playful striptease dance also foregrounds artistry, in this case the construction of layered imagery that presents, among other things, Bayram's refusal to be trapped by governmental regulations, as well as the production's attempt to create non-voyeuristic access to strangers.

A similar mixing of Authenticity-Effects and self-reflexive artistry in ways that create an interplay of being brought close to, and being kept at a distance from, people occurs in *Blackmarket* No. 7. For example, seemingly real and genuine dialogues are cut short by the reverberating thirty-minute gong that brings them to an abrupt end, and while the *Schwarzradio* live transmissions permit the spectAuditors a form of immediate access to some of the talks and conversations, the multiplication of a vast number of dialogue partners creates a concrete and metaphorical beehive of knowledge that cannot be fully accessed or grasped. Similarly, the Mobile Academy staff – some of whom in the Graz (2007), Vienna (2008), and Turku (2011) productions sported elaborate retro hair-dos that could be read as taking the beehive imagery to a new level – performed the role of an alternate service industry that both brought its clients to their preferred experts, and assigned them to consultations on topics outside their comfort zones. One consequence was a thwarting of the client's ability to fully grasp and master unfamiliar people and knowledges.

As our analysis of approaches to the presentation and reception of culturally unfamiliar real people has demonstrated, both productions exemplify a form of intercultural theatre that invites encounter with people and their expertise that are insufficiently known or invisible, and in ways that seek to transcend hierarchical structures of social relation or fetishistic voyeurism. In *Blackmarket* No. 7, opportunities for encounter with culturally diverse people and unfamiliar knowledges are made possible through a range of strategies: non-exclusive casting of both experts and clients; the inclusion of multiple, heterogeneous, and non-knowledge topic areas; booking systems that generate unexpected matches; and the broad distribution of audio-texts through the *Schwarzradio* and online sound archive. In *Mr Dağaçar*, similar opportunities for encounter are opened up through a collaborative cross-cultural staging of people who are often made invisible in society and/or theatre: unofficial and socially excluded managers of city waste, the shadow-play puppeteer who is normally concealed during a show, and the (female) dramaturgical assistant and translator who also usually remains behind the scenes.

In both productions, spectators or participants are brought close to these people through textual strategies that are a key source of Authenticity-Effects. In Mobile Academy's work, these include both spontaneous and intimate face-to-face dialogue and its live transmission, and also personalized narrations, all of which cause and allow a physical experience of the labour and corporeal investments involved in getting-to-know strangers. These Authenticity-Effects themselves, because they open up the subjective, incomplete, and flawed nature of both communications with people and access to knowledge, tend to trouble a sense of our ability to fully know and understand the unfamiliar.

Maintenance of partial proximity is also ensured through temporal and spatial artistry, such as the timed slot that allows only a certain percentage of knowledge exchange, and the mass choreography of a humming beehive of interlocutors, only a fragment of which can be taken in. In Rimini Protokoll's production, the textual Authenticity-Effects include self-representational narratives delivered in native languages, semi-translated improvised dialogue, and self-reflexive meta-text that exposes the production's preparatory processes and social relations. While effects such as dialogue that has only been partially translated create an experience of incomplete proximity that we are likely to be familiar with from everyday life, in *Mr Dağaçar* many of these effects are also destabilized in ways that further foreground the incomplete nature of our access to the (un)familiar. For example, in Rimini Protokoll's production, an impression of the genuine is destabilized by the removal of authorship signposts, thereby creating uncertainty about who has said or created what. This uncertainty has the potential to emulate the 'never-ending processes of getting to know one another' (Regus 2009: 11), or to draw attention to (assumptions about the) power relations involved in theatre production.

Through the interweaving of Authenticity-Effects with destabilizations of a sense of the genuine and unmediated, and the use of self-reflexive artistry, both Theatre of Real People productions create an interplay of closeness to and distance from unfamiliar real people that has the potential to challenge the controlling gaze of theatre artists and spectators. In this and other ways, they offer an alternative to the presentation of mastery that tends to mark illusionist theatre. In so doing, they contribute to the development of postcolonial curatorship and spectatorship fostered by Lilienthal at the HAU, and move towards Ahmed's preferred model of ethical communication. Such communication involves a getting closer that yet takes up 'the impossibility of that very gesture, at one and the same time' (Ahmed 2000: 148), a paradoxical endeavour that Theatre of Real People is well placed to pursue.

Conclusion

Authenticity-Effects and encounter with the unfamiliar at the HAU

Theatre of Real People produced by or hosted at the Hebbel am Ufer (HAU) during Matthias Lilienthal's period of leadership was frequently marked by an experience of the complex, ambiguous or paradoxical that was often generated by a particular approach to what we call Authenticity-Effects. We have defined these effects as, first, techniques that generate and sometimes destabilize a *sense* of the sincere and genuine, referential truthfulness and veracity, and unmediated and intimate contact with people. Second, these effects are also the perceptual experiences that result from such techniques. We have also used the concept of the Authenticity-Effect as an analytical tool for assessing and questioning the relation to social reality of both performers and spectators in Theatre of Real People.

In the HAU productions we have examined, a sense of authenticity was especially connected with the real people – from a variety of cultural backgrounds, and usually without prior performance training – who were featured in these works, and who also contributed to encounter with the unfamiliar outside of and within one's own culture, city, and self. These people helped destabilize a sense of the authentic, in ways that invited fresh perspectives on personal identity and social phenomena. For example, in one of the works examined in this book, Rimini Protokoll's *100% Melbourne* (2012), a young City of Melbourne statistician who seemed genuine when he stated his interest in seeing the unfamiliar faces behind his numbers, appeared slightly less so when he declared he had only ever been on stage once before in his life. The ninety-nine other Melbournians, cast according to demographic criteria, also often seemed sincere and truthful. However, many of them would signal the rehearsed and stage-managed nature of their presentations, and openly admit at the end of each show that they had lied when answering survey questions during the performance, thereby underlining the production's invitation to reflect on both the complexity of identity and representational democracy.

In the 2004 version of Lilienthal's *X-Apartments*, under the dramaturgy of Shermin Langhoff and Arved Schultze, the protagonists included Frau Barthelmess, who lived in a rough-looking concrete apartment block in Berlin's Lichtenberg. Against the backdrop of a pink and pastel-coloured décor, she gave poetry readings about her deceased cat. Coming straight after an episode in a neighbouring corridor where youths (played by actors) thuggishly demanded a toll from participants, her reading and setting may have appeared artificial to some by comparison. This juxtaposition of figures and scenarios had the capacity to both trigger prejudices about the violent and dangerous nature of the suburb, and to encourage critical appraisal of them. In Rimini Protokoll's 2005 discovery tour *Call Cutta: Mobile Phone Theatre*, genuinely dissimulating Indian call-centre workers guided participants through a part of Berlin by means of intimate chat and narratives that blend facts and fiction, thereby unsettling knowledge about German-Indian relations and Germany's Nazi past, as well as shaping new perspectives on intercultural experiences. The seventh version of Mobile Academy's *Blackmarket for Useful Knowledge and Non-Knowledge* (2007) featured 100 experts who engaged in narratives and one-on-one dialogues with audience members about migration and mobility in a way that provided an experience of the partial nature of knowledge, and ethical potential of accepting the never fully graspable nature of anything or anyone. In *Mr Dağaçar and the Golden Tectonics of Trash* (2010–) by Rimini Protokoll, rubbish-recyclers working in Istanbul delivered meta-text that challenged both the artists' and the spectators' rights to the position of authority, and 'the relations of force and authorization embedded in the desire to know (more) about strangers' (Ahmed 2000: 63).

Some of the most significant forms of destabilization that we have discovered or foregrounded include the following. First, those which create uncertainty about what is genuine and true through means such as: a mixing and blurring of truths and lies; guides and interlocutors who are both dependable and unreliable; and a demonstration of the inability to distinguish between authentic and performed selves, or between on- and off-stage rhetoric. Second, those destabilizations which unsettle the spectators' sense that they know the origins and authors of the spoken texts during the performance event, such as are produced by passages of everyday speech delivered by real people that seem to indicate rhetorical and aesthetic shaping by artists, or by moments where complex meta-text on the production's artistic processes is delivered by and attributed to real people. Third, forms of destabilization which challenge a sense that there is a stable and fixed essence to the self through, for example, presenting autobiographical text that lacks 'retrospective teleology' (Brockmeier 2001: 252) and instead presents a fractured selfhood. And finally, those forms which undermine the audience's capacity to distinguish between theatre and non-theatre by, for example: unfolding events in everyday urban sites in ways that produce unclear or missing frames of reference; or the creation of a conflict for participants between the role of theatre spectator and another role, such as that of house guest.

One of the likely effects of these strategies is the demonstration and experience of the complex, contradictory, and unexpected nature of individuals and social reality. This effect has the capacity to challenge participant expectations that stem from schemata and cognitive scripts, and thereby also draw critical attention to one's own resentments (Behrendt 2004) as well as to the associated clichés, stereotypes, and prejudices. As a citizen performer in *100% Melbourne* observed, 'People aren't what they seem' (Humphrey, in Garde 2015: 269), and as Rimini Protokoll themselves noted, the number of Melbournians in favour of the death penalty was unexpectedly high given the seemingly peaceful and laid-back nature of the city (Haug, in Bowen et al. 2015: 308). Lilienthal has approvingly spoken of the way in which Rimini Protokoll's work shows how reality is often quite different from what one imagines it to be, and does so while 'pointing out the constructed nature of their theatre' (auf die Gemachtheit ihres Theaters [...] verweisen: Baecker et al. 2012: 17). Such an observation could be made of all of the formats and productions examined in this book.

In many of the works we have analysed here, a number of the Authenticity-Effects that destabilize a sense of authentic identity also contribute to a troubling of the histories and patterns of encounter with strangers (Ahmed 2000: 8) that are marked by hierarchy and involve fixing the stranger in a subordinate place or as an fetishized other. In *Mr Dağaçar*, for example, giving the meta-text to the rubbish recyclers to speak in the first person – a text that seemed to contain authentic and insightful information about the production's preparatory processes and politics – assisted the observed subjects to also assume the position of knowing observer, a position that in theatre is often reserved for artists and spectators. In Nurkan Erpulat's 2008 project for *X-Apartments*, Authenticity-Effects were destabilized in ways that were likely to disrupt the viewing position of a sensation-seeking cultural tourist who perceives 'the world as food for sensibility' (Baumann 1998: 94). In *X-Apartments*, many of the real-people performers in each project were actual residents of the apartments visited by the spectators. In Erpulat's project, an ambiguous female figure wearing a black headscarf and westernized clothing, and serving glasses of water – ambiguous because her familiarity with the lived-in apartment suggested but did not clarify that she resided there and was a real-people performer – provided and prohibited access to a peephole view of a veiled woman who undressed and posed naked on a sofa, smoking a cigarette. Not only did the woman serving water subversively take the place of the colonial male European artist who historically controlled access to the figure of desire, but her multifaceted cultural markers embodied and invited reflection on a crossing of what some viewers might perceive to be East and West cultural boundaries. In these and many other instances, Theatre of Real People at the HAU brought a sceptical approach to bear on authenticity in ways that invited encounters with strangers, including the insufficiently known or marginalized, and encounters that sought to transcend hierarchical structures of social relation in both theatre and society.

A further finding of our investigation is that the destabilization of a sense of the authentic that helped create complex and ambiguous figures and encounters, also contributed significantly to an experience of ungraspability. As commentators on (intercultural) encounter have pointed out, the experience and practice of failing to grasp the full meaning of an other, or to fully understand an encounter with an unfamiliar person, can lead to the insight not only that complete understanding is never possible, but that it might not be desirable (Ahmed 2000: 148, 157; Regus 2009: 11). Our production analyses have demonstrated that a sense of ungraspability is most likely to arise when a destabilization of a sense of the authentic occurs through an illumination of the *partial* nature of the proximity to people offered by the performance event. That is an illumination of the incomplete, flawed, and/or biased nature of proximity. Such foregrounding may consist in no more than a subtle glimpse, such as in the case of the autobiographical narrative by Vietnam veteran Stephen Black in *100% Melbourne*, where signs of aesthetic reframing and of the unsaid disrupt the assumption that the narrative gives direct, complete, and objective access to his true self.

In the case of the *Blackmarket* format, some of the Authenticity-Effects – such as the unfinished dialogues between expert and client that bring to mind the nature of much real-life everyday dialogue – arguably have the potential to generate a sense of the partial nature of knowledge and of proximity to the people who deliver it without any need for destabilizing interventions other than the framing of the event as performance. However, in most cases within Mobile Academy's format, a sense of partial proximity is achieved or underlined through artistic interventions that unsettle habitual perception, including: the arrangement of multiple simultaneous talks in one intimate space that makes it impossible to fully grasp each and every story; the overtly subjective and strictly timed nature of the narratives; and the management of each expert/client encounter through check-in staff manoeuvres and a booming gong. One vivid instance of overtly staged partial proximity is the cheeky striptease number in *Mr Dağaçar*, in which trash recycler Bayram Renklihava removes the Beyoglu uniform that the municipal authorities think will make him look more official to the tourists, but does not strip completely naked, a gesture that resists a voyeuristic or authoritarian desire to master the unfamiliar. This, and many other instances in the Theatre of Real People we have explored, demonstrate that such a mode of performance is ideally suited to pursuing that ethical (and paradoxical) model of communication that involves a getting closer while acknowledging 'the impossibility of that very gesture, at one and the same time' (Ahmed 2000: 148).

Lilienthal and his team's artistic and management approach at the HAU successfully set the scene for a production house and a Theatre of Real People that provided a relevant and innovative model for engagement with the unfamiliar in the context of our contemporary intercultural situation. As this study has shown, the success of the HAU model was due to attitudes and initiatives that fostered a realist aesthetic and its intertwining with (inter)cultural innovation. Lilienthal and his team's unique realist credo was expressed in a commitment to integrating aesthetic with societal discourse, and in combining numerous arts disciplines and media in ways that challenged conventional approaches to art and its relation to social reality.

This challenge was manifest in two ways. On the one hand, the HAU's early engagement with various migrant generations offered a model of how a cultural institution can act as a motor for social change at a time when, at least until Neco Çelik's 2006 production of Feridun Zaimoglu and Günter Senkel's play *Black Virgins* (*Schwarze Jungfrauen*) at the HAU, the 'city theatre' (Stadttheater) had ignored this topic (Khuon 2010: 17). On the other hand, the HAU's engagement with the culturally unfamiliar did not make the migrant the sole focal point, and was characterized instead by a willingness to acknowledge the complexity of difference and positive potential of cultural diversity and globalization. This acknowledgment was evident in the HAU's dedication to: attracting new and culturally diverse artists and audience members; curating projects and festivals that did not focus on national or ethnic origins and cultural practices but were oriented around themes to which everyone involved could contribute in his or her own way; and the pursuit of an institutional-network approach that encouraged non-hierarchical intercultural collaborations.

While there have been some shifts in emphasis since 2012, when Lilienthal was replaced by Annemie Vanackere, former artistic director of the Schouwburg in Rotterdam, the HAU has continued to fuel the reality trend. Christine Wahl, for example, reflecting on Vanackere's first two seasons, has noted the following: a move away from site-specific work in diverse urban locations and a return to performance in theatre buildings; an interest in turning inwards to closely examine the nature of theatre; and a heightened appreciation of choreographic work. However, Wahl also observed that many of the artists supported by Lilienthal continue to have a prominent profile under Vanackere (2014: 47). These include influential contributors to Theatre of Real People such as Werner Kroesinger, Gob Squad, She She Pop, and Rimini Protokoll. Indeed, the latter remain based at the HAU and their 2014 piece *Situation Rooms*, co-produced with the HAU, was invited to the prestigious Berliner Theatertreffen. Another point of continuity has been the practice of working with culturally diverse artists, as exemplified by the HAU's 2014 mini-festival Staging Cambodia. One talking point at the festival was the video work *Galaxy Khmer/Portrait Series Battambang*, co-produced by Belgian director-choreographer Michael Laub together with the HAU and Phare Performing Social Enterprise, a Cambodian NGO. In addition to the rock band The Cambodian Space Project, dancers from Cambodia, and visual material by Cambodia-based German filmmaker Marc Ebele, the work featured diverse people not professionally trained in screen performance – including a night-watchman, male fashion model, sex workers, young circus artists, and single mothers – who presented personal stories, in many cases about traumatic experiences and circumstances. The presentation of these narratives in an episode in which five females were simultaneously pictured telling their stories and weeping – an episode described by one reviewer as 'peculiarly comical and alienating' (Wildermann 2014) – provided a discomforting experience that invited reflection on artists' exploitation of what appeared to be the authentic misfortune of strangers. Here the self-reflexive and sceptical approach to Authenticity-Effects involving real and unfamiliar people continues the socially engaged practices of Theatre of Real People at the HAU.

Theatre of Real People and socio-political potential: some criticisms and opportunities

In a criticism of contemporary art, Bernd Stegemann postulates that seeking authenticity is part of a (bourgeois) mechanism for overcoming current alienation by promising access to a genuine self and the true essence of an other (2015: 93–5). As our discussion of complexity and ungraspability has made clear, the HAU productions we have examined did not seek to offer such an authentic encounter with an other. The assumption that all Theatre of Real People tends to pursue such an essentialist approach has been part of a broader misunderstanding of this mode of performance in some circles in Germany. Stegemann and Frank M. Raddatz in particular have subsumed many Theatre of Real People productions under the label 'Theatre of the Authentic' (Das Theater des Authentischen), which they have also repeatedly presented as synonymous with postdramatic theatre (Raddatz 2010: 139, 159). This subsumption is relevant to our case studies, as Raddatz has associated several regular contributors to programmes at the HAU, including Rimini Protokoll and She She Pop, with an authenticity 'hype' (2014b: 89). Dismissing what he regards as a self-indulgent postdramatic interest in the nature of reality, he has also criticized Lilienthal's *X-Apartments* for putting 'the exploration of the relationship between reality indices and simulation' (die Erkundung des Verhältnisses von Wirklichkeitsindex und Simulation) as its key agenda, to which end it sends audience members into 'the homes of complete strangers' (das Zuhause wildfremder Menschen: Raddatz 2014b: 90).

According to Raddatz, this wave of enthusiasm for the 'Theatre of the Authentic' is superficial and will soon be brought to an end (2011: 384) by what he characterizes as a fascination with the unformed and raw, a concomitant shallowness and lack of literariness (2011: 376), and diminished possibilities for making multi-layered texts and creating alternative worlds (2011: 378). When illustrating this rawness, Raddatz quotes a comment by Daniel Wetzel on Rimini Protokoll's preference for working with real people who have not become overly accustomed to the theatre environment (2011: 376). However, he does not contextualize this remark by providing information about Rimini Protokoll's careful editorial work. This work includes textual interventions that shape the protagonists' words beyond what Stefan Kaegi refers to as 'the requirements of tellability' (Kaegi, in Bowen et al. 2015: 306), and diverges from the practice of the unelaborated ready-made (Dreysse 2004: 35) that Raddatz (2007: 25) and Stegemann (2015: 137) associate with such theatre. Our analyses of *Call Cutta* and *100% City* have shown the merits of the editorial elaborations, which include processes of fictionalization that invite a surplus of meaning and multifaceted interpretations. Rich meaning-making also occurs in those productions that use the simultaneous presence of multiple experts to open out diverse perspectives on a given issue. In *100% City*, for example, where a large mass of citizens take different and sometimes contradictory positions in response to survey questions.

Rather than engaging in what Stegemann has characterized as a pointless perceptual oscillation (2015: 20), the theatre productions analysed in this book often set in motion an interplay between fostering and disturbing the audience's sense of authenticity that has the capacity to confront spectators with their own expectations and generate an awareness of the schemata that shape their reception. Unlike the version of the authentic that Stegemann describes in his *Lob des Realismus* (translatable as *In Praise of Realism*, 2015: 93, 97), the version created by the HAU productions we have examined did not erase or cover up socio-political contradictions and injustices. Instead, it invited audiences to engage with intercultural tensions and created ways to address the inequitable power relations and voyeurism that can result from publically presenting real people. In a commentary on Stegemann's criticism of postmodern performance, including Theatre of the Authentic, as well as an interview with Stegemann, Raddatz implicitly endorses what he frames as Stegemann's plea to turn theatre again into 'an art capable of criticism in a late capitalist public sphere' (Theater wieder zu einer kritikfähigen Kunst in der spätkapitalistischen Öffentlichkeit zu machen: Stegemann in Raddatz 2014b: 90; Raddatz 2014a: 27). In *Lob des Realismus*, Stegemann advocates a new realism in the arts that works with a Brechtian defamiliarization and serves dialectical purposes ('dialektische Verfremdung': Stegemann 2015: 132) in order to engage critically with social injustice and political problems. In asking whether postdramatic theatre is compatible with politics, Stegemann and Raddatz join a number of other scholars (Jürs-Munby, Carroll and Giles 2013). However, they tend to make generalizing statements about what they present as clearly separable dramatic and postdramatic theatre strands. By contrast, in his analysis of Rimini Protokoll's *Black Tie*, Johannes Birgfeld (2015) argues for the importance of engaging with specific theatre productions rather than establishing a strand dichotomy. Birgfeld's analysis provides a historical context for the current German discussion by pointing to Birgit Haas's (2007) earlier plea for a dramatic theatre, and refutes several of Raddatz and Stegemann's claims, including the assertion that the experts in Rimini Protokoll's theatre generally lack the capacity to disrupt illusion and to create distancing effects or defamiliarization (*Verfremdung*).

Stegemann's call for *Verfremdung* within a dialectical framework (2015: 131–42) raises two questions in particular: first, whether it is still possible to return to a way of making theatre that follows immediately in Brecht's footsteps; and second, whether a single approach to making socially and/or politically engaged theatre is desirable. David Barnett provides a nuanced response to the first question by acknowledging both the historical changes that have affected the nature and outcomes of the 'dialectic in postmodernity' and the 'knowable details' of the world we live in (2013: 52). He also proposes a distinction between postdramatic and 'post-Brechtian' theatre. Barnett's conceptualization of the latter takes into account the impact on theatre of more recent epistemological and ideological developments on potential insights into and certainties about the world. It acknowledges that post-Brechtian theatre has at 'its core both a dissatisfaction with the narrowness of the Brechtian dialectic and a desire to expand its remit to address concrete social problems' (2013: 66).

With regard to the second question, in a keynote address to the Australian Theatre Forum 2015, one of the issues raised by Belgian festival director and curator Frie Leysen was the necessity in 'times of right-wing nationalism, extremism, racism and intolerance', where 'we take down the borders but raise them soon again' (2015), to develop multiple artistic responses. Her comment suggests the ongoing pertinence of endeavours to invite encounters with unfamiliar people – both from close by and from far afield – and to change the perspectives of all involved, an endeavour pursued by Lilienthal and his HAU team. As curators, neither Leysen nor Lilienthal avoid the tensions, risks, and adventures that might come with their striking openness to both content and aesthetics. Prior to the Autumn 2015 season, Lilienthal, in his new role as artistic director of the Münchener Kammerspiele, one of Germany's leading state-funded 'city theatres' (Stadttheater), presented a vision statement that confirmed his ongoing commitment to experimentation on multiple fronts with socially engaged performance that would serve and be made by culturally diverse people. The statement, which appeared in both German and English on the Kammerspiele website, outlined that the theatre aimed to provide English subtitles for as many performances as possible in order to make its work more accessible to both the international employees of Munich's successful business companies, and the '[m]any refugees who come to the city from the crisis regions on Europe's external borders and even beyond' (Lilienthal, on Münchener Kammerspiele website). In addition, Lilienthal indicated his intention to tackle the local issue of the lack of affordable housing in *Shabby Shabby Apartments*, a co-production with the collective of architects known as raumlaborberlin, which would take place prior to the opening of the official season and provide opportunities for interested parties to stay overnight in inexpensive architect-designed temporary accommodation. Located at diverse city sites, this production continued an earlier project for the Theatre of the World Festival 2014 in Mannheim, a festival curated by Lilienthal and for which he had also commissioned similar apartments in order to offer a space for reflection on the relation between self and other (Lilienthal, in Mand 2014).

In his vision statement for the Kammerspiele, Lilienthal also announced his plan to continue his collaboration with artists with whom he had worked at the HAU, and among the names he mentioned were practitioners who have contributed to Theatre of Real People, such as Rimini Protokoll, She She Pop, Gob Squad, and Rabih Mroué. The inclusion of these artists underlines his commitment to this mode of performance. However, he also introduced, as his first in-house director, Nicolas Stemann, renowned for his staging of Elfriede Jelinek's texts and interest in contemporary interpretations of classical drama. And he named the actors who together would make up a culturally diverse ensemble, a mix of newcomers and old hands from the Kammerspiele. The appointment of Stemann builds upon Lilienthal's recent experience of working with the director at the Theatre of the World 2014 festival, for which Stemann staged Elfriede Jelinek's *The Wards* (*Die Schutzbefohlenen*). This controversial and acclaimed production featured both professional actors and real asylum-seekers. Lilienthal's choice of a director, who is not only highly experienced in working with an ensemble and staging plays, but also skilled in testing the limits of these practices, demonstrates his ongoing openness to experimentation with boundaries between modes of performance in pursuit of a theatre that engages with a culturally diverse society. It was exactly this engagement that informed the influential application of Authenticity-Effects to encounters with the unfamiliar in Theatre of Real People at the HAU under Lilienthal.

Bibliography

Ahmed, S. (2000), *Strange Encounters: Embodied Others in Post-Coloniality*, London: Routledge.

Albrecht, C. (2003), 'Fremdheit', in A. Wierlacher and A. Bogner (eds), *Handbuch interkulturelle Germanistik*, Stuttgart: Metzler, 232–8.

Anderson, M. and Wilkinson, L. (2007), 'A Resurgence of Verbatim Theatre: Authenticity, Empathy and Transformation', *Australasian Drama Studies*, 50: 153–69.

Assmann, A. (2003), *Erinnerungsräume: Formen und Wandlungen des kulturellen Gedächtnisses*, München: Beck.

Auslander, P. (2008), *Liveness: Performance in a Mediatized Culture*, London: Routledge.

Baecker, D. (2011), 'Wer ist WIR? Theater in der interkulturellen Gesellschaft: Vortrag auf der Jahreskonferenz der Dramaturgischen Gesellschaft 2011 am Theater Freiburg am 26. Januar 2011', 26 January [www.dirkbaecker. com; accessed 1 April 2014].

Baecker, D., Lilienthal, M. and Müller, T. (2012), 'Hoffnung auf Ereignishaftes in der Erwartungserfüllungsanstalt', in K. Hehmeyer and M. Pees (eds), *Import Export: Arbeitsbuch zum HAU Berlin*, Berlin: Theater der Zeit, 11–19.

Bailes, S. J. (2011), *Performance Theatre and the Poetics of Failure: Forced Entertainment, Goat Island, Elevator Repair Service*, London: Routledge.

Barnett, D. (2001), 'Documentation and its Discontents: The Case of Heinar Kipphardt', *Forum for Modern Language Studies*, 37 (3): 272–85.

Barnett, D. (2013), 'Performing Dialectics in an Age of Uncertainty, or: Why Post-Brechtian ≠ Postdramatic', in J. Carroll, S. Giles and K. Jürs-Munby (eds), *Postdramatic Theatre and the Political: International Perspectives on Contemporary Performance*, London: Methuen, 47–66.

Barnett, D. (2015), 'Sampling the Stasi with a GPS Device in Berlin: *50 Aktenkilometer* and the Recent German Past', in J. Birgfeld, U. Garde and M. Mumford (eds), *Rimini Protokoll Close-Up: Lektüren*, Hannover: Wehrhahn, 94–114.

Barthes, R. (1986), 'The Reality Effect', in R. Barthes, *The Rustle of Language*, trans. R. Howard, New York: Hill & Wang, 141–8.

Barton, B. (1987), *Das Dokumentartheater*, Stuttgart: Metzler.

Baudrillard, J. (1994), *Simulacra and Simulation*, Ann Arbor, MI: University of Michigan Press.

Baumann, Z. (1998), *Globalization: The Human Consequences*, New York: Columbia University Press.

Behrendt, E. (2004), 'Prinzip Pferdewette', *Theater heute*, Jahrbuch 2004 [http://www.archiv.hebbel-am-ufer.de/de/tdj.html; accessed 1 April 2014].

Behrendt, E. (2008), 'Stadterkundungsparcours: "X Wohnungen" wird zum Exportschlager', *Frankfurter Rundschau*, 11 June [http://www.fr-online.de/kultur/stadterkundungsparcours–x-wohnungen–wird-zum-exportschlager,1472786,3324754.html; accessed 25 January 2013].

Behrendt, E. (2012), 'Hundert Prozent Gegenwart – Pro HAU', *Theater heute*, 4: 32–3.

Benjamin, W. (2008), *The Work of Art in the Age of its Technological Reproducibility, and Other Writings on Media*, Cambridge, MA: Harvard University Press.

Bensmaia, R. (2010), 'Reality Effect', in D. Herman, M. Jahn and M.-L. Ryan (eds), *Routledge Encyclopedia of Narrative Theory*, London: Routledge, 492.

Beyond Belonging Translokal (2009), 'Program', *Die Tageszeitung*, n.d. [http://www.kanak-attak.de/ka/down/pdf/beyondbelonging_tazBeilage2.pdf; accessed 2 March 2014].

Bhabha, H. K. (1994), *The Location of Culture*, London: Routledge.

Bharucha, R. (2014), 'Hauntings of the Intercultural: Enigmas and Lessons on the Borders of Failure', in E. Fischer-Lichte, T. Jost and S. I. Jain (eds), *The Politics of Interweaving Performance Cultures: Beyond Postcolonialism*, New York: Routledge, 179–200.

Billington, M. (2011), 'Don't Mention the Phwoar: The Future of German Theatre', *The Guardian*, 14 March [http://www.theguardian.com/world/2011/mar/13/german-theatre-new-europe-berlin; accessed 15 October 2014].

Birgfeld, J. (2015), '*Black Tie*. Ein Monodrama, oder: Deliterarisierung des Theaters?', in J. Birgfeld, U. Garde and M. Mumford (eds), *Rimini Protokoll Close-Up: Lektüren*, Hannover: Wehrhahn, 36–56.

Birgfeld, J., Garde, U. and Mumford, M. (eds) (2014), *Rimini Protokoll Close-Up: Lektüren*, Hannover: Wehrhahn.

Birkenhauer, T. (2008), 'Nicht Realismus, sondern Realität', in A. Kleihues (ed.), *Realitätseffekte*, Munich: Fink, 115–33.

Bishop, C. (2012), *Artificial Hells: Participatory Art and the Politics of Spectatorship*, London: Verso Books.

Blythe, A. (2008), 'Alecky Blythe', in W. Hammond and D. Steward (eds), *Verbatim Verbatim*: *Contemporary Documentary Theatre*, London: Oberon Books, 78–102.

Boal, A. (1998), *Theater of the Oppressed*, trans. C. A. McBride and M.-.O. L. McBride, London: Pluto Press.

Boenisch, P. (2008), 'Other People Live: Rimini Protokoll and their Theatre of Experts – An Interview', *Contemporary Theatre Review*, 18 (1): 107–13.

Bojadžijev, M. (2007a), 'Kleine Einführung in die Theorie des Rassismus I', *Mobile Academy*: *Blackmarket-Archiv*, 10 March [http://blackmarket-archive.com/#; accessed 29 June 2015].

Bojadžijev, M. (2007b), 'Kleine Einführung in die Theorie des Rassismus III', *Mobile Academy*: *Blackmarket-Archiv*, 10 March [http://www.blackmarket-archive.com/#; accessed 28 June 2015].

Bolter, J. D. and Grusin, R. (2000), *Remediation*: *Understanding New Media*, Cambridge, MA: MIT Press.

Bottoms, S. (2006), 'Putting the Document into Documentary: An Unwelcome Corrective?', *The Drama Review* 50 (3): 56–68.

Bourriaud, N. (2002), *Relational Aesthetics*, Dijon: Les presses du réel.

Bowen, J., Garde, U., Griffith, A., Guglielmo, V., Haug, H., Kaegi, S., Mumford, M. and Watts, R. (2015), 'Panel Discussion 100% Melbourne: Contemporary Documentary Performance that Puts "Real Melbournians" on the Stage', in J. Birgfeld, U. Garde and M. Mumford (eds), *Rimini Protokoll Close-Up*: *Lektüren*, Hannover: Wehrhahn, 302–17.

Boyd, C. (2012), 'Numbers Don't Add Up To a City in *100% Melbourne*', *The Australian*, 7 May [http://www.theaustralian.com.au/arts/stage/numbers-dont-add-up-to-a-city/story-fn9d344c-1226348078985; accessed 20 May 2012].

Brandl-Risi, B. (2010), 'Moving and Speaking through the Event, Once More: Participation and Reenactment in Jeremy Deller's *The Battle of Orgreave* and Rimini Protokoll's *Deutschland 2*', *Theater*, 40 (3): 54–65.

Brecht, B. (1991), 'Zu *Das Badener Lehrstück vom Einverständnis*: Anmerkung', in W. Hecht, J. Knopf, W. Mittenzwei and K.-D. Müller (eds), *Werke*: *Große kommentierte Berliner und Frankfurter Ausgabe*, Berlin and Frankfurt am Main: Aufbau and Suhrkamp, 24: 90–1.

Brecht, B. (1993), 'Kleines Organon für das Theater', in W. Hecht, J. Knopf, W. Mittenzwei and K.-D. Müller (eds), *Werke*: *Große kommentierte Berliner und Frankfurter Ausgabe*, Berlin and Frankfurt am Main: Aufbau and Suhrkamp, 23: 65–97.

Brecht, B. (2015), 'The German Drama: Pre-Hitler', in M. Silberman,
    S. Giles and T. Kuhn (eds), *Brecht on Theatre*, London: Bloomsbury,
    119–24.
Brendel, G. (2010), 'Chor trifft Krise: Drei Theaterstücke in Athen kreisen um
    den Prometheus-Mythos und seine Aktualität', *Deutschlandradio Kultur*,
    15 July [http://www.deutschlandradiokultur.de/chor-trifft-krise.1013.de.
    html?dram:article_id=170725; accessed 10 October 2014].
Brockmeier, J. (2001), 'From the End to the Beginning: Retrospective
    Teleology in Autobiography', in J. Brockmeier and D. Carbaugh (eds),
    Narrative and Identity: Studies in Autobiography, Self and Culture,
    Amsterdam: John Benjamins, 247–80.
Brooker, P. (1994), 'Key Words in Brecht's Theory and Practice of Theatre', in
    P. Thomson and G. Sacks (eds), *The Cambridge Companion to Brecht*,
    Cambridge: Cambridge University Press, 185–200.
Brown, P. (ed.) (2010), *Verbatim: Staging Memory and Community*, Sydney:
    Currency Press.
Bruss, E. W. (1976), *Autobiographical Acts: The Changing Situation of a Literary
    Genre*, Baltimore, MD: Johns Hopkins University Press.
Butler, J. (1988), 'Performative Acts and Gender Constitution: An Essay in
    Phenomenology and Feminist Theory', *Theatre Journal*, 40 (4): 519–31.
Calcutt, L., Skrbis, Z. and Woodward, I. (2009), 'Conceptualizing Otherness:
    An Exploration of the Cosmopolitan Schema', *Journal of Sociology*, 45 (2):
    169–86.
Carp, S. (2012), 'Im postkolonialen Raum: Überlegungen zum politischen
    Kuratieren', in K. Hehmeyer and M. Pees (eds), *Import Export: Arbeitsbuch
    zum HAU Berlin*, Berlin: Theater der Zeit, 96–9.
Casson, J. W. (2000), 'Living Newspaper: Theatre and Therapy', *The Drama
    Review*, 44 (2): 107–22.
Çelik, N. (2007), 'Von der fortschreitenden Islamisierung und von der Kunst
    sie zu genießen I', 10 March [http://www.blackmarket-archive.com/#;
    accessed 28 June 2015].
Çelik, N. (2012), '"Oberspezialisten für die türkischen Herkunft. Oder: Warum
    ich gerne Kleist inszenieren würde", transcription by Michaela
    Schlangenwerth', in K. Hehmeyer and M. Pees (eds), *Import Export:
    Arbeitsbuch zum HAU Berlin*, Berlin: Theater der Zeit, 48–51.
Cheesman, T. (2012), 'Nathan without the Rings: Postmodern Religion in
    Nathan Messias', in T. Cheesman and K. E. Yeşilada (eds), *Feridun
    Zaimoglu*, Bern: Lang: 117–44.

Cheesman, T. and Yeşilada, K. E. (eds) (2012), *Feridun Zaimoglu*, Oxford: Peter Lang.

City of Melbourne (2012), '*100% Melbourne*: Our City, on Stage' [http://www.melbourne.vic.gov.au/AboutMelbourne/ArtsandEvents/ArtsParticipation/Pages/100percentMelbourne.aspx; accessed 12 May 2013].

Connolly, K. (2010), 'Bundesbank Executive Provokes Race Outcry with Book', *The Guardian*, 31 August [http://www.theguardian.com/world/2010/aug/30/bundesbank-executive-book-race-row; accessed 12 May 2014].

Cornish, M. (2013), 'Rooms for Sight: The Artificial Everyday Theater of Rimini Protokoll', in R. DeRosa (ed.), *Simulation in Media and Culture: Believing the Hype*, Lanham, MD: Lexington Books, 165–75.

Croggon, A. (2012) '100% Melbourne', 24 May [theatrenotes.blogspot.com; accessed 30 May 2012].

Culler, J. (1988), *Framing the Sign: Criticism and its Institutions*, Oxford: Blackwell.

Cvejić, B. (2006), 'Trickstering, Hallucinating and Exhausting Production: The Blackmarket of Useful Knowledge and Non-Knowledge', *31: Das Magazin des Instituts für Theorie der Gestaltung und Kunst Zürich*, 8/9: 11–18.

Deck, J. and Sieburg, A. (2008), *Paradoxien des Zuschauens: Die Rolle des Publikums im zeitgenössischen Theater*, Bielefeld, transcript.

Derrida, J. (1979), 'The Parergon', *October*, 9: 3–41 (trans. C. Owens).

Deutschlandradio (2008), 'Dahin gehen, wo es weh tut: Matthias Lilienthal und sein Realo-Theater "X-Wohnungen"', *deutschlandradio*, 5 June [http://www.deutschlandradiokultur.de/dahin-gehen-wo-es-weh-tut.1013.de.html?dram:article_id=168003; accessed 30 October 2014].

De Waal, A. (2015), 'Staging Wounded Soldiers: The Affects and Effects of Post-Traumatic Theatre', *Performance Paradigm*, 11: 16–31.

Diederichsen, D. (2012), 'Der Imperativ des Authentischen', *polar – Politik|Theorie|Alltag*, 13: Aufstand [http://www.polar-zeitschrift.de/polar_13.php?id=615#615; accessed 20 November 2014].

Dovey, J. (2000), *Freakshow: First Person Media and Factual Television*, London: Pluto Press.

Draeger, V. (2006), 'Frei sein wie ein Wald: *Meine Melodie* eröffnete Stückreihe um Migration', *Metropol*, 11 January: 13.

Dreysse, M. (2004), 'Spezialisten in eigener Sache', *Forum Modernes Theater*, 19 (1): 27–42.

Dreysse, M. and Malzacher, F. (eds) (2007), *Experten des Alltags: Das Theater von Rimini Protokoll*, Berlin: Alexander Verlag.

Dreysse, M. and Malzacher, F. (eds) (2008) *Experts of the Everyday: The Theatre of Rimini Protokoll*, Berlin: Alexander Verlag.

Dürr, A. (2008), 'Dokumentar-Theater: Das Unfassbare fassen', 5 July [http://www.spiegel.de/kultur/gesellschaft/dokumentar-theater-das-unfassbare-fassen-a-563905.html; accessed 19 May 2015].

Eagleton, T. (2000), *The Idea of Culture*, Oxford: Blackwell.

Edgar, D. (2008), 'Doc and Dram', *The Guardian*, 28 September [http://www.theguardian.com/stage/2008/sep/27/theatre.davidedgar].

Eiermann, A. (2012), 'Welcher Wal? Auf der Suche nach einer Metapher für die Arbeit von Rimini Protokoll und ihrer Bedeutung für die Angewandte Theaterwissenschaft', in A. Matzke (ed.), *Das Buch von der angewandten Theaterwissenschaft*, Berlin: Alexander Verlag, 248–79.

Emcke, C. (2012), 'Theater der Themen und Formate', in K. Hehmeyer and M. Pees (eds), *Import Export: Arbeitsbuch zum HAU Berlin*, Berlin: Theater der Zeit, 6–7.

Emmott, C. and Alexander, M. (2015), 'Schemata', in P. Hühn, J. C. Meister, J. Pier and W. Schmid (eds), *The Living Handbook of Narratology*, Hamburg: Hamburg University [http://www.lhn.uni-hamburg.de/article/schemata; accessed 5 May 2015].

Ernst, W. (2000), 'The Concept of the Original in the Age of the Virtual World', in R. Mißelbeck and M. Turck (eds), *Video Arts in the Museum. Restoration and Preservation. New Methods of Presentation. The Idea of the Original*, Cologne: Museum Ludwig.

Erven, E. van (2001), *Community Theatre: Global Perspectives*, London: Routledge.

European Commission (n.d.) 'European Capitals of Culture' [http://ec.europa.eu/programmes/creative-europe/actions/capitals-culture_en.htm; accessed 25 June 2015].

Favorini, A. (1994a), 'Introduction: After the Fact. Theater and the Documentary Impulse', in A. Favorini (ed.), *Voicings: Ten Plays from the Documentary Theater*, Hopewell, NJ: Ecco Press, vi–xxxiv.

Favorini, A. (1994b), 'Introduction to *In Spite of Everything! Historical Revue of the Years 1914 to 1919 in Twenty-Four Scenes with Intermittent Film*', in A. Favorini (ed.), *Voicings: Ten Plays from the Documentary Theater*, Hopewell, NJ: Ecco Press, 1.

Festjens, T. and Martens, G. (2015), 'Chronik des angekündigten Untergangs einer Fluggesellschaft: *Sabenation. Go home & follow the news*', in J. Birgfeld, U. Garde and M. Mumford (eds), *Rimini Protokoll Close-Up: Lektüren*, Hannover: Wehrhahn, 128–47.

Fischer-Lichte, E. (2006), 'Perzeptive Multistabilität und ästhetische Wahrnehmung', in E. Fischer-Lichte, B. Gronau, S. Schouten and C. Weiler (eds), *Wege der Wahrnehmung: Authentizität, Reflexivität und Aufmerksamkeit im zeitgenössischen Theater*, Berlin: Theater der Zeit, 129–39.

Fischer-Lichte, E. (2007), 'Theatralität und Inszenierung', in E. Fischer-Lichte, C. Horn, I. Pflug and M. Warstat (eds), *Inszenierung von Authentizität*, Tübingen: A. Francke, 9–28.

Fischer-Lichte, E. (2008), 'Reality and Fiction in Contemporary Theatre', *Theatre Research International*, 33 (1): 84–96.

Fischer-Lichte, E. (2014), 'Introduction: Interweaving Performance Cultures – Re-thinking 'Intercultural Theatre': Toward an Experience and Theory of Performance beyond Postcolonialism', in E. Fischer-Lichte, T. Jost and S. I. Jain (eds), *The Politics of Interweaving Performance Cultures: Beyond Postcolonialism*, New York: Routledge, 1–21.

Fischer-Lichte, E., Horn, C., Pflug, I. and Warstat, M. (eds) (2007), *Inszenierung von Authentizität*, Tübingen: A. Francke.

Fitzel, T. (2004), *Audio Recordings for Radio SWR2*, unpublished.

Forrest, T. (2008), 'Mobilizing the Public Sphere: Schlingensief's Reality Theatre', *Contemporary Theatre Review*, 18 (1): 90–8.

Forrest, T. and Scheer, A. (2010), *Christoph Schlingensief: Art without Borders*, Bristol: Intellect.

Forsyth, A. (2009), 'Performing Trauma: Race Riots and Beyond in the Work of Anna Deavere Smith', in A. Forsyth and C. Megson (eds), *Get Real: Documentary Theatre Past and Present*, Basingstoke: Palgrave Macmillan, 140–50.

Forsyth, A. and Megson, C. (eds) (2009), *Get Real: Documentary Theatre Past and Present*, Basingstoke: Palgrave Macmillan.

Freeman, M. and Brockmeier, J. (2001), 'Narrative Integrity, Autobiographical Identity and the Meaning of the "Good Life"', in J. Brockmeier and D. Carbaugh (eds), *Narrative and Identity: Studies in Autobiography, Self and Culture*, Amsterdam: John Benjamins, 75–99.

Fuchs, E. (1985), 'Presence and the Revenge of Writing: Re-thinking Theatre after Derrida', *Performing Arts Journal*, 9 (2/3): 163–73.

Funk, W., Gross, F. and Huber, I. (2012), 'Exploring the Empty Plinth: The Aesthetics of Authenticity', in W. Funk, F. Gross and I. Huber (eds), *The Aesthetics of Authenticity: Medial Constructions of the Real*, Bielefeld, transcript: 9–21.

Garde, U. (2010a), 'Interview with Helgard Haug', 18 September, Berlin, unpublished.

Garde, U. (2010b), 'Interview mit Madhusree Mukerjee', 29 September, Sydney, unpublished.

Garde, U. (2011), 'Spotlight on the Audience: Collective Creativity in Recent Documentary and Reality Theatre from Australia and Germany', in G. Fischer and F. Vaßen (eds), *Collective Creativity: Collaborative Work in the Sciences, Literature and the Arts*, Amsterdam: Rodopi, 313–28.

Garde, U. (2012), 'Interview with Kirsten Hehmeyer', 11 July, Berlin, unpublished.

Garde, U. (2013a), 'Destabilising Notions of the Unfamiliar in Australian Documentary Theatre: version 1.0's *CMI* (*A Certain Maritime Incident*)', *Portal: Journal of Multidisciplinary International Studies*, 10 (1) [http://epress.lib.uts.edu.au/journals/index.php/portal/article/view/2450/3392; accessed 12 March 2013].

Garde, U. (2013b), 'Reality and Realism in Contemporary German Theatre Performances', in D. Birke and S. Butter (eds), *Realisms in Contemporary Culture: Theories, Politics and Medial Configurations*, Berlin: De Gruyter, 178–94.

Garde, U. (2013c) 'Interview with Arved Schultze', 29 June, Sydney, unpublished.

Garde, U. (2015), 'Ein Spiel mit der Stadt. Die spielerische Durchbrechung von Schemata in *100% Melbourne*', in J. Birgfeld, U. Garde and M. Mumford (eds), *Rimini Protokoll Close-Up: Lektüren*, Hannover: Wehrhahn, 254–77.

Garde, U. and Mumford, M. (2010), 'Interview with Hannah Hurtzig', 10 August, Berlin, unpublished.

Garde, U. and Mumford, M. (2013), 'Postdramatic Reality Theatre and Productive Insecurity: Destabilising Encounters with the Unfamiliar in Theatre from Sydney and Berlin', in J. Carroll, S. Giles and K. Jürs-Munby (eds), *Postdramatic Theatre and the Political: International Perspectives on Contemporary Performance*, London: Methuen, 147–64.

Garde, U., Mumford, M. and Wake, C. (2010), 'A Short History of Verbatim Theatre', in P. Brown (ed.), *Verbatim: Staging Memory and Community*, Sydney: Currency Press, 9–17.

Gardner, C. (2014), 'The Losey–Moscow Connection: Experimental Soviet Theatre and the Living Newspaper', *New Theatre Quarterly*, 3: 249–68.

Geisler, S. (2010), 'Auferstanden aus Vorurteilen', *Berliner Morgenpost*, 27 October [http://www.morgenpost.de/printarchiv/berlin/article1433978/Auferstanden-aus-Vorurteilen.html; accessed 9 July 2013].

Glauner, M. (2005), 'Und das Telefon sagt Du', *Der Freitag*, 15 April.

Glauner, M. (2012), 'Kurz vor Schluss: Matthias Lilienthal', *zitty*, 9 January [http://www.zitty.de/matthias-lilienthal.html; accessed 25 January 2014].

Goebbels, H. (2012) *Theater der Abwesenheit*, Berlin: Theater der Zeit.

Goethe-Institut Max Mueller Bhavan Kolkata website (n.d.) Archive of Events [http://www.goethe.de/ins/in/en/bag/acv.cfm?fuseaction=events. detail&event_id=4048257; accessed 3 March 2015].

Graton, E. (2007a), 'Einmal Wissen, bitte', *Zuender. Zeit Online*, 8 March [http://zuender.zeit.de/2007/11/mobile-academy-02; accessed 28 June 2015].

Graton, E. (2007b), 'Neue Orte des Lernens erfinden', interview with Hannah Hurtzig, *Zuender. Zeit Online* [http://zuender.zeit.de/2007/11/interview-hanna-hurtzig; accessed 25 June 2015].

Grehan, H. (2009), *Performance, Ethics and Spectatorship in a Global Age*, New York: Palgrave Macmillan.

Griffiths, G. (2006), 'The Myth of Authenticity', in B. Ashcroft, G. Griffiths and H. Tiffin (eds), *The Post-Colonial Studies Reader*, London: Routledge, 165–8.

Gronau, B. (2006), 'Wege zu einer neuen Authentizität? Strategien der Realitätskonstruktion, a discussion with Dirk Cieslak, Annemarie M. Matzke, Arved Schultze and Daniel Wetzel', in E. Fischer-Lichte, B. Gronau, S. Schouten and C. Weiler (eds), *Wege der Wahrnehmung: Authentizität, Reflexivität und Aufmerksamkeit im zeitgenössischen Theater*, Berlin: Theater der Zeit, 14–27.

Gronau, B., Hochleichter, C. and Hurtzig, H. (2006), 'Schwarzmarkt für nützliches Wissen und Nicht-Wissen. Eine Installation von Hannah Hurtzig', *Dramaturgie. Zeitschrift der Dramaturgischen Gesellschaft*, 1: 7–11 [http://www.dramaturgische-gesellschaft.de/assets/Uploads/dramaturgie/dramaturgie-2006-01.pdf; accessed 28 June 2015].

Grotowski, J. (1976), *Towards a Poor Theatre*, London: Eyre Methuen.

Gudrun Herrbold website [http://www.gudrunherrbold.de; accessed 1 June 2015].

Gutjahr, O. (2010), 'Interkulturalität als Forschungsparadigma der Literaturwissenschaft: Von den Theoriedebatten zur Analyse kultureller Tiefensemantiken', in D. Heimböckel, I. Honnef-Becker, G. Mein and H. Sieburg (eds), *Zwischen Provokation und Usurpation: Interkulturalität als (un)vollendetes Projekt der Literatur- und Sprachwissenschaften*, München: Fink, 17–39.

Haas, B. (2007), *Plädoyer für ein dramatisches Drama*, Wien: Passagen.

Habermas, J. (1987), *The Philosophical Discourse of Modernity: Twelve Lectures*, Cambridge: Polity Press.

Hammond, W. and Steward, D. (eds) (2008), *Verbatim Verbatim: Contemporary Documentary Theatre*, London: Oberon Books.

Hare, D. and Stafford-Clark, M. (2008), 'David Hare and Max Stafford-Clark', in W. Hammond and D. Steward (eds), *Verbatim Verbatim: Contemporary Documentary Theatre*, London: Oberon Books, 45–75.

HAU (2004), '*X-Wohnungen* Berlin 2004 – Theater in privaten Räumen', HAU website [http://www.archiv.hebbel-am-ufer.de/archiv_de/kuenstler/ kuenstler_1868.html; accessed 25 January 2013].

HAU (2008), '*X-Wohnungen* Neukölln', HAU website [http://www.archiv. hebbel-am-ufer.de/archiv_de/kuenstler/kuenstler_12762.html; accessed 25 January 2013].

Hauck, M. (2008), 'So nett soll Berlin sein?', *Frankfurter Allgemeine Sonntagszeitung*, 3 February [http://www.rimini-protokoll.de/website/de/ article_2677.html; accessed 25 January 2013].

Heddon, D. (2008), *Autobiography and Performance*, Basingstoke: Palgrave Macmillan.

Hehmeyer, K. and Pees, M. (eds) (2012), *Import Export: Arbeitsbuch zum HAU Berlin*, Berlin: Theater der Zeit.

Hill, A. (2005), *Reality TV: Audiences and Popular Factual Television*, London: Routledge.

Hintze, D. (2014), 'Die Bürgerbühne erobert das Stadttheater. Nachrichten aus der Wirklichkeit', *Neue Zürcher Zeitung*, 1 September [www.nzz.ch/ feuilleton/buehne/nachrichten-aus-der-wirklichkeit-1.18374184; accessed 9 June 2015].

Irmer, T. (2006), 'A Search for New Realities: Documentary Theatre in Germany', *The Drama Review*, 50 (3): 16–28.

Iser, W. (1993), *The Fictive and the Imaginary: Charting Literary Anthropology*, Baltimore, MD: Johns Hopkins University Press.

Iser, W. (2006), 'Reception Theory', in W. Iser (ed.), *How to Do Theory*, Malden, MA: Blackwell, 57–69.

Jackson, S. (2013), 'Reality's Referents: Forms of the Real Across the Arts', in S. Forberg and M. Frandsen (eds), *Monsters of Reality: A Performance Festival on 'Dramaturgies of the Real'*, Oslo: Siri Forberg and Copenhagen: The Danish National School of Performing Arts – Continuing Education,

123–35 [http://www.teaterskolen-efteruddannelsen.dk/PDF/MOR-PublicationOnline.pdf].

Jürs-Munby, K. (2006), 'Introduction', in H.-T. Lehmann, *Postdramatic Theatre*, London: Routledge, 1–15.

Jürs-Munby, K., Carroll, J. and Giles, S. (eds) (2013), *Postdramatic Theatre and the Political: International Perspectives on Contemporary Performance*, London: Bloomsbury.

Kaegi, S. (2012), 'Mein HAU', *Theater heute*, 4: 28.

Kanak Attak website [http://www.kanak-attak.de/ka/about/manif_eng.html; accessed 28 June 2015].

Karschnia, A. (2007a), 'THEATeRReALITÄT: REALITY CHECK ON STAGE: Wirklichkeitsforschungen im zeitgenössischen Theater', in K. Tiedemann and F. M. Raddatz (eds), *Reality Strikes Back: Tage vor dem Bildersturm*, Berlin: Theater der Zeit, 146–59.

Karschnia, A. (2007b), '"Vom richtigen Leben." Interview with Lukas Matthaei and Josh Fox', in K. Tiedemann and F. M. Raddatz (eds), *Reality Strikes Back. Tage vor dem Bildersturm*, Berlin: Theater der Zeit, 175–89.

Kaup-Hasler, V. and Philipp, C. (2007), 'An Image of the Mass and of Collective Learning', conversation with Hannah Hurtzig [http://www.mobileacademy-berlin.com/englisch/bm_texte/interview.html; accessed 2 April 2015].

Kavka, M. (2008), *Reality Television, Affect and Intimacy: Reality Matters*, New York: Palgrave Macmillan.

Keim, K. (2010), 'Der Einbruch der Realität ins Spiel: Zur Synthese von Faktizität und Fiktionalität im zeitgenössischen semi-dokumentarischen Theater und den Kulturwissenschaften', in K. Tiedemann and F. M. Raddatz (eds), *Reality Strikes Back II: Tod der Repräsentation: Die Zukunft der Vorstellungskraft in einer globalisierten Welt*, Berlin: Theater der Zeit, 127–38.

Khuon, U. (2010), 'Theater als Forum der letzten Fragen', in W. Sting, N. Köhler, K. Hoffmann, W. Weiße and D. Grießbach (eds), *Irritation und Vermittlung: Theater in einer interkulturellen und multireligiösen Gesellschaft*, Berlin: LIT, 9–19.

Kirby, M. (1984), 'On Acting and Not-Acting', in G. Batcock and R. Nickas (eds), *The Art of Performance*, New York: Dalton, 97–117.

Kitamura, K. (2010), '"Recreating Chaos": Jeremy Deller's *The Battle of Orgreave*', in I. McCalman and P. A. Pickering (eds), *Historical Reenactment: From Realism to the Affective Turn*, Basingstoke: Palgrave Macmillan, 39–49.

Knaller, S. and Müller, H. (2005), 'Authentisch/Authentizität', in K. Barck,
    M. Fontius, D. Schlenstedt, D. Steinwachs and F. Wolfzettel (eds), *Historisches
    Wörterbuch der äesthetischen Grundbegriffe*, Stuttgart: Metzler, 40–65.

Knowles, R. (2010), *Theatre and Interculturalism*, Basingstoke: Palgrave
    Macmillan.

Kolesch, D. (2005), 'Natürlichkeit', in E. Fischer-Lichte, D. Kolesch and M.
    Warstat (eds), *Metzler Lexikon Theatertheorie*, Stuttgart: Metzler, 220–3.

Kolesch, D. (2012), 'Austauschverhältnisse: Die Geburt des modernen Subjekts
    auf dem Theater', in F. Kreuder, M. Bachmann, J. Pfahl and D. Volz (eds),
    *Theater und Subjektkonstitution: Theatrale Praktiken zwischen Affirmation
    und Subversion*, Bielefeld, transcript: 21–39.

Kosnick, K. (2009), 'Conflicting Mobilities: Cultural Diversity and City
    Branding in Berlin', in S. Donald, E. Kofman and C. Kevin (eds), *Branding
    Cities: Cosmopolitanism, Parochialism, and Social Change*, New York:
    Routledge, 28–41.

Krampnitz, D. (2005), 'Auf indischer Schnitzeljagd durch Berlin-Kreuzberg',
    Welt am Sonntag, 3 April [http://www.welt.de/print-wams/article126068/
    Auf-indischer-Schnitzeljagd-durch-Berlin-Kreuzberg.html; accessed 23
    March 2014].

Kranz, O. (2004), 'Laube, Pieper, Hoffnung. Nicht ohne meinen Gartenzwerg:
    Roland Brus modelt eine Berliner Schreberkolonie zur Bühne um', *Die
    Welt*, 11 August [www.welt.de/print-welt/article333326/Laube-Pieper-
    Hoffnung.html; accessed 19 May 2015].

Krottenthaler, K. (2004), *Rohschnitte aus X-Wohnungen Spezial
    (Videodokumentation)*, Berlin: HAU.

Langellier, K. M. (2001), 'Personal Narrative', in M. Jolly (ed.), *Encyclopedia of
    Life Writing: Autobiographical and Biographical Forms*, London: Routledge,
    699–701.

Langhoff, S. (2009), 'Beyond Belonging 2009 Festival Programm', *Die
    Tageszeitung* [http://www.kanak-attak.de/ka/down/pdf/beyondbelonging_
    tazBeilage.pdf; accessed 20 May 2013].

Laudenbach, P. (2004), 'Die Reichtumsfalle', *Der Tagesspiegel*, 6 February
    [http://www.tagesspiegel.de/kultur/die-reichtumsfalle/488164.html;
    accessed 3 March 2014].

Laudenbach, P. (2010a), 'Die Globalisierung steht an der Pforte', *Süddeutsche
    Zeitung*, 24 August.

Laudenbach, P. (2010b), 'Wir können auch anders: Künstler machen mit
    Kreuzberger Schülern richtig Theater', *Süddeutsche Zeitung*, 3 July: 14.

Laudenbach, P. (2012), 'Matthias Lilienthals Intendanz am HAU endet 2012', *Tip Berlin*, 23 January 2012 [http://www.tip-berlin.de/kultur-und-freizeit-theater-und-buehne/fortsetzung-matthias-lilienthals-intendanz-am-hau-endet-2012; accessed 12 July 2014].

Leggewie, C. and Zifonun, D. (2010), 'Was heißt Interkulturalität?', *Zeitschrift für interkulturelle Germanistik*, 1: 12–31.

Lehmann, H.-T. (1999), *Postdramatisches Theater*, Frankfurt am Main: Verlag der Autoren.

Lehmann, H.-T. (2006), *Postdramatic Theatre*, London: Routledge.

Lehmann, H.-T. (2008), 'Theory in Theatre? Observations on an Old Question', in M. Dreysse and F. Malzacher (eds), *Experts of the Everyday: The Theatre of Rimini Protokoll*, Berlin: Alexander Verlag, 152–67.

Lehmann, H.-T. (2012), 'Impromptu', in K. Hehmeyer and M. Pees (eds), *Import Export: Arbeitsbuch zum HAU Berlin*, Berlin: Theater der Zeit, 171.

Lei, D. (2011), 'Interruption, Intervention, Interculturalism: Robert Wilson's HIT Productions in Taiwan', *Theatre Journal*, 63 (4): 571–86.

Lerner, M. (n.d.) 'Dr. Mark Lerner: Productions' [http://www.realitytheatreproductions.com/IN_SESSION/REALITY_THEATRE_PRODUCTIONS.html#!about/c22ca; accessed 30 June 2015].

Lethen, H. (1996), 'Versionen des Authentischen: Sechs Gemeinplätze', in H. Böhme and K. R. Scherpe (eds), *Literatur- und Kulturwissenschaften: Positionen, Theorien, Modelle*, Reinbek: Rowohlt, 205–31.

Leysen, F. (2015), 'Embracing the Elusive. Or, the Necessity of the Superfluous'. Closing Keynote for the Australian Theatre Forum, 23 January [http://www.australiantheatreforum.com.au/atf-2015/documentation/transcripts/closing-keynote-frie-leysen/; accessed 4 April 2015].

Lilienthal, M. (2003), 'Das voyeuristische Erschrecken: Zu Idee und Konzept von *X Wohnungen*', in A. Schultze and S. Wurster (eds), *X Wohnungen, Duisburg: Theater in privaten Räumen*, Berlin: Alexander Verlag, 9–12.

Lilienthal, M. (2015), 'Liebes Publikum / Dear Audience' [http://www.muenchner-kammerspiele.de/; accessed 1 August 2015].

Lo, J. (2014), 'Dancing for the Dead', in E. Fischer-Lichte, T. Jost and S. I. Jain (eds), *The Politics of Interweaving Performance Cultures: Beyond Postcolonialism*, New York: Routledge, 119–37.

Lo, J. and Gilbert, H. (2002), 'Toward a Topography of Cross-Cultural Theatre Praxis', *The Drama Review*, 46 (3): 31–53.

Lunau, K. (2011), 'Mimikry und verwandte Phänomene in Natur und Kultur: Definitionen und Begriffe in der Biologie und in den Kulturwissenschaften', in A.-R. Meyer and S. Sielke (eds), *Verschleierungstaktiken: Strategien von eingeschränkter Sichtbarkeit, Tarnung und Täuschung in Natur und Kultur*, Frankfurt am Main: Lang, 193–224.

Macras, C. (2012), 'Mein HAU', *Theater heute*, 4: 27.

Malzacher, F. (2005), 'Das Flirten der Servicegesellschaft', *Frankfurter Rundschau*, 5 April.

Malzacher, F. (2007), 'Dramaturgien der Fürsorge und der Verunsicherung', in M. Dreysse and F. Malzacher (eds), *Experten des Alltags. Das Theater von Rimini Protokoll*, Berlin: Alexander Verlag, 14–43.

Malzacher, F. (2008), 'Dramaturgies of Care and Insecurity: The Dramaturgy of Rimini Protokoll', in M. Dreysse and F. Malzacher (eds), *Experts of the Everyday: The Theatre of Rimini Protokoll*, Berlin: Alexander Verlag, 14–43.

Mand, B. (2014), 'Erlebnisraum als Performance', interview with Matthias Lilienthal, *Morgenweb*, 29 January [http://www.morgenweb.de/nachrichten/kultur/kultur-allgemein/erlebnisraum-als-performance-1.1379872; accessed 6 August 2015].

Mansmann, N. (2004), '*X Wohnungen* Berlin 2004 – Theater in privaten Räumen', *Brainstorms: Berlins bessere Seiten* [http://www.brainstorms42.de/artikel/x-wohnungen.php; accessed 7 July 2013].

Martin, C. (2006), 'Bodies of Evidence', *The Drama Review*, 50 (3): 8–15.

Martin, C. (2010), 'Introduction: Dramaturgy of the Real', in C. Martin (ed.), *Dramaturgy of the Real on the World Stage*, Basingstoke: Palgrave Macmillan, 1–26.

Martin, C. (2013), *Theatre of the Real*, Basingstoke: Palgrave Macmillan.

matthaei-und-konsorten website (2006) [matthaei-und-konsorten.de/en; accessed 23 May 2015].

Matzke, A. (2006), 'Von echten Menschen und wahren Performern', in E. Fischer-Lichte, B. Gronau, S. Schouten and C. Weiler (eds), *Wege der Wahrnehmung: Authentizität, Reflexivität und Aufmerksamkeit im zeitgenössischen Theater*, Berlin: Theater der Zeit, 39–47.

Matzke, A. (2014), 'Independent Theatre in Germany: In Search of New Forms of Theatre', February, Goethe-Institut e. V., Internet-Redaktion (ed.), trans. J. Uhlaner, February [https://www.goethe.de/en/kul/tut/gen/tup/20376514.html; accessed 15 October 2014].

McBeth, S. (1993), 'Myths of Objectivity and the Collaborative Process in Life History Research', in C. B. Brettell (ed.), *When They Read what We Write: The Politics of Ethnography*, Westport, CT: Bergin & Garvey, 145–62.

Meierhenrich, D. (2005), 'Spaziergang im Denkschritt', *Berliner Zeitung*, 5 April.

Meierhenrich, D. (2008), '100 Jahre Hebbel: Rimini Protokoll und Matthias von Hartz feiern mit: Camouflage des Theaters', *Berliner Zeitung*, 4 February [http://www.berliner-zeitung.de/archiv/100-jahre-hebbel–rimini-protokoll-und-matthias-von-hartz-feiern-mit-camouflage-des-theaters,10810590,10536632.html; accessed 2 August 2014].

Meinecke, T. and Gurk, C. (2012), 'Extraraum', in K. Hehmeyer and M. Pees (eds), *Import Export: Arbeitsbuch zum HAU Berlin*, Berlin: Theater der Zeit, 72–9.

Metzger, S. (2010), *Theater und Fiktion: Spielräume des Fiktiven in Inszenierungen der Gegenwart*, Bielefeld, transcript.

Mobile Academy website [http://www.mobileacademy-berlin.com/; accessed 3 June 2015].

Morris, P. (2003), *Realism: The New Critical Idiom*, London: Routledge.

Müller, K. B. (2004), 'Die Kunst des Teetrinkens', *Die Tageszeitung*, 2 June [http://www.taz.de/1/archiv/print-archiv/printressorts/digi-artikel/?ressort=ku&dig=2004%2F06%2F02%2Fa0269&cHash=9ca4495c37; accessed 30 October 2014].

Müller, K. B. (2008a), 'Deutsch kaputt: Tamer Yigit und Branka Prlic bringen mit ihrem *Warngedicht* im HAU ein Stück über vier migrantische Jugendliche auf die Bühne', *Die Tageszeitung*, 4 October [https://www.taz.de:443/1/archiv/print-archiv/printressorts/digi-...?ressort=ku&dig=2008%2F10%2F04%Fa0226&cHash=abOfadf31a&type=98; accessed 4 September 2014].

Müller, K. B. (2008b), 'Durch ein fremdes Leben', *Die Tageszeitung*, 2 January [www.taz.de/!10326/; accessed 5 February 2012].

Mumford, M. (2000), 'Brecht on Acting for the 21st Century: Interrogating and Re-inscribing the Fixed?', *Communications from the International Brecht Society*, 29 (1/2): 44–9.

Mumford, M. (2001), 'Gestic Masks in Brecht's Theatre: A Testimony to the Contradictions and Parameters of a Realist Aesthetic', *The Brecht Yearbook*, 26: 143–71.

Mumford, M. (2003), 'Verfremdung', in D. Kennedy (ed.), *The Oxford Encyclopedia of Theatre and Performance*, Vol. 2, Oxford: Oxford University Press, 1404–5.

Mumford, M. (2009), *Bertolt Brecht*, London: Routledge.

Mumford, M. (2010a), *Mr Dağaçar and the Golden Tectonics of Trash*, Rehearsal Notes, 6 October, Podewil, Berlin, unpublished.

Mumford, M. (2010b), *Post-Rehearsal Conversation with Sebastian Brünger*, Podewil, Berlin, 6 October, unpublished.

Mumford, M. (2011), 'Fluid Collectives of Friendly Strangers: The Creative Politics of Difference in the Reality Theatre of Rimini Protokoll and Urban Theatre Projects', in G. Fischer and F. Vaßen (eds), *Collective Creativity: Collaborative Work in the Sciences, Literature and the Arts*, Amsterdam: Rodopi, 329–43.

Mumford, M. (2013), 'Rimini Protokoll's Reality Theatre and Intercultural Encounter: Towards an Ethical Art of Partial Proximity', *Contemporary Theatre Review*, 23 (2): 153–65.

Mumford, M. (2014), 'Towards Transculturality in Reality Theatre from Berlin and Sydney: A Study of the Nomad in Rimini Protokoll's *Cargo Sofia-X* and the "Spiritual Medium" in *Fast Cars and Tractor Engines* by Urban Theatre Projects', in A. Corkhill and A. Lewis (eds), *Intercultural Encounters in German Studies*, St. Ingbert: Röhrig, 181–96.

Mumford, M. (2015), '*100% City* and Popular Factual Television: A New Game Plan for Managing Proximity to People?', in J. Birgfeld, U. Garde and M. Mumford (eds), *Rimini Protokoll Close-Up: Lektüren*, Hannover: Wehrhahn, 278–301.

Mündel, B. and Mackert, J. (2010), 'Das Prinzip für die ganze Gesellschaft: Ein Beitrag zur Debatte Theater in der Migrationsgesellschaft', *Theater heute*, 43: 37–43.

Nichols, B. (1991), *Representing Reality: Issues and Concepts in Documentary*, Bloomington, IN: Indiana University Press.

Norris, C. (1991), *Deconstruction: Theory and Practice*, London: Routledge.

OED (2000), *Oxford English Dictionary Online*, Oxford: Oxford University Press [http://www.oed.com; accessed 4 March 2015].

Orvell, M. (1989), *The Real Thing: Imitation and Authenticity in American Culture*, Chapel Hill, NC: University of North Carolina Press.

Oskamp, K. (2004), 'Warten mit Konzept', *Berliner Zeitung*, 7 June [http://www.berliner-zeitung.de/archiv/warten-mit-konzept,10810590,10182794.html; accessed 25 January 2015].

Paget, D. (1987), 'Verbatim Theatre: Oral History and Documentary Techniques', *New Theatre Quarterly*, 3 (12): 317–36.

Paget, D. (1990), *True Stories? Documentary Drama on Radio, Screen and Stage*, Manchester: Manchester University Press.

Paget, D. (2007), 'Acting with Facts: Actors Performing the Real in British Theatre and Television Since 1990. A Preliminary Report on a New Research Project', *Studies in Documentary Film*, 1: 165–76.

Paget, D. (2009), 'The "Broken Tradition" of Documentary Theatre and its Continued Powers of Endurance', in A. Forsyth and C. Megson (eds), *Get Real: Documentary Theatre Past and Present*, Basingstoke: Palgrave Macmillan, 224–38.

Pailer, G. and Schößler, F. (2011), *GeschlechterSpielRäume: Dramatik, Theater, Performance und Gender*, Amsterdam: Rodopi.

Pauls, A. (2010), 'Kidnapping Reality: An Interview with Vivi Tellas', in C. Martin (ed.), *Dramaturgy of the Real on the World Stage*, Basingstoke: Palgrave Macmillan, 246–58.

Pavis, P. (1990), 'Interculturalism in Contemporary Mise en Scène: The Image of *India* in *The Mahabharata* and the *Indiade*', in E. Fischer-Lichte, J. Riley and M. Gissenwehrer (eds), *The Dramatic Touch of Difference: Theatre, Own and Foreign*, Tübingen: Gunter Narr, 52–72.

Pavis, P. (1992), *Theatre at the Crossroads of Culture*, London: Routledge.

Peters, N. (2011), 'Die Umkehrung des eigenen Blicks: Beobachtungen und Bekundungen aus dem Blickwinkel Berliner Theater', in W. Schneider (ed.), *Theater und Migration: Herausforderungen für Kulturpolitik und Theaterpraxis*, Bielefeld, transcript: 169–76.

Pewny, K. (2011), *Das Drama der Prekären: Über die Wiederkehr der Ethik in Theater und Performance*, Bielefeld, transcript.

Pilz, D. (2006) 'Organisiertes Chaos', 8 December [http://www.nzz.ch/aktuell/ startseite/articleEPVSS-1.81497; accessed 25 January 2015].

Pinto, Alexander (2012), 'Stadt / Land / Theater – Tendenzen regionaler Entwicklung', *Hildesheimer Thesen*, 4 [http://www.nachtkritik.de/index. php?option=com_content&view=article&id=7453:hildesheimer-thesen-iv-stadtlandtheater-tendenzen-regionaler-entwicklung&catid=669:hildeshei mer-thesen&Itemid=60; accessed 1 April 2014].

Piscator, E. (1980), *The Political Theatre*, London: Eyre Methuen.

Puchner, M. (2006), *Poetry of the Revolution: Marx, Manifestos, and the Avant-Gardes*, Princeton, NJ: Princeton University Press.

Raddatz, F. M. (2007), 'Boris Groys im Gespräch. Zur Situation des Geschmacks in unserer Zeit oder Wie der Schauspieler zum Ready-made wird', in K. Tiedemann and F. M. Raddatz (eds), *Reality Strikes Back: Tage vor dem Bildersturm*, Berlin: Theater der Zeit, 21–35.

Raddatz, F. M. (2008), 'Hau 1, 2, 3 – Spielstätten sozialer Plastik: Matthias Lilienthal im Gespräch', *Theater der Zeit*, 2: 16–20.

Raddatz, F. M. (2010), 'Authentische Rezepte für ein unvergessliches Morgen: Der Wunsch nach dem Echten in Zeiten globalen Wandels', in K. Tiedemann and F. M. Raddatz (eds), *Reality Strikes Back II: Tod der Repräsentation: Die Zukunft der Vorstellungskraft in einer globalisierten Welt*, Berlin: Theater der Zeit, 139–62.

Raddatz, F. M. (2011), 'Die Vertreibung der Dichtung durch das Authentische', in A. Pelka and S. Tigges (eds), *Das Drama nach dem Drama. Verwandlungen dramatischer Formen in Deutschland seit 1945*, Bielefeld, transcript: 373–84.

Raddatz, F. M. (2014a), 'Das Ende der Versöhnung: Schuld, Schmerz und Widersprüche sicht- und fühlbar zu machen ist die Zukunftsaufgabe des Theaters, ein Gespräch mit dem Theaterdenker Bernd Stegemann', *Theater der Zeit*, 4: 7–8.

Raddatz, F. M. (2014b), 'Erobert Euer Grab! Die Zukunft des Theaters nach der Rückkehr aus der Zukunft', *Lettre International*, 26 (104): 84–91.

Rancière, J. (2009), *The Emancipated Spectator*, London: Verso.

RATTEN 07 website [www.ratten07.de/; accessed 19 May 2015].

Rau, M. (2013), 'Genau so: Realitätseffekte in Die letzten Tage des Ceauşescus', in U. Daur (ed.), *Authentizität und Wiederholung: Künstlerischen und kulturelle Manifestationen eines Paradoxes*, Bielefeld, transcript: 185–98.

Regus, C. (2009), *Interkulturelles Theater zu Beginn des 21. Jahrhunderts: Ästhetik – Politik – Postkolonialismus*, Bielefeld, transcript.

Reinelt, J. (2006), 'Toward a Poetics of Theatre and Public Events: In the Case of Stephen Lawrence', *The Drama Review*, 50 (3): 69–87.

Reinelt, J. (2009), 'The Promise of Documentary', in A. Forsyth and C. Megson (eds), *Get Real: Documentary Theatre Past and Present*, Basingstoke: Palgrave Macmillan, 6–23.

Ridout, N. (2013), *Passionate Amateurs: Theatre, Communism and Love*, Ann Arbor, MI: University of Michigan Press.

Rimini Protokoll (2005), *Call Cutta*, unpublished script.

Rimini Protokoll (2008), *100% Berlin*. Program Notes. Berlin: HAU.

Rimini Protokoll (2010), *Mr Dağaçar and the Golden Tectonics of Trash*, 14 October, unpublished script.

Rimini Protokoll (2012a), *ABCD. Saarbrücker Poetikdozentur für Dramatik*, ed. J. Birgfeld with an afterword by J. Birgfeld. Berlin: Theater der Zeit.

Rimini Protokoll (2012b), *100% Melbourne*, May, unpublished script.

Rimini Protokoll (2013), *Call Cutta*. Video in English with German Subtitles. Vimeo, uploaded 27 March [https://vimeo.com/62794689; accessed 24 July 2013].

Rimini Protokoll website (n.d.), 'Call Cutta: Mobile Phone Theatre' [http://www.rimini-protokoll.de/website/en/project_143.html; accessed 12 July 2010].

Rimini Protokoll website [www.rimini-protokoll.de; accessed 12 July 2010].

Roselt, J. (2006), 'Die Arbeit am Nicht-Perfekten', in E. Fischer-Lichte, B. Gronau, S. Schouten and C. Weiler (eds), *Wege der Wahrnehmung*, Berlin: Theater der Zeit, 28–38.

Roselt, J. (2008), *Phänomenologie des Theaters*, Paderborn: Wilhelm Fink.

Roselt, J. (2012), 'Hildesheimer Thesen III – Was die unfreiwillige Gemeinsamkeit zwischen Stadttheater und Freier Szene bringen kann: Nachahmung ist im Theater kein Frevel', nachtkritik [http://www.nachtkritik.de/index.php?view=article&id=7426:hildesheimer-thesen-iii-&option=com_content&Itemid=84; accessed 14 August 2015].

Roselt, J. (2015), 'Rimini Protokoll and Bürgerbühne Theatre: Institutions, Challenges and Continuities', *Performance Paradigm*, 11: 76–87.

Roslyn Oades website [www.roslynoades.com; accessed 23 May 2015].

Ruesch, M. (2007a), '*Call Cutta* – bei Anruf Kunst', in A. Kotte (ed.), *Theater im Kasten. Rimini Protokoll – Castorfs Video – Beuys & Schlingensief – Lars von Trier*, Zürich: Chronos, 161–217.

Ruesch, M. (2007b), 'Interview mit Stefan Kaegi', in A. Kotte (ed.), *Theater im Kasten. Rimini Protokoll – Castorfs Video – Beuys & Schlingensief – Lars von Trier*, Zürich: Chronos, 331–4.

Rule, A. (2009), 'The Blackmarket', 26 July [http://blog.frieze.com/the_blackmarket/; accessed 28 June 2015].

Said, E. (1993), *Culture and Imperialism*, New York: Knopf.

Saldaña, J. (2005), *Ethnodrama: An Anthology of Reality Theatre*, Walnut Creek, CA: Rowman Altamira.

Salverson, J. (1996), 'Performing Emergency: Witnessing, Popular Theatre, and the Lie of the Literal', *Theatre Topics*, 6 (2): 181–91.

Schäfer, A. (2008), 'Luftschloss aus Stein', *Der Tagesspiegel*, 26 January [http://www.tagesspiegel.de/politik/geschichte/theaterhaus-luftschloss-aus-stein/1150176.html; accessed 6 March 2014].

Schaper, R. (2004), 'Der Faktor X', *Der Tagesspiegel*, 20 June [http://www.tagesspiegel.de/kultur/der-faktor-x/525034.html; accessed 7 July 2013].

Schechner, R. and Wolford, L. (eds) (1997), *The Grotowski Sourcebook*, Abingdon: Routledge.

Schipper, I. (2013), 'Staging Authenticity', in S. Forberg and M. Frandsen (eds), *Monsters of Reality: A Performance Festival on 'Dramaturgies of the Real'*, Oslo: Siri Forberg and Copenhagen: The Danish National School of Performing Arts – Continuing Education, 59–69 [http://www.teaterskolen-efteruddannelsen.dk/PDF/MOR-PublicationOnline.pdf].

Schlagenwerth, M. (2008), 'Gegen die Wand: Tamer Yigit and Branka Prlic inszenieren *Ein Warngedicht*, ein Stück über migrantisches Leben', *Berliner Zeitung*, 30 September [http://www.berliner-zeitung.de/archiv/tamer-yigit-und-branka-prlic-inszenieren--ein-warngedicht---ein-stueck-ueber-migrantisches-leben-gegen-die-wand,10810590,10589914.html; accessed 4 September 2014].

Schlagenwerth, M. (2010), 'Die fremde Nachbarschaft: Das "X-Schulen"-Projekt des HAU: 21 Künstler und 120 Jugendliche bespielen eine Kreuzberger Gesamtschule', *Berliner Zeitung*, 1 July [http://www.berliner-zeitung.de/archiv/das--x-schulen--projekt-des-hau--21-kuenstler-und-120-jugendliche-bespielen-eine-kreuzberger-gesamtschule-die-fremde-nachbarschaft,10810590,10726904.html; accessed 15 November 2014].

Schmidt, A. C. (2008), 'High-Speed-Flaneure wider Willen', *goon-magazin*, 17 June.

Schößler, F. (2013), *Drama und Theater nach 1989: Prekär, Interkulturell, Intermedial*, Hannover: Wehrhahn.

Schouten, S. (2011), *Sinnliches Spüren: Wahrnehmung und Erzeugung von Atmosphären im Theater*, Berlin: Theater der Zeit.

Schreiber, D. (2004), 'Sehnsucht nach Alltag: Die Realitätsspiele des Rimini Protokolls', *Theater der Zeit*, 3: 40–2.

Schuller, G. (2009), 'The Encyclopaedic Fragmentation of Knowledge as Theatre', interview with Hannah Hurtzig in Vienna on 18 May 2008, in G. Schuller (ed.), *The World as Flatland – Report 1: Designing Universal Knowledge*, Zurich: Lars Müller, 128–33.

Schultze, A. (2003), 'Theater und Realität: Die Inszenierung des Fremden', in A. Schultze and S. Wurster (eds), *X Wohnungen, Duisburg: Theater in privaten Räumen*, Berlin: Alexander Verlag, 13–19.

Schultze, A. (2005), 'Dramaturgie', *Zeitschrift der dramaturgischen Gesellschaft*, 2: 34.

Schütt, H.-D. (2008), 'Weltherrscher ohne Arbeit: Rimini Protokoll bot im HAU drei Abende lang *100% Berlin*', *Neues Deutschland*, 8 February [https://www.neues-deutschland.de/artikel/123629.weltherrscher-ohne-arbeit.html; accessed 15 March 2014].

Seidler, U. (2006), 'Sehen und Sagen', *Berliner Zeitung*, 3 April [http://www.berliner-zeitung.de/archiv/weltbedeutendes-theater-kann-so-einfach-sein--alvis-hermanis-gastierte-mit-seinen–lettischen-geschichten--im-hau-sehen-und-sagen,10810590,10375926.html; accessed 2 August 2014].

Sellar, T. (2014a), 'A Change Has Totally Taken Place', interview with Matthias Lilienthal, *Theater*, 44 (2): 72–9.

Sellar, T. (2014b), 'The Dramaturg as Globalist', in M. Romanska (ed.), *Routledge Companion to Dramaturgy*, New York: Routledge, 113–17.

Şenocak, Z. (2011), *Deutschsein. Eine Aufklärungsschrift*, Hamburg: Körberstiftung.

She She Pop website [http://www.sheshepop.de/en; accessed 15 January 2015].

Shields, D. (2010), *Reality Hunger: A Manifesto*, New York: Alfred Knopf.

Siegmund, G. (2008), 'The Art of Memory: Fiction as Seduction into Reality', in M. Dreysse and F. Malzacher (eds), *Experts of the Everyday: The Theatre of Rimini Protokoll*, trans. D. Belasco Rogers et al., Berlin: Alexander Verlag, 188–211.

Singer, W. (2014), 'Wie entsteht Kunst im Gehirn?', *Frankfurter Allgemeine Zeitung*, 11 September [http://www.faz.net/aktuell/wissen/hirnforschung-wie-entsteht-kunst-im-gehirn-13148167.html; accessed 12 September 2014].

Singleton, B. (2014), 'Performing Orientalist, Intercultural and Globalized Modernities: The Case of *Les Naufragés du Fol Espoir* by the Théâtre du Soleil', in E. Fischer-Lichte, T. Jost and S. I. Jain (eds), *The Politics of Interweaving Performance Cultures: Beyond Postcolonialism*, New York: Routledge, 77–95.

Slevogt, E. (2008), 'Volk oder nicht Volk', *nachtkritik*, 1 February [http://www.nachtkritik.de/index.php?option=com_content&view=article&id=974:100-prozent-berlin-100-berliner-und-rimini-protokoll-feiern-das-100jaehrige-hebbel-theater&catid=55:hau-berlin; accessed 2 August 2014].

Soans, R. (2008), 'Robin Soans', in W. Hammond and D. Steward (eds), *Verbatim Verbatim: Contemporary Documentary Theatre*, London: Oberon Books, 15–44.

Spohn, C. (ed.) (2006), *Zweiheimisch: Bikulturell leben in Deutschland*, Hamburg: Körber-Stiftung.

Stegemann, B. (2015), *Lob des Realismus*, Berlin: Theater der Zeit.

Straub, J. (2012), 'Introduction: The Paradoxes of Authenticity', in J. Straub (ed.), *Paradoxes of Authenticity: Studies on a Critical Concept*, Bielefeld, transcript: 9–19.

Terkessidis, M. (2010), *Interkultur*, Berlin: Suhrkamp.

The Grassmarket Project website [www.grassmarketproject.org/; accessed 20 May 2015].

Theater heute Redaktion (2012), 'Das Globalisierungsbarometer', interview with K. Hehmeyer and M. Lilienthal, *Theater heute*, 4: 24–6, 29–30.

Tiedemann, K. (2007), 'Vorwort', in K. Tiedemann and F. M. Raddatz (eds), *Reality Strikes Back. Tage vor dem Bildersturm. Eine Debatte zum Einbruch der Wirklichkeit in den Bühnenraum*, Berlin: Theater der Zeit, 6–9.

Tiedemann, K. and Raddatz, F. M. (eds) (2007), *Reality Strikes Back. Tage vor dem Bildersturm: Eine Debatte zum Einbruch der Wirklichkeit in den Bühenraum*, Berlin: Theater der Zeit.

Tiedemann, K. and Raddatz, F. M. (eds) (2010), *Reality Strikes Back II: Tod der Repräsentation*, Berlin: Theater der Zeit.

Tomlin, L. (2013), *Acts and Apparitions: Discourses on the Real in Performance Practice and Theory, 1990–2010*, Manchester: Manchester University Press.

Ulbricht, M. (2007), 'Im Licht der Aufklärung: "Schwarze Jungfrauen" von Feridun Zaimoglu und Günter Senkel bei den "Stücken". Autor fordert Sitz für Muslima in Islamkonferenz', *Westdeutsche Allgemeine*, 19 May.

United Nations Human Development Report (2009) [http://hdr.undp.org/en/media/HDR_2009_EN_Summary.pdf; accessed 18 January 2010].

van Alphen, E. and Bal, M. (2009), 'Introduction', in E. van Alphen, M. Bal and C. Smith (eds), *The Rhetoric of Sincerity*, Stanford, CA: Stanford University Press, 1–16.

van Erven, E. (2001), *Community Theatre: Global Perspectives*, London: Routledge.

Varney, D. (2010), '"Right now Austria looks ridiculous": *Please Love Austria!* – Reforging the Interaction Between Art and Politics', in T. Forrest and A. T. Scheer (eds), *Christoph Schlingensief: Art Without Borders*, Bristol: Intellect, 105–21.

Visser, A. (2012), 'A Smack on the Nose', interview with Matthias Lilienthal, *Berlin&I*, 3: 25–6.

Vollmer, A. (2004), 'Hebbel am Ufer / HAU 1–3', discussion with Matthias Lilienthal, in A. Vollmer (ed.), *Die Zukunft der Berliner Theater. Konkurrenz oder Reform? Event oder Ensemble?, Dokumentation der Vierten Theater-Anhörung, 4 February 2004*, Berlin: 47–50.

Wahl, C. (2008a), '100 Jahre Theater Hebbel am Ufer: Bierbank-Rentner und Ballett-Mädchen', *Der Spiegel*, 2 February [http://www.spiegel.de/kultur/gesellschaft/0,1518,532757,00.html; accessed 23 November 2010].

Wahl, C (2008b), 'Stochern im schwarzen Loch: Hau 3 Miriam Yung Min Stein wagt in *Black Tie* einen mikroskopischen Blick aufs eigene Leben', *Der Tagesspiegel*, 27 November [www.rimini-protokoll.de/website/de/ article_3889.html; accessed 23 November 2010].

Wahl, C. (2012), 'Die fünf Revolutionen des Matthias Lilienthal', *Spiegel Online*, 1 June [http://www.spiegel.de/kultur/gesellschaft/hau-wie-matthias-lilienthal-in-berlin-das-theater-revolutionierte-a-836247.html; accessed 16 December 2014].

Wahl, C. (2014), 'Die ersten 600 Tage', *Theater heute*, 55 (8/9): 47–9.

Wahl, C. (n.d.), 'Hans-Werner Kroesinger', *50 Directors Working at German Theatres* [http://www.goethe.de/kue/the/reg/reg/hl/kro/enindex.html; accessed 19 March 2015].

Wake, C. (2013a), 'Headphone Verbatim Theatre: Methods, Histories, Genres, Theories', *New Theatre Quarterly*, 29 (4): 321–35.

Wake, C. (2013b), 'To Witness Mimesis: The Politics, Ethics and Aesthetics of Testimonial Theatre in *Through the Wire*', *Modern Drama*, 56 (1): 102–25.

Weiler, C. (2006), 'Nichts zu inszenieren. Arbeit am Unsichtbaren', in E. Fischer-Lichte, B. Gronau, S. Schouten and C. Weiler (eds), *Wege der Wahrnehmung: Authentizität, Reflexivität und Aufmerksamkeit im zeitgenössischen Theater*, Berlin: Theater der Zeit, 58–71.

Weiler, C. (2015), 'Theatre and Diversity in the Berlin Republic', in S. Colvin (ed.), *The Routledge Handbook of German Politics and Culture*, Abingdon: Routledge, 218–28.

Welsch, W. (1999), 'Transculturality – the Puzzling Form of Cultures Today', in M. Featherstone and S. Lash (eds), *Spaces of Culture: City, Nation, World*, London: Sage, 194–213.

Wenger, E. (1998), *Communities of Practice: Learning, Meaning and Identity*, Cambridge: Cambridge University Press.

Wenner, D., Regus, C., Hehmeyer, K. and Pees, M. (2012), 'Die Welt und Königs Wusterhausen', in K. Hehmeyer and M. Pees (eds), *Import Export: Arbeitsbuch zum HAU Berlin*, Berlin: Theater der Zeit, 61–5.

Wetzel, J. (2006), '"Fremde" in den Medien', *Bundeszentrale für politische Bildung*, 13 January [http://www.bpb.de/izpb/9694/fremde-in-den-medien?p=0; accessed 2 March 2015].

Wetzel, D. (2008), 'Zuschauertheater. Regieführen bei Rimini Protokoll', in *Eigensinn zeigen. Das Körber Studio für junge Regie*, Hamburg: Körber-Stiftung, 69–71.

Wildermann, P. (2010), 'Für Sitzenbleiber: HAU mal so: "X-Schulen" in der
    Kreuzberger Hector-Peterson-Oberschule', *Der Tagesspiegel*, 3 July.
Wildermann, P. (2014), 'Weep as Loud As You Can', *Der Tagesspiegel*, 16 January,
    in Michael Laub / Remote Control Productions [http://www.michael-laub.
    com; accessed 8 August 2015].
Wille, F. (2012), 'Im Selbstwiderspruch – Contra HAU', *Theater heute*, 4: 34–5.
Willett, J. (1986), *The Theatre of Erwin Piscator: Half a Century of Politics in
    the Theatre*, London: Methuen.
Yamaguchi, M. (2009), 'Berlin's HAU as an Epicenter of the Performing Arts',
    interview with Matthias Lilienthal, *Performing Arts Network Japan*, 24 July
    [http://www.performingarts.jp/E/pre_interview/0906/1.html; accessed
    24 May 2014].
Yeşilada, K. E. (2012), '"God's Warriors": A Green Thread in the Work of
    Feridun Zaimoglu', in T. Cheesman and K. E. Yeşilada (eds), *Feridun
    Zaimoglu*, Oxford: Lang, 145–66.
Young, S. (2009), 'Playing with Documentary Theatre: *Aalst* and *Taking Care of
    Baby*', *New Theatre Quarterly*, 25 (1): 72–87.
Zaimoglu, F. (2001), *Kopf und Kragen: Kanak- Kultur-Kompendium*, Frankfurt
    am Main: Fischer.
Zaimoglu, F. (2008), 'Gottes Krieger', in F. Zaimoglu, *Zwölf Gramm Glück*,
    Köln: Kiepenheuer & Witsch, 122–56.
Žižek, S. (2002) *Welcome to the Desert of the Real: Five Essays on 11 September
    and Related Dates*, London: Verso.

Index

Prometheus in Athens, 113, 116
Psimenou, Peyé, 175
public, and private, 31–2
Puchner, Martin, 47

Raddatz, Frank, 10, 206–8
RATTEN 07, 37
Rau, Milo, 67
real
    and authentic, 28
    definition, 6
    and fiction, 82, 87
    HAU approach, 53–5
    hyperreal, 48
    and media, 7
    and performance, 55–7, 82
    and spectacle, 48
    and staged, 81
    and theatre, 7, 82, 194
real people
    and audience, 104
    audience vs performers, 16, 62–3
    and authenticity, 5, 67, 105
    and Authenticity-Effects, 167
    and *Blackmarket*, 183–4
    and *Call Cutta*, 149–50, 154
    definition, 5, 52, 93
    and engagement, 27
    HAU's interest in, 55, 67
    and *Mr Dağaçar*, 181, 193–7
    as performers, 23–31, 44
        on HAU agenda, 52
    resurgence of, 39
    and Rimini Protokoll, 207
    and uncertainty, 80
    and the unfamiliar, 191
    unpredictability of, 122
    and *X-Apartments*, 56
    See also non-professional
        performers; performers;
        Theatre of Real People
reality
    and *100% City*, 123
    and art, 85, 129
    and authenticity, 127

    and capitalism, 50
    complexity of, 201–2
    definition, 6
    and engagement, 146
    and HAU, 53–4
    and hyperreal, 48
    Lilienthal's interest in, 2, 53, 126
    reality effect (Barthes), 9, 18, 85–6
    reality hunger, 47
    and theatre, 126, 129–30, 159
    and Theatre of Real People, 69
    X-Apartments, 55–7
Reality Theatre, 4, 9
Reality TV, 47
Recorded Delivery, 43
refugees, 6, 44, 93, 171, 175, 209
    See also asylum seekers; migration;
        mobility
Reich (Frau), 135
Reinelt, Janelle, 49, 54
Renklihava, Bayram, 180, 190, 192–5,
    204
Ridout, Nicholas, 45–6
Rimini Protokoll, 1, 4, 18, 97, 205, 210
    and casting, 192
    and democracy, 116
    influence of, 61–4
    Lilienthal on, 123
    open-mindedness of, 166
    and performers, 122
    preparatory research, 182
    and real people, 207
    and rhetorical devices, 160
    theatre of experts, 38
    and the unfamiliar, 91
    See also 50 Aktenkilometer; 100%
        Berlin; 100% City; 100%
        Melbourne; An Enemy of the
        People in Oslo; Black Tie; Call
        Cutta; experts; *Deutschland*
        2; Karl Marx: Capital,
        Volume One; Mr Dağaçar;
        Prometheus in Athens;
        Situation Rooms; Wallenstein:
        A Documentary Play